UNDERSTANDING THE BALTIC STATES

T0386792

CHARLES CLARKE

(*editor*)

Understanding the Baltic States

Estonia, Latvia and Lithuania since 1991

HURST & COMPANY, LONDON

First published in the United Kingdom in 2023 by
C. Hurst & Co. (Publishers) Ltd.,
New Wing, Somerset House, Strand, London, WC2R 1LA
© Charles Clarke and the Contributors, 2023
All rights reserved.

Distributed in the United States, Canada and Latin America by
Oxford University Press, 198 Madison Avenue, New York, NY 10016,
United States of America.

The right of Charles Clarke and the Contributors to be identified as the
authors of this publication is asserted by them in accordance with the
Copyright, Designs and Patents Act, 1988.

A Cataloguing-in-Publication data record for this book
is available from the British Library.

ISBN: 9781787389410

This book is printed using paper from registered sustainable
and managed sources.

www.hurstpublishers.com

CONTENTS

PART VII
FUTURE NEW CHALLENGES

LIST OF ABBREVIATIONS

BNR	Belarusian Democratic Republic
CBS	Council of the Baltic States
CDU	Christian Democratic Union (*Christlich Demokratische Union Deutschlands*)
CIS	Commonwealth of Independent States
COMECON	Council for Mutual Economic Assistance
CPSU	Communist Party of the Soviet Union
CPU	Communist Party of Ukraine
CSCE	Commission on Security and Cooperation in Europe
CSDP	Common Security and Defence Policy
EEC	European Economic Community
FCO	Foreign and Commonwealth Office
FDP	Free Democratic Party (*Freie Demokratische Partei*)
FSB	Federal Security Service of the Russian Federation (*Federal'naya sluzhba bezopasnosti Rossiyskoy Federatsii*)
Helcom	Helsinki Commission
IME	Self-Managing Estonia (*Ise Majandav Eesti*)

LIST OF ABBREVIATIONS

INM	Institute of National Memory (Ukraine)
JEF	UK Joint Expeditionary Force
KGB	Committee for State Security (*Komitet Gosudarstvennoy Bezopasnosti*)
MRP	Molotov-Ribbentrop Pact
NATO	North Atlantic Treaty Organization
OMON	Special Purpose Mobile Unit (*Otryad Mobil'nyy Osobogo Naznacheniya*)
OUN	Organisation of Ukrainian Nationalists
PDRU	Party of Democratic Revival of Ukraine
PiS	Law and Justice (*Prawo i Sprawiedliwość*)
PJC	Permanent Joint Council
PPS	Paris Peace Conference
RSFSR	Russian Soviet Federative Socialist Republic
SDSR	Strategic Defence and Security Review
SNP	Scottish National Party
SS	Protection Squadron (*Schutzstaffel*)
TNA	The National Archives (United Kingdom)
UKMIS	The United Kingdom Mission to the United Nations
USSR	Union of Soviet Socialist Republics
VAK	Environmental Protection Club (*Vides Aizsardzības Klubs*)

CHRONOLOGY

1988–1991

Dr John Freeman

13 April 1988	Edgar Savisaar announces support for perestroika and launches the idea of Eestimaa Rahvarinne or The Popular Front of Estonia.
14 May 1988	Alo Mattiisen unveils his series 'Five Patriotic Songs' at the Tartu Pop Festival.
3 June 1988	Founding of Sąjūdis, the Popular Front of Lithuania.
10–11 June 1988	Spontaneous singing demonstrations take place at Tallinn Song Festival Grounds, prompting the Estonian activist and artist Heinz Valk to proclaim a 'Singing Revolution.'
16 June 1988	Karl Vaino ousted as the First Secretary of the Communist Party of Estonia and is replaced by the relatively liberal Vaino Väljas.

CHRONOLOGY

28 June–1 July 1988	Nineteenth All-Union Conference of the Communist Party of the Soviet Union held, in which Mikhail Gorbachev calls for the democratisation of the Union. The Party relinquishes its monopoly of economic power in the Soviet Union.
23 August 1988	Rallies are held in the Baltic States on the forty-ninth anniversary of the Molotov-Ribbentrop Pact which placed the Baltic States in the Soviet sphere of influence.
11 September 1988	An estimated 300,000 people gather at Tallinn Song Festival Grounds to sing patriotic songs and listen to proponents of the independence movement.
1 October 1988	Eestimaa Rahvarinne holds its founding conference.
9 October 1988	Latvijas Tautas Fronte, or the Popular Front of Latvia, is established at its first conference.
19 October 1988	Ringaudas Songaila resigns as the First Secretary of the Communist Party of Lithuania having ordered the forcible dispersal of a pro-independence rally in Vilnius the previous month. He is replaced by Algirdas Brazauskas, a reformer.
22 October 1988	Gorbachev announces amendments to the Soviet constitution which would form a new democratically elected legislature, the Soviet Congress of People's Deputies,

as well as restricting the rights of the republics to secede.

22–23 October 1988 Sąjūdis holds its founding conference.

16 November 1988 The Supreme Soviet of Estonia declares itself sovereign, although not independent.

18 November 1988 The flag and national anthem of Lithuania are legalised whilst the Lithuanian language is given primacy over Russian. Similar changes to Estonian and Latvian language laws are also implemented in this month.

26 November 1988 Mikhail Gorbachev rejects the Estonian Communist Party's declaration of sovereignty, claiming that there was no legal basis for such a move.

26 March 1989 The first round of elections to the Soviet Congress of People's Deputies is held across the Soviet Union.

9 April 1989 The second round of elections to the Soviet Congress of People's Deputies confirms eighty-seven percent of the available seats for the Communist Party. Boris Yeltsin wins a place in the Congress against a Communist Party endorsed candidate.

25 May 1989 First session of the Soviet Congress of People's Deputies.

25 June 1989 The first congress of the Belarusian People's Front, known as Revival (*Adradzhennie*) is held in Vilnius.

23 August 1989	The Baltic Way, a human chain of approximately two million people, stretches 690 kilometres from Tallinn to Vilnius. It marks the fiftieth anniversary of the Molotov-Ribbentrop Pact.
9 September 1989	Rukh, the Ukrainian People's Front is founded.
28 September 1989	Volodymyr Shcherbytsky, a staunch hardline conservative, is removed as First Secretary of the Communist party of Ukraine. It follows a purge of the Politburo of the Soviet Union by Gorbachev, in which Shcherbytsky also lost his position.
9 November 1989	The Berlin Wall falls, marking the lifting of the Iron Curtain.
2–3 December 1989	The Cold War is declared at an end by Gorbachev and President George Bush at the Malta Summit. Bush warns Gorbachev not to use force against secession campaigners.
December 1989	Sweden establishes a diplomatic office in Tallinn. It is followed by an equivalent in Riga, in May 1990.
24 December 1989	The Soviet Congress of Deputies approves a motion, condemning the secret protocols of the Molotov-Ribbentrop Pact, in which the Soviet Union and Nazi Germany defined spheres of influence, as illegal.
24 December 1989	After mass protests, the Communist Party

of Lithuania declares itself separate from the Communist Party of the Soviet Union, leading to it rebranding as the Democratic Labour Party of Lithuania.

21 January 1990 — To mark the *Act Zluky* which confirmed Ukrainian unity in 1919, Rukh organises a human chain from Lviv to Kyiv.

16 February 1990 — Death of Volodymyr Schcherbytsky.

24 February 1990 — Free and democratic elections held in Lithuania for the Supreme Soviet. Sąjūdas-backed candidates win an outright majority.

11 March 1990 — Lithuania declares the re-establishment of its independence, the first of the Soviet republics to do so. The Supreme Soviet in Lithuania elects one of the founding members of Sąjūdis, Vytautas Landsbergis, as its chairman.

29 May 1990 — Boris Yeltsin selected as Chairman of the Supreme Soviet of the Russian SFSR.

12 June 1990 — The Russian SFSR declares state sovereignty.

12 July 1990 — Yeltsin resigns from the Communist Party of the Soviet Union.

16 July 1990 — The Ukrainian Soviet declares state sovereignty.

2 August 1990 — Iraq invades Kuwait, leading to the start of the Gulf War.

3 August 1990 — Ukraine adopts a law announcing economic independence.

CHRONOLOGY

August 1990	Sweden announces its intention to apply for membership to the European Economic Community (EEC).
28 October 1990	Rukh changes policy by backing Ukrainian independence rather than reform.
22 November 1990	Margaret Thatcher forced to resign as Prime Minister of the United Kingdom, signalling a more welcoming British attitude towards German reunification and independence for the Baltic States.
2 January 1991	The state police body OMON occupies Press House in Riga.
10 January 1991	Gorbachev sends an ultimatum, demanding that the constitutions of the Soviet Union and the Lithuanian Socialist Soviet Republic be restored. In his speech, he threatens to impose presidential rule on Lithuania.
11 January 1991	After the Lithuanian rejection of Gorbachev's ultimatum, the Soviet military begins to seize state institution buildings in Vilnius.
13 January 1991	Tanks and soldiers surround the TV tower in Vilnius. They attack a crowd of civilians, killing fourteen.
13 January 1991	The Latvian Popular Front barricades key buildings in Riga to protect the continuation of the elected government.
17 January 1991	Commencement of Operation Desert Storm, in which a US-led coalition attempts to end Iraqi occupation of Kuwait.

9 February 1991	Referendum for Lithuanian independence held. Ninety-three percent vote in favour.
28 February 1991	End of the Gulf War with Iraq's withdrawal from Kuwait.
3 March 1991	Latvia and Estonia follow Lithuania in holding an independence referendum. In Latvia, seventy-five percent vote in favour, whilst in Estonia the figure is seventy-eight percent.
17 March 1991	A Soviet referendum is held asking voters if they approve of 'a renewed federation of equal Soviet states.' Seventy-eight percent do but the Baltic republics, along with Georgia, Armenia and Moldova, boycott the vote.
12 June 1991	Yeltsin wins the first ever Russian presidential election.
1 July 1991	Sweden applies to join the EEC, ending Cold War neutrality.
5 July 1991	Ukraine institutes the role of president.
1 August 1991	George Bush gives the so-called 'Chicken Kiev' speech, urging Ukrainians not to succumb to 'suicidal nationalism.'
19 August 1991	Hardliners within the Communist Party launch a coup, detaining Gorbachev in his dacha, and moving troops into Moscow. The coup faces resistance from Yeltsin and other protestors. It collapses on 22 August.
20 August 1991	The Supreme Council in Estonia confirms

its independence. In Latvia, a similar resolution is made the following day.

22 August 1991   Iceland becomes the first nation to recognise the independence of all the Baltic States, having recognised Lithuanian independence on 11 February 1991.

24 August 1991   Ukrainian parliament backs a declaration of independence with a vote of 346 to 1.

1 September 1991   British Prime Minister John Major meets Baltic leaders in Moscow.

6 September 1991   The Soviet Union recognises the independence of the Baltic States.

1 December 1991   The Ukrainian referendum on independence delivers a result ninety-two percent in favour.

8 December 1991   The President Yeltsin of Russia and President Leonid Kravchuk of Ukraine, along with the leader of Belarusian parliament, Stanislav Shushkevich, sign the Belovezh Accords, forming the Commonwealth of Independent States (CIS).

25 December 1991   Gorbachev resigns as President of the USSR.

26 December 1991   The Soviet Union ceases to exist.

PART I

INTRODUCTION

THE IMPORTANCE OF THE BALTIC

Rt Hon Charles Clarke

The origins of this book lie in the establishment of the Cambridge University Baltic Geopolitics Programme.[1] This Programme was formally launched in January 2021 and has since organised a substantial range of different events, both online and in person, which have addressed many of the current geopolitical challenges which the Baltic Sea region faces. Our ambition is to build greater academic strength in Cambridge itself since we are extremely conscious of the very limited study of the Baltic Sea region which currently takes place in British universities.

Our Programme is seeking to remedy this important weakness both because of the historic relationship between the UK and the Baltic Sea region, which I describe below, and of course because the current geopolitical situation threatens all of us and the often precarious security which Europe had enjoyed for decades. In Britain we need to understand, better than we often do, what is driving change, how it affects us and how we can relate to it. Brexit makes this even more important.

The Programme's central organising principles are that we need to learn from history, to focus upon the whole Baltic Sea region and upon the British-Baltic relationship, to engage both academics and practitioners, and to examine the whole range of issues—from energy and climate change to migration and economic growth—which have significant geopolitical implications. We are massively assisted by the network of nineteen universities from across the region which we have established, and which combine powerful expertise and knowledge about the issues.

Our Programme is in its early stages. Our first major in-person event was a symposium which took place on 23 March 2022. This was entitled 'The Baltic Contribution to the Dissolution of the Soviet Union in 1991' and, thirty years on, it addressed the momentous events which led to the destruction of the Soviet Union and the re-establishment of the independent Baltic states of Estonia, Latvia and Lithuania. The event brought together leading academic analysts of the field, historians, diplomats, journalists and first-hand observers from a variety of geographical locations and professional standpoints.

Obviously, the Russian invasion of Ukraine on 24 February 2022 bestowed a hugely increased salience upon the issues that we were discussing and emphasised the importance of understanding far better than we generally do the motivations of Russia (not only those of Vladimir Putin) and the experience of the Baltic Sea region.

The March symposium proved to be very interesting and worthwhile, including many stimulating perceptions. It reflected a range of differing perspectives and led to fruitful discussion. We therefore decided to produce this book, of which the participants' contributions and presentations form the core. We have added other valuable insights like the history of the region prior to these events as well as analyses of the maritime security issues and the intriguing position of Kaliningrad.

We believe that this book adds significantly to our understanding of the way in which the Baltic States, and indeed the wider region, have emerged into contemporary times. For example, the Cold War concept of the 'British Army on the Rhine' has now been replaced by the UK operational deployment to Estonia ('Operation Cabrit') within NATO's 'Enhanced Forward Presence', established at its 2016 NATO Summit and following the establishment of the UK Joint Expeditionary Force in 2012. And the 2022 decisions of Sweden and Finland to join NATO are massive changes to a foreign policy approach which had lasted over seventy years

From a British point of view, I think this book also offers a welcome reorientation of our wider thinking about European politics—away from the focus on the Franco-German relationship, which seems to me to have dominated a lot of our thinking, and towards the German-Russian relationship. This interaction has been so decisive for an enormous swathe of the continent as the border marking the influence of these two great powers has shifted over the last 200 years.

A word of particular explanation is needed about two important dimensions of the Symposium, and therefore of this book.

The first is the British relationship with events in the Baltic which is reflected in a number of the chapters. It is worth setting out at a little length the history and importance of the relationship between the UK and the Baltic. This is an important aspect of the work of the Baltic Geopolitics Programme.

The second is the increasing importance of the use of history as a driver of contemporary geopolitical behaviour which is of course so apparent in the behaviour of Vladimir Putin, and which so influences attitudes to Russia across the Baltic Sea region and has done for decades.

UNDERSTANDING THE BALTIC STATES

The UK and the Baltic[2]

On 16 March 2021, the United Kingdom government published *'Global Britain in a Competitive Age': The Integrated Review of Security, Defence, Development and Foreign Policy.*[3] It set out how, after Brexit, the UK would embrace its 'global' destiny, including a substantial shift towards the challenges of the Indo-Pacific.

However, in fact, Britain's relationship with the rest of Europe will not only continue to be very important, it will actually become more so. The European Union remains the UK's most significant neighbour and of course the reverse is also true—despite Brexit, Britain remains far more important to the EU than any other neighbouring state.

This is because of the intertwined history of our relationships over centuries and the Baltic Sea is central to that. For more than a millennium the relationships between Britain and the Baltic have been characterised by conflict and cooperation.

The British-Baltic connection really took off during the early Middle Ages, when much of northern and eastern England and Scotland bore the brunt of Viking raids, mostly mounted from Denmark. This is when the phrase 'Danegeld' entered the English language, first as a financial tribute paid to buy off the attackers, and then as a tax levied to fund the defence of the realm against them. In the later Middle Ages, many British east coast towns, such as Boston, King's Lynn, Aberdeen and Edinburgh were 'staple towns' of the Hanseatic League, the dominant economic ordering system in the area (today sometimes compared with the EU).

Over the next 300 years or so, relations between England and Scotland (and later Great Britain) and the Baltic remained important but became more geopolitical. During the Thirty Years War in the first half of the seventeenth century, many looked to the Swedish King Gustavus Adolphus to defend the

'Protestant Cause' in Germany. During the eighteenth century, the Baltic became a source of critical naval supplies, such as ships' masts and hemp. The trade produced its own tensions. Catherine the Great of Russia, for example, complained that the British were 'always exceedingly jealous of the trade carried on with her, and seldom binds herself by treaties with other states, and depends upon no other laws than her own.'

An important British national interest was to keep any hostile power out of the Baltic, be it the Catholic League in the Holy Roman Empire, Tsarist Russia, or France under Napoleon. This involved seeing off hostile coalitions such as the Leagues of Armed Neutrality, intended to break Britain's maritime dominance, or the Continental System, designed to exclude her from the mainland European economy.

Throughout this period, the Baltic Sea states themselves became increasingly weak within the international system. Sweden and Denmark, which had previously exercised a role well beyond the region, lost ground. They were caught in the crossfire of the great powers, for example when Napoleon forced the Swedes and the Danes to take his side against London. Wisely, the British did not always react. When in 1810 Napoleon pressured Sweden into declaring war on Britain, the Royal Navy commander in the region, Admiral Saumarez, treated the government in Stockholm with respect and ignored the challenge.

During the nineteenth and early twentieth centuries, Britain continued to shape the Baltic. Most of the time, it tried to keep the Russians, whether Tsarist or Soviet, hemmed in. When the Crimean War broke out, the Royal Navy attacked Russian forts off Finland. After the Russian Revolution, British forces were sent to support the new anti-Bolshevik states which emerged from the wreckage. In the first half of the twentieth century, the British also sought to keep Imperial Germany and the Third Reich boxed into the Baltic.

In the course of these operations, Britain became a leading guarantor of the Baltic States. Estonian independence after 1918 was very much assisted by the shelter of Royal Navy guns. General Johan Laidoner, Commander in Chief of the Estonian armed forces at the time, stated that he 'was sure that without the arrival of the British fleet in Tallinn, in December 1918, the fate of our country and our people would have been very different.'

Britain's relationship with the Baltic has had its problematic and traumatic moments. During the Napoleonic Wars, Britain attacked Denmark twice, both times with dubious legality and to devastating effect. In 1801, the Royal Navy destroyed most of the Danish fleet to prevent it from falling into French hands. Six years later, the British emphasised the point by attacking the capital of Denmark itself. One hundred and forty years later the Royal Air Force wrecked two of the most beautiful German cities in the Baltic, Lübeck and Rostock.

Of course, there were limits to British power. When London was outraged by the partition of Poland in 1772, satirists asked whether the navy would sail up the Vistula from Danzig (modern-day Gdansk) to Warsaw in order to bring Russia, Prussia and Austria to heel. In 1864 Bismarck called Britain's bluff when Palmerston threatened to intervene to support Denmark over Schleswig-Holstein. If the (then small) British army landed in Germany, he quipped, he would have it arrested. And having acted as midwife to the Baltic States in 1918–1921, the Royal Navy was unable to prevent the Soviet Union from annexing them in 1940 and again in 1944.

After the Second World War, Britain remained engaged in the Baltic and, as part of the NATO alliance, was responsible for the defence of the German coastline there. The objective was to contain the Soviet Union.

Since 1945 immigration to the UK from the region has been significant, especially of Poles, Latvians, Lithuanians and

Estonians, when many refugees came to work in Britain from those countries. After their accession to the EU in 2004 the number of immigrants from these countries grew substantially and remains the subject of political controversy.

In 1973 the relationship gained a new dimension when the United Kingdom joined the European Economic Community. Economic relations between Denmark and Britain at that time were so close that Denmark decided to join on the same day. The UK's membership of what became the European Union was seen by many countries in the region as an important counter-weight to the power of France and Germany—the Common Market's original founders. Britain was strongly committed to steady enlargement of the European Union to include the Baltic countries (Eastern Germany in 1990, Finland and Sweden in 1995 and Poland and the Baltic States in 2004).

Over the next forty-seven years of Britain's membership of the EU, her relationship with the Baltic developed along diverging axes. On the one hand, as the states of the region integrated with the rest of Europe the proportion of their trade with Britain declined. On the other hand, the political, geopolitical and demographic connections grew. In general, these countries tended to align with the UK in major EU policy debates. London built on these preferences to try to minimise Franco-German dominance of the bloc. This was the background to the Conservative-Liberal Democrat coalition government's 'Northern Future' initiative in 2011.

The UK's Brexit referendum vote in 2016 was difficult for most Europeans, but it was particularly traumatic for the strongly anglophile Scandinavians and Balts whose worries about security, especially in the Eastern Baltic, were also very concrete.

Britain was militarily the most important of the three non-Baltic 'framework' European NATO nations delivering deterrence in the Baltic Sea region. After Putin annexed the Crimea in 2014 these links deepened, for example through the establishment and then development of the UK Joint Expeditionary Force together with Baltic and Scandinavian countries. Relations became even deeper after Putin's invasion of Ukraine in February 2022 with intensified military co-operation, increased intensity of ministerial visits, both in the UK and in the Baltic, and the written security guarantees which Britain agreed with Sweden and Finland as they decided to join NATO in July 2022.

As we look to the future the UK's strategy depends on the assumption that the western Baltic remains friendly territory. In this context, the post-Brexit relationship to the European Union will be critical. Britain has no interest in undermining the EU as the principal politico-legal ordering system in the Baltic. At the same time, the UK must ensure that the region remains an economically shared space and it must not allow the EU's security pretensions from disrupting NATO. So far, London has not linked her relationship with the EU to the defence of Europe through NATO and hopefully it will not do so despite the post-Brexit failure so far to agree a satisfactory UK/EU foreign policy relationship.

The realities of geopolitics remain. The UK mattered and will matter in Europe, especially in the Baltic. We share with those countries commitments to sustainability, particularly in energy, to the rule of law and human rights, and to social stability and cohesion, excluding political extremism. These common values will matter even more as the post-Ukraine future works itself out. The UK needs to think systematically about its relationship to a very important part of its own continent.

The Weaponising of History and Memory

In July 2021 Vladimir Putin published his important article 'On the Historical Unity of Russians and Ukrainians.'[4] The principal purpose of this narrative was to validate the Russian approach to

Ukraine and so to attempt to justify both the annexation and invasions of 2014, the attack in February 2022 and the annexations in September 2022. The article is a classic example of the weaponising of a particular historical narrative in order to attempt to excuse military and geopolitical action. The narrative attempts both to offer a quasi-legal justification for the stance that Russia has taken and to bolster support for this action amongst the Russian people up to and including the imposition of 'partial mobilisation' of the Russian people in September 2022. It is Putin's fundamental rationalisation for what he has been doing and it enables him to refer back to the history of World War Two and to frame the whole conflict as a question of NATO, even fascist, attacks on Russia rather than anything else.

As far as the Baltic States are concerned, he described in this article the events of 1988 to 1991 as a 'parade of sovereignties' and goes on to say 'Of course, inside the USSR, borders between republics were never seen as state borders; they were nominal within a single country which ... was highly centralised. But in 1991 all those territories and, which is more important, people found themselves abroad overnight, taken away, this time indeed, from their historical motherland.'

It is hardly surprising that this historical formulation, combined with the bitter history of Soviet domination from 1940 to 1991, dominates attitudes in the Baltic to this day and leads to some probably unjustified fears of the loyalty of Russian ethnic minorities in the event of Russian aggression.

Whatever other motivations could be thought to explain the Russian interventions against Ukraine in 2014 and 2022, the importance of Putin's historical narrative, as deployed in this article, together with related narratives, should not be underestimated.

Putin's use of history is certainly not the only example of the deployment of particular historical accounts for contemporary political and strategic purposes.

For example, much of Britain's Brexit campaign in 2016 was dominated by perceptions of British history—some balanced, some highly partial. These understandings were as important a factor in determining people's final referendum votes as the widespread rejection of contemporary politics and 'globalisation' and the important present-day economic and political choices whose outcome those votes determined.

Such perceptions of history reinforced those nationalist and populist narratives which maintained that the post-1945 internationalist economic and political model had failed whole communities and countries. The economic decline of traditional industries and immigration were for them notable illustrations of the failures of 'globalisation' and these accounts fired a sense of impotence in millions of people about their own ability to control the world in which they live.

These feelings of helplessness contribute to the depressing spirit of the times as those who believed that they had lost out turned towards political leaders who spoke out against the status quo. A whole set of political movements from the extremes have been able to thrive in this climate, whether Brexit and Jeremy Corbyn in the UK, the Tea Party, Donald Trump and Bernie Sanders in the US, or Marine Le Pen and the Swedish Democrats, Syriza and Podemos in continental Europe.

In each of these cases versions of national history are used, and often abused, to validate the points of views of the various campaigners in the arguments that they present. These accounts are now also supplemented by 'fake news', fabricated to illustrate the central theme. Such 'debates' are playing a major role in defining our future history.

Though the way in which Putin is weaponising his version of the history of Russia (and incidentally also intervening in other countries' national political and strategic debates) is exceptional, the whole process does place immense responsibility on academic historians to do their very best to describe accurately the motivations and aspirations of the various players at moments at moments of historical change. This is extremely difficult and of course there can never be an 'objective' view of the way in which history has played out. Historical discussion must give proper weight to the various differing points of view about what happened and its meaning for today.

But these issues are now far sharper than in the past, and the responsibility of historians is greater, largely because the communications media, including social media, enable versions of false historical truth to be disseminated very rapidly, and in a very influential way, without any moderation by reference to factual accounts of what actually happened.

This is a challenge for politicians and government leaders as well as historians. They have the obligation to hold as closely as they can to reasonably accurate descriptions of history as well as to current real-world choices. It is unsurprising that the study of historical memory is an increasingly important academic discipline, notably in the countries of central and eastern Europe, and our book reflects the importance of this.

The welfare of democratic society requires that public debate is based upon accurate accounts of history. Our hope is that in its commitment to engaging genuine historians of the region that the Baltic Geopolitics Programme can help to achieve that at a time when secure democracy is needed more than ever. This book is a contribution to that end in regard to a very significant period of modern geopolitical history which still has strong contemporary implications.

Acknowledgements and Thanks

There are many contributors without whom this book could not have happened.

I firstly want to thank Professor Brendan Simms, the Director of the Centre for Geopolitics at Cambridge University, for his support in the establishment of the Baltic Geopolitics Programme, the organisation of the Symposium of 23 March 2022 and for his commitment to our ambitions.

And with him Donatas Kupčiūnas, a Research Associate at the Centre, whose detailed knowledge of the region and his academic focus have been indispensable.

Brendan and Donatas have both contributed chapters to this book and it is indeed the support of the range of very distinguished chapter authors which make the book what it is. They come from a variety of different professional backgrounds and geographical locations, and their involvement has come in many different forms. I am extremely grateful for all of their efforts and inspiration.

John Freeman's excellent editorial work has enabled this book to happen so proficiently and effectively.

And Michael Dwyer of Hurst Publishing, and his team, have taken this idea from an idea to a reality, for which we will always be grateful.

I would also like to thank those who provided financial support for our Symposium which made the event, and so this book, possible.

Charles Clarke

2

A HISTORY OF THE BALTIC REGION

1860–1991

Neil Taylor

It is the first duty of any historian of the Baltic countries to stress their differences rather than any similarities. Such similarities that did occur usually resulted from outside pressures rather than from any cooperation between them. The Baltic Germans imposed Protestantism on areas that centuries later would become Estonia and Latvia; Swedish rule in the seventeenth century ensured this religious continuity. Lithuania, being linked to Poland from 1569–1795, stayed Catholic, with the founding by the Jesuits of Vilnius University in 1579 reinforcing this. The Russian Empire would impose Orthodoxy on all three in the late nineteenth century. In the second half of the twentieth century, the Soviet Union would impose orthodoxy in a very different sense of the word, being keen to prevent any cultural and intellectual diversity outside a socialist straitjacket.

The period from 1918 to 1940 was the first time that the three countries had their own governments beholden to none of the great powers or to any religious authority. All three did abandon democracy for a mild form of authoritarianism but at different times and for different reasons. They rarely worked together, which greatly accelerated their demise when the Soviet Union, partially in 1939, and then fully in 1940, took control. Apart from the four years 1941–5, when Germany ruled the area, this control remained until 1991, the year that the Soviet Union collapsed. The independence restored in that year has of course survived, but any links have been with larger bodies, such as the EU and NATO, and not just between the three.

The late nineteenth century saw the start of nationalist movements in the Baltic region, and also industrial activity which would lead to the formation of unions and left-wing activity similar to that taking place throughout Europe. In Lithuania, there would be constant concern at the supposed threat of Poland again taking the upper hand, with opposition to the Poles as strong as that towards the Russians. The start of the national movement there can be given a specific year, 1864, when the Russian government insisted on the printing of Lithuanian texts only in the Cyrillic alphabet, a policy that would last until 1904. It was a complete failure as publishers in neighbouring Prussia were more than happy to print books in the Roman script and to help with smuggling them into Lithuania. The abolition of serfdom in 1861 was supposed to garner support for the Russian government, but this failed too, as working conditions in fact changed very little for Lithuanian farmers.

The year 1864 was similarly significant in Estonia as it was the year the first nationally circulating newspaper *Eesti Postimees* was published in Tartu. This was followed, again in Tartu, by the first Song Festival which took place in 1869; with no works being sung in Russian or in German, its contribution to the nationalist movement is clear. By now Lydia Koidula (1843–86), Estonia's most famous poet, could write in Estonian and no longer in German. Similarly, her plays could also be performed in her native language.

In Latvia there is no specific date that can be quoted from this time, but from the 1860s, an increasing number of publications appeared in Latvian. It has to be stressed, however, that pressures were more cultural than national. There was little thought that Latvia would ever be anything apart from a province in the Russian Empire. This period would also see a great population movement towards the two industrial towns of Riga and Daugavpils. Particularly in Riga, the Baltic Germans dominated trade and manufacturing, but Latvians would slowly be able to enter these fields and not be restricted to purely manual labour. Architecturally, this Baltic-German legacy remains throughout Riga. On a smaller scale there was a similar movement to Tallinn from the Estonian countryside.

Nonetheless, the Baltic Germans, who had been settled for 600 years, still dominated the two capitals until after World War I. Unlike in Lithuania, the Russians were able to delegate the running of these two areas to the Baltic Germans, who ensured regular tax payments and, above all, built the railways which would link the Baltics to the affluent cities of St Petersburg and Moscow, engendering international trade in both directions. The port at St Petersburg could be blocked by ice for several months each winter whereas such blockages were of a much shorter period in Riga and Tallinn. The link to Riga was completed in 1861, to Tallinn in 1870 and to Tartu in 1877. Riga undoubtedly benefitted from having this link ten years prior to the port which was its major competitor. An earlier railway was completed in 1862 through Lithuania to Warsaw, but this was probably seen more as a tool for political control by the imperial Russian authorities than one for potential trading links, so it did not involve the Baltic Germans.

Lithuania's political diversity at the end of the nineteenth century is perhaps best shown by the fact that Felix Dzerzhinsky (1877–1926), Józef Piłsudski (1867–1935) and Pyotr Stolypin (1862–1911) all grew up in Vilnius and attended the same school. Dzerzhinsky would become notorious as the Director of the Cheka, the forerunner of the KGB, after having been expelled from the school for political activism and then spending many years in prison, in Siberia and in exile. Piłsudski achieved appropriate fame as the Polish commander for his defeat of Soviet forces in 1920–1 before becoming Poland's 'strong man' until his death in 1935. Stolypin began his political career in local government in Kovno, now Kaunas, before rising to become Prime Minister of Russia in 1906.

Aware of the various, but totally uncoordinated resistance movements within the Baltics, the Russian government attempted to impose greater use of the Russian language and to convert Lutheran communities into Orthodox ones. The assassination of Alexander II in 1881 was a convenient pretext for intensifying this activity and for adding anti-Semitism to it. For instance, at Tartu University an attempt was made in 1887 to switch the language of tuition from German to Russian and to re-introduce the Russian name for the town, Juriev. This was only partially successful, like so many other attempts at maintaining rigid imperial control. The 'Bloody Sunday' demonstration in St Petersburg in January 1905 was the most famous outburst against the Russian regime and it would be followed by similar activity in the Baltics, manifested in northern Latvia by the destruction of many manor houses. Amongst those forced into exile after January 1905 was Konstantin Päts, the future leader of Estonia. Edward VII of Great Britain paid an official visit to Tsar Nicholas II in 1908, but this took place in Tallinn harbour as a visit on land was considered too dangerous, either there or in St Petersburg.

Fighting between Russian and German troops took place on Baltic territory during World War I but with nothing like the intensity of the battles along the Western front. As the Soviet government needed to concentrate on eliminating its domestic opponents, it was keen to withdraw from fighting the Germans which resulted in the signing of the Treaty of Brest-Litovsk on 3 March 1918. The Treaty in theory gave independence to the three Baltic provinces but in fact it allowed them to fall into German hands. In February of that year both Lithuania and Estonia had declared independence and Latvia would do the same in November, but in all three cases it would be well into 1919 before serious areas of land came under the control of the new regimes. Only in 1920 were treaties signed with Soviet Russia confirming their borders. At times during 1919, the military situation in all three countries suggested that a permanent Soviet occupation was very likely. The British navy, freed in November 1918 from duties in the North Sea, provided both military and civilian aid to Estonian and Latvian forces. General Laidoner, the Estonian commander, would later write that 'without the arrival of the British fleet in December 1918, the fate of our country would have been very different and we would have found ourselves in the hands of the Bolsheviks.'

The signing of the Armistice at Compiegne on 11 November 1918 is usually seen in the West as representing the end of World War I, but in fact it signalled only the end of the fighting on the Western Front. In Eastern Europe, intense fighting would continue until 1920, involving not only the nascent Baltic countries but Germany, Poland, Ukraine, Soviet and White Russian forces as well. In early 1919 much of the Latvian countryside was in German hands, whilst Riga was ruled by Bolshevik sympathisers. The German forces under General Rüdiger von der Goltz might well have seized Latvia and Estonia, but were in the end defeated by a combined Estonian and Latvian attack at Cēsis in northern

Latvia on 22 June 1919, a date which is still celebrated in Estonia as 'Victory Day.'

There was however no formal German surrender on the Eastern Front and in fact no final peace treaty at all in that area, just a series of treaties signed in 1920 and 1921 between the different belligerents. The most famous of these treaties was the one signed in Tartu on 4 February 1920 under which Soviet Russia recognised the independence of Estonia in perpetuity. In return, Estonia was the first country to grant diplomatic recognition to Soviet Russia. Britain would follow suit only in 1924 with recognition of what was by then the Soviet Union. It would be 1933 before the USA would act likewise. Jaan Poska, who headed the Estonian delegation at Tartu, commented that Estonia 'would not be bothered by Bolsheviks again' whereas Lenin saw the treaty as a temporary arrangement before the Estonian people would overthrow their government. In Lithuania he saw socialism as being postponed, not abandoned. He was presumably encouraged in this optimism by the success of Soviet forces in Ukraine and Georgia where short-lived attempts at independence were quickly and ruthlessly suppressed.

Estonia had the least difficult emergence into independence, being able through early 1919 to drive the Soviet forces back towards Russia and to ensure that the Germans would not return. That year was more brutal in Latvia and in Lithuania. The three countries are often rightly praised for what they achieved when they were suddenly able to re-establish their governments in August 1991. It is often forgotten how their predecessors in 1918–20 deserve similar praise for setting up viable countries in the immediate aftermath of World War I, with minimal help from outside countries and with the continuing threats from Soviet Russia, and after 1924, from the Soviet Union. Each had signed separate peace treaties with Russia in 1919/20, similar to the Tartu Treaty mentioned above, when

Russia was at its weakest fighting Poland, and so could secure terms much more favourable than would have been the case had negotiations dragged on into 1921. Of future significance was the fact that the Moscow Treaty signed between Soviet Russia and Lithuania in July 1920 recognised Vilnius and the surrounding area as being part of Lithuania.

There were minor disputes between the three Baltic countries about the borders between them, but both of these were resolved by a British arbitrator. Stephen Tallents, who would later achieve fame in Britain as the founder of the Institute of Public Relations, divided Valga/Valka between Estonia and Latvia along a border which both sides reluctantly accepted at the time, but which they are now happy to live with. The Latvians and Lithuanians both claimed Palanga, and both had valid grounds for so doing, but the Siberian explorer turned diplomat, James Alexander Simpson, ruled in favour of Lithuania, largely to ensure that this new country had an outlet to the sea.

More serious was the issue of Vilnius, which the Lithuanians claimed as their historic capital but where the vast majority of the population saw themselves as Polish or Jewish. 1917–20 saw fighting there between German, Soviet, Lithuanian and Polish forces, resolved finally by the Polish occupation in October 1920 which would last until the autumn of 1939. In fact, the Poles also seized territory stretching to the Latvian border. Kaunas would become the 'provisional' capital of Lithuania and although there was little actual fighting between the Poles and the Lithuanians, a formal state of war remained until 1938, with travel between the two only being possible via Germany or Latvia. Estonia and Latvia did not wish to take a formal position on the Vilnius issue, maintaining cordial diplomatic relations with the Poles throughout the interwar period. As a result, there could be no serious cooperation between the three countries, or alliances with neighbouring ones which would have strengthened potential bargaining positions with any of the great powers which threatened them.

Under the terms of the Versailles Treaty, the former German towns of Danzig (now the Polish town Gdansk) and Memel (now the Lithuanian town Klaipeda) were to be administered by the newly-founded League of Nations. This arrangement worked in Danzig until the German invasion that started World War II. In 1923, the Lithuanians took advantage of the sleepy French occupation force based in Memel to seize the town and to incorporate it along with its largely German-speaking population. Whilst nothing was ever said publicly, the hope of the major powers was that the Lithuanians would accept Memel as a consolation prize for Vilnius staying in Polish hands. Considerable autonomy would be granted to the German speakers, but not enough to prevent a German re-occupation in March 1939, proclaimed in person by Hitler himself with the same fervour that he had shown in Vienna a year earlier. His welcome in Memel was equally ecstatic as for years previously the local German-language newspaper, the *Memeler Dampfboot* had been printing extracts from *Mein Kampf.*

By the early 1930s Kaunas was de facto seen as Lithuania's permanent capital with churches, banks, museums and a presidential palace all built in an appropriately monumental style. The Lithuanian author Tomas Venclova compares the situation with Ireland, suggesting that had the British held Dublin and the Irish formed a government in Galway, this would have been a parallel situation to that faced by the Lithuanians. Perhaps a comparison with post-war Bonn and Berlin is more appropriate, with few foreseeing during the 1960s and 1970s a time when Bonn would no longer be a capital city.

Although the Jewish population formed a sizable minority in both Latvia and Lithuania, it wisely took little part in the independence movements during the late nineteenth century or in the fighting that followed the collapse of the Tsarist regime. Many had felt forced to flee following the pogroms that began throughout the Russian Empire in the 1880s. Similarly, they did not take sides between Poland and Lithuania, or in the independence struggles to the north. Many of those prominent in Russian revolutionary activity were Jewish, but this did not influence the local Baltic communities although other groups sometimes used this as a pretext for anti-Semitism.

The Bund, founded in Vilnius in 1897, aimed to unite Jewish workers across the Russian Empire. It was associated with a number of social-democratic movements but wisely it did not link itself to any particular one at that stage. It specifically did not link itself with Zionism, the other Jewish movement founded that year.

Jews, in common with many other communities, moved from the countryside into the towns, where the new industries and a burgeoning middle class offered greater job prospects. The language problem would in due course hinder their progress in local and national administrations, as so few would be able to master a Baltic language at a time when knowledge of German and/or Russian would not be seen as an acceptable substitute. This Jewish community had found themselves part of the Russian Empire after the division of Poland began under Catherine the Great. The Pale of Settlement prevented them from moving north into what would become Estonia and northern Latvia. Even when these restrictions came to be lifted during the nineteenth century, few moved to Estonia, so between the Wars the Jewish population there stayed at around 4,000. The figure was however large enough for them to be granted considerable rights under The Cultural Autonomy Law passed in Estonia in 1925, which enabled them to run schools and to apply for government subsidies for many of their activities.

Whilst Lithuanians have been attacked for alleged complicity in the Holocaust following the German invasion of the USSR, it is often forgotten that, when Memel was seized by the Nazis in March 1939, any Jewish resident there was granted asylum in Lithuania, at a time when most other European countries were refusing admission to them. They felt very fortunate at a time when it was of course impossible for them to foresee their fate in 1941.

Whilst threats from the Soviet Union could easily be contained, those from right-wing movements within became ever more significant in all three countries. Through the 1920s, coalition governments would form and dissolve every few months, providing ample ammunition to those seeking to impose an authoritarian regime, on the grounds that stability was needed. Similar pressures were of course being exerted in most European countries at that time, with the most egregious examples being Italy, Germany and Spain. In the Soviet Union, terror in a different format started with the Holodomor in Ukraine in 1932 and would continue with the purges of the late 1930s. One individual leader dominated each of the three Baltic countries between 1920 and 1940, first working within the democratic system and then subverting it to stay in power. These three were Konstantin Päts in Estonia, Kārlis Ulmanis in Latvia and Antanas Smetona in Lithuania. All would have periods in prison and in exile before coming to power. Soviet historians simply described them as 'fascists' as a justification for their overthrow.

Smetona first came to international prominence when he gave a speech in Berlin in November 1917 proposing an independent Lithuania; its territory would encompass areas where Lithuanian was the predominant language, so there would be no attempt to renew the Polish-Lithuanian Commonwealth which had combined the two nations from 1569 to 1795. However, his stance would shortly be contradicted when he signed the Declaration of Independence in February 1918 in Vilnius, which insisted that Vilnius would be the capital of the new country. Historically, there was a logic to this in that the Grand Dukes presided there through the fourteenth and fifteenth centuries when Lithuanian control stretched to the Black Sea, but by the start of the twentieth century Lithuanian speakers comprised only about 2% of the population, a percentage given in an 1897 census and in one carried out in 1916 during the German occupation. (Polish and Yiddish speakers each comprised 40–50% of the population in both censuses).

Smetona was elected as a provisional president between 1919 and 1920 but then worked largely as a journalist until the coup in 1926 which brought him to power. This coup was planned quickly and Smetona was the clear choice for leader of those involved. For ten years or so, he could rule largely as he pleased, but he was compelled to establish diplomatic relations with Poland in 1938 at a time when frequent demonstrations in the countryside obliged him to increase payments to farmers. The 'loss' of Klaipeda/Memel to Germany in March 1939 was seen as a further sign of weakness and therefore forced him to broaden his cabinet. There would be no subsequent threats to his power until the Soviet invasion in June 1940. He tried to win cabinet support for armed resistance to the Soviet forces, but when this was not forthcoming, he fled with his family firstly to Germany and then to the USA.

Kārlis Ulmanis started planning for his coup in 1931, three years before it took place in May 1934. He was frustrated at what he saw as the slow pace of government, given the plethora of political parties, but it is unlikely that there would have been much opposition to the policies he introduced during his six years as a dictator. Having spent six years of his exile in Nebraska as a student and then as a lecturer in agricultural science, he was clear about the policies needed to support Latvian farmers.

In Estonia, Konstantin Päts acted more quickly; under pressure from VAPS, the League of Freedom Fighters, he allowed a referendum to take place in October 1933 which would grant near dictatorial powers to the president. The League hoped that General Laidoner, the hero of the war against the Russians in 1919, would stand on their behalf, but he did not wish to associate himself with an organisation clearly showing Nazi sympathies. This presidential election never in fact took place, as Päts staged a coup on 12 March 1934 and proclaimed a state of emergency to prevent the election taking place. VAPS was dissolved and 500 of its members were arrested, although they were all released within a few months.

The three leaders hardly knew each other but once they had each seized power, their regimes shared many similarities. The Soviets would justify their removal in 1940 by calling them 'fascists'. At a pinch, this term could perhaps be used for Kārlis Ulmanis, who took ideas for some of his municipal buildings from Italy and liked to describe himself as *Vadonis* ('leader') which had no equivalent in Estonian or in Lithuanian, but which could be seen as a translation of the Italian *Duce*. However, both Päts and Ulmanis specifically proscribed organisations which could be called fascist, VAPS in Estonia and Perkonkrusts in Latvia. Each of these organisations might well have staged a coup had not the two leaders acted first.

In other respects, the label fascist is totally incorrect: mild authoritarianism is perhaps the best description. The three neutered parliament and opposition parties; cultural life was left unscathed, and there was toleration of all religions and minority languages. There were no grand palaces or majestic parades across the country. The three calmly got on with their work and could take advantage of the worldwide economic improvement which followed the depression of the early 1930s. By looking after their agricultural communities and encouraging small businesses in the towns, there was little scope for dissenting voices to gain support. The Baltic-German communities, having been settled in Estonia and Latvia for over 500 years, saw little need to leave after the defeat of the German armies in 1919 and likewise did not feel threatened after the two coups. They could not keep their large estates but could keep their manor houses and their businesses in the major towns. Particularly in the aftermath of World War I, the uncertain future of the Weimar Republic was hardly an attractive proposition given what independent Estonia and Latvia seemed likely to offer. Equally, German attempts to encourage Nazi support groups during the 1930s largely failed, so there were no threats to the Jewish communities.

The three leaders acquiesced in Soviet demands for 'mutual assistance' pacts in the autumn of 1939, which amounted to the acceptance of Soviet garrisons along the coast. This involved the displacement of several local communities, but in other respects a false sense of security endured as the Soviet troops stayed in their barracks and normal life continued. The Molotov-Ribbentrop Pact suggested that there would be no further military activity in Eastern Europe after Poland had been divided between Germany and the Soviet Union, but of course the crucial clause 'allowing' the Baltic countries to fall into the Soviet field of influence was kept secret from them. The Lithuanians were comforted by the return of Vilnius and the surrounding countryside, which the Soviets had just conquered from the Poles.

Few foresaw the further intrusion of June 1940. The Soviet government anticipated minimal, if any, resistance, and the fact that in Latvia and in Estonia the presidents stayed put, suggested that some form of autonomy would continue. Both presidents would soon be taken to the Soviet Union and would die in captivity there. Ruthless and speedy Sovietisation was ended not by local activity but by the German invasion in June 1941. The bitterness of that first year of the Soviet occupation, which culminated in the 14 June 1941 deportations, has remained until this day. It settled the pattern for the occupation regime that would be imposed in 1944 and which lasted until 1991. In 1918–20 the three countries in their different ways were able to exploit the weakness of the German and Russian empires to establish independence. Neither of the successors of these two empires was able to disturb Baltic independence until 1939. The end of this independence was a result of the renewed strength of these two empires and their cooperation detailed in the Molotov-Ribbentrop Pact of 23 August 1939, in which they carved up Eastern Europe into two different spheres of influence. That the three Baltic countries found themselves in the Soviet sphere would dictate their fate until independence was re-established in August 1991.

Given the brutality of the Soviet occupation from June 1940 to June 1941, it is not surprising that the German forces were considered by many outside the Jewish community as liberators. This brutality reached its height on 14 June 1941, just a week before the German invasion, when about 65,000 people were deported from the three countries, largely to Siberia. When the Germans attacked, there was minimal Soviet resistance with Lithuania falling to them within hours; Riga was then reached on 1 July. By the time the Germans reached Estonia, some Soviet resistance was organised but, by the end of August, the whole mainland was occupied. Whilst Soviet troops retreated hurriedly and chaotically, looting and destroying as they did so, German forces are remembered for paying for whatever they needed. They were soon able to delegate administration to locals who had survived the Soviet purges and they allowed small-scale private enterprise and a return to cultural diversity. However, the Jewish population would immediately be made to suffer at an intensity which would only reach the rest of occupied Europe after the Wannsee Conference in January 1942. The burning of the Great Choral Synagogue in Riga on 4 July, with the congregation and refugees inside it, was the precursor to mass killings which would take place in concentration camps set up in each of the three countries.

The return of the Red Army early in 1944 was resisted strongly by both the Germans and local forces. Much of Western Latvia was in fact never conquered during the war, only falling into Russian hands after the German surrender in May 1945. This resistance gave time for many local people to flee by boat to Sweden or to retreat with the German forces. Between 18 October and 22 October 1944, Tallinn was in Estonian hands, the Germans having left, and the Soviets not yet having arrived. This meant that Soviet forces overthrew an Estonian government, not a German occupation, a fact which subsequent Soviet and Russian historians would always ignore.

In the early years of the Soviet reoccupation, there was an expectation that Western countries would help to liberate the Baltics. This was not on their agenda, with support being limited to recognition of the Baltic governments now in exile, who were allowed to maintain their embassies. In what were now three Soviet provinces, resistance was entirely local and largely in the hands of the Forest Brothers, guerrilla bands based in the countryside who could rely on supplies and discretion from the local population. The frequent references in the government-controlled press to 'bandits' show how effective they were in the immediate aftermath of the war. However, by the early 1950s, with the Soviet authorities controlling every aspect of work and private life, it was impossible for anyone to have an unregistered existence and the few who tried to were eventually arrested and sentenced to long terms of imprisonment.

The First Secretaries imposed from Moscow were from the local communities but usually had a background in pre-War communist activity and some had retreated with the Soviet forces in 1941. They therefore had extensive training in what was required of them. Few are remembered now as anything more than 'Yestonians' in all three countries, such was their acceptance of diktats from Moscow and the dullness of their public speeches.

Perhaps Antanas Sniečkus, First Secretary in Lithuania from 1940 until his death in 1974, deserves a mention. Whilst more Stalinist than Stalin until the mid 1950s in his enthusiasm for deportations and killings, he then mellowed and succeeded in keeping out an influx of Russian speakers and the industrialisation of Lithuania which would have changed the country irrevocably. Karl Vaino, the totally inert First Secretary in Estonia from 1978 to 1988, had to suffer the indignity of 150,000 people turning out to celebrate his dismissal. (His grandson, Anton Vaino, became Putin's Chief of Staff in 2016, a post he still holds at the time of writing, October 2022).

Estonia and Lithuania in different ways managed from the 1960s to establish links with the outside world. A ferry link twice a week was established in 1965 between Helsinki and Tallinn. Of course, very few Estonians were allowed to use it, but the regular influx of Finnish tourists ensured that dissident literature and locally unavailable consumer goods could reach the local population. Soon afterwards, it became possible to receive Finnish television in much of the country, so every evening Estonians were brought in touch with Western politics and culture. The staging in Tallinn of the sailing events linked to the Moscow Olympics in 1980 introduced many Estonians to foreigners for the first time.

In Lithuania, Catholicism remained strong despite Soviet attempts to marginalise it. Religious tracts could be brought in from Poland and Keston College in the UK became a crucial link with churches abroad for the local brave clergy, ensuring that whatever samizdat literature could be smuggled out of the country would be widely circulated. Solidarity activity in Poland from the 1970s became known in Lithuania and could give hope for change after the crushing of the Prague Spring in 1968 suggested the opposite. Latvia had no equivalent to any of these links which its neighbours could establish. Riga, which had been the largest and busiest of the Baltic ports in the interwar period, was now the most isolated.

The policies of perestroika and glasnost, introduced by Gorbachev from 1985, were immediately taken up in the three countries. Thanks to television, the regular appearance of the old national flags at demonstrations became an illustration of the changes underway which could then be seen around the world. However, the Moscow government would never understand, or perhaps would never want to understand, why the three Baltic provinces could not accept this status and why only full independence was their goal. The failed coup against Gorbachev in August 1991 provided the catalyst that was needed. The still existing Soviet government and the emerging Russian one both gave immediate recognition to the three Baltic governments. The restoration of independence was now finally assured.

PART II

THE INTERNATIONAL CONTEXT

3

THE BALTIC STATES, RUSSIA AND EUROPE'S ORDER

1917–1991–2022

Professor Kristina Spohr

In early spring 2022, war once more returned to Europe.

Thirty years had passed since the peaceful disintegration of the Soviet empire; thirty years since the re-establishment of Baltic independence.

Hope had bloomed in 1992 for a new departure in European and indeed world politics. It seemed that the world had exited the Cold War in a genuine spirit of cooperation. Diplomacy and dialogue had triumphed.

Russia's new leader, Boris Yeltsin, and US President George H.W. Bush had proclaimed a new era of 'friendship and partnership' founded on 'mutual trust and respect' and a 'common commitment to democracy and economic freedom' as they declared a formal end to seven decades of rivalry. Yeltsin went even further speaking of America and the West not merely as 'partners' but even 'allies.'[1]

Yeltsin explicitly called 'for cooperation, cooperation for the whole world,' because, he said, 'if the reform in Russia goes under, that means there will be a cold war', which then 'is going to turn into a hot war.'[2] Sadly, his words have come true.

Three decades on, all dreams of a Russo-Western Alliance have long evaporated, and there is no talk of partnership. Far from it. On 24 February 2022, Russia's armed forces invaded Ukraine. This blatant act of aggression marked a major escalation of a conflict that first erupted in 2014 with Russia's annexation of the Crimea and its backing of the separatist territories in the Donbass.

Putin's real target, however, is the European order, that of a 'Europe whole and free and at peace,'[3] created under American aegis after the end of the Cold War. To Putin, it is an 'empire of lies', one, so he said on the first day of war, that has tried to 'put the final squeeze on us, finish us off, and utterly destroy us.'[4]

To countries like Estonia, Latvia, and Lithuania—Baltic states that struggled for much of the twentieth century to escape Russian domination—that European order is the touchstone of their freedom.

It was during the 'hinge years' of 1989–1991, as the world *peacefully* moved out of the Cold War and Mikhail Gorbachev sought to reform the USSR, that the Baltics seized the chance to re-establish their independence—statehoods first gained in 1918 after the Russian Revolution, then lost as a consequence of the 1939 Hitler-Stalin Pact. Beyond their legalistic approach to restore full sovereignty over their territories, theirs was famously the 'Singing Revolution',[5] a non-conflictual, political-cultural assertion of nationhood and self-determination.[6]

It was after the failed August coup in 1991 that they finally regained international recognition as independent states—a couple of months before the USSR disintegrated altogether.[7] In 2004, Estonia, Latvia and Lithuania were welcomed into the 'institutional West'—becoming members of both the EU and NATO.

But now in 2022, yet again they fear for their existence. Because they believe that Ukraine is only a part of Putin's brutal *Anschluss*-agenda. Next might well be other parts of the Russian 'near abroad', the rim of former Soviet republics with significant Russian minorities (among which Putin counts the Balts).[8]

This is something Estonians, Latvians and Lithuanians have feared for three decades—that Russia might again impose its 'empire', by force. And yet, there are two key differences compared with nineteenth and early twentieth century imperial power politics.

First, that Western umbrella. In the 1930s the United States refused to get entangled with Europe. Now, its security frontier is Estonia, Latvia, and Lithuania. Then Britain recoiled from protecting Czechoslovakia in its struggle against Nazi Germany— described by Neville Chamberlain in September 1938 as 'a quarrel in a faraway country, between people of whom we know nothing.'[9] Today a British Cabinet Minister can say that his country will go to war if a 'single Russian toecap' enters NATO territory.[10]

So, let me look briefly at what these Baltic contested borderlands have meant and mean for Russia and for the West in 1917–1991–2022. For it is here, in the lands of still young nation-states founded just over a century ago, that the age-old question arises—now even more acutely—of where the line is to be drawn between East and West, between Russia's sphere of influence and the space dominated by Western great powers, and more recently Western institutional structures and values.

After all, in the course of the twentieth and twenty-first centuries, they came to epitomise the significance of universal recognition of the equal rights and independent agency of small states in the community of nations, the values of the UN Charter of 1945 and the Helsinki Final Act of 1975. Will these still be upheld in our troubled successor century?

* * *

Only five years ago, Britain fixated not on 1991, but on the centenary of the Russian Revolution of 1917 and the ending of the First World War in 1918. Ironically, there was very little awareness here of the crucial significance of those years for people in Estonia, Latvia, and Lithuania. For these nations 1917 and 1918 are supremely the years of independence. They fought brutal wars against the Red Army to avoid being pulled back into the Russian Empire, now dressed up in Soviet colours. Indeed, only in 1920, did the USSR formally recognize the existence of the three Baltic States *de jure* by signing peace treaties. Yet, their independence remained tenuous, as they faced the challenge of constructing independent, stable and prosperous democracies. What ensued was state-building—in the multiple realms of culture, society, economics, and politics.[11]

These largely agrarian societies underwent modernisation and industrialisation. Land reforms swept away the German barons in Estonia and Latvia, likewise the Polish gentry in Lithuania. Although the export staples of these countries remained grain, timber, flax and livestock, new industries and new currencies facilitated a turn to Western markets. With Britain and Germany as the major trading partners, this new triangle reflected the Baltics' ability to act freely from Russia and underlined how much they were becoming part of the European system.

The political scene, however, was very unstable in the interwar Baltic arena. In all three states, multiparty coalitions were short-lived and kept breaking apart. And by the late 1920s—as in East-Central Europe but unlike the pattern in Finland—nationalist authoritarian regimes began to emerge. In Estonia and Latvia these were partly intended to head off embryonic fascist movements—notably the *Pērkonkrusts*. But in Lithuania, the ultra-nationalist *Tautininkai*, which formed the ruling party from 1926 to 1940, itself spawned a fascist movement known as the Iron Wolf.

The Baltic Three found it difficult to achieve viable security cooperation, because Estonia and Latvia were status quo powers, while Lithuania was locked in territorial disputes with Poland. Lithuanians also had an elevated sense of their past, dating back to the huge Polish-Lithuanian Commonwealth of the early-modern era which, at its largest extent in the seventeenth century, stretched from the Baltic virtually to the Black Sea. Lithuania's Catholic heritage further distinguished it from the largely Protestant and more northern-oriented Estonians and Latvians, who traditionally had looked to Sweden and the Baltic Sea, with a strong German overlay from the days of the Teutonic Knights and the Hanseatic League.[12]

Yet the Baltic trio's fundamental problem was geopolitics. Their aspirations for neutrality were almost doomed to failure because these were small countries trapped between two assertive and revisionist powers, Nazi Germany and Stalinist Russia, each of whom—for much of the 1930s—seemed on the verge of destroying the other.

The fate of the Baltics was eventually determined by great-power politics. First, the failure of talks for an Anglo-French alliance with the Soviet Union during spring and early summer of 1939, and then the surprise conclusion of the Hitler-Stalin Pact in August 1939. The latter, crucially, handed over the three Baltic States, together with Finland and eastern Poland, to the Soviets. The Poles were gobbled up by Germany and Soviet Russia in September 1939; the Finns, by contrast, managed to resist the USSR in the Winter War of 1939/40 and maintained their independent statehood through the Continuation War of 1941/44 and beyond, though not without significant territorial losses in Karelia and Petsamo.

The three Baltic States, by 'silently submitting,' allowed a swift Soviet annexation in June 1940. For them, the rest of the Second World War constituted a 'double occupation'—first Soviet rule until June 1941, then German control until the spring of 1944, when the Red Army's Baltic campaign brought them once more back into the Soviet orbit. The Soviet 'annexation occupation' (*Annexionsbesetzung*) of 1945 was never recognized *de jure* by most Western governments, while the Kremlin treated them as constituent republics of the Soviet Union.[13]

* * *

As a consequence of war and occupation, the population of the Baltics had shrunk by a quarter. Between 1940 and 1953 some ten percent of the native Balts had been deported to the gulags or forcibly resettled to Siberia. Meanwhile, in a deliberate strategy to destroy the Baltic nations (not just stealing their statehood) Stalin 'Russified' Baltic lands.[14]

Between 1945 and 1991, the Baltic peoples—to survive culturally as much as politically—responded to Soviet occupation by leading double lives. It was a tactic that ultimately played an important role in hastening the Soviet Union's demise and therefore needs some closer examination.

To be sure, from the Kremlin's perspective Estonia, Latvia and Lithuania represented a kind of 'Soviet West'—a place of privilege and relative prosperity within the Union. But for Moscow, the Baltic nations also served to demonstrate the richness of Soviet culture—'socialist in content and national in form.' This was the Union's diversity of folklore the Communist Party liked to showcase, both at home and abroad. So, the Soviet system left a strong imprint on daily life in the Baltic republics.

Crucially, in the relative privacy of the home, the Baltic peoples kept alive their native languages and traditions and memories of life in the inter-war republics. They cherished, even idealised, the concept of independence like a lost paradise. This perspective was enhanced by ties to the outside world. On a human level there were close contacts to the Baltic émigré communities in North America and Western Europe. What's more, Estonians along the coast could watch Finnish TV, while Latvians held onto their strong cultural ties with German Balts; likewise Lithuanians with Poland and the Catholic Church. The Cold War iron curtain was distinctly permeable.[15]

In the Baltics, this double life played a central role in the unraveling of the Soviet experiment. Gorbachev saw the Baltic showcase as a prime laboratory for his policy of perestroika—trying out radical economic restructuring and allowing the republics greater autonomy in introducing market reforms. Encouraged by perestroika and glasnost, Baltic intellectuals seized the opportunity to organize themselves politically. Ironically, Gorbachev's political devolution allowed the burgeoning national independence movements to gain political legitimacy, thereby soon posing a serious challenge to the Kremlin.

As in the inter-war years of state-building, national consciousness was fostered by linguistic reassertion (the new language laws in 1988/89 giving primacy to Estonian, Latvian and Lithuanian over Russian). And glasnost also allowed space for memory politics. History wars ensued between Moscow and Tallinn, Riga and Vilnius—most evident in the massive Baltic chain demonstration of August 1989 to publicly commemorate the fiftieth anniversary of the Hitler-Stalin Pact and the resulting Soviet annexation of the three republics in 1940. Indeed, their political claims for re-establishing independence were grounded in carefully formulated legal arguments. The central assertion was that, despite 1940, the Baltic States had never lost their status as subjects of international law. Theirs was a historical *de jure* claim that had been rhetorically supported throughout the Cold War by the key Western states.[16]

Not that Western governments ever proactively pursued a Baltic policy or sought to interfere in intra-Soviet affairs. As in the case of Budapest 1956, Berlin 1961, Prague 1968, Warsaw 1980/81, America and its allies focused by and large on Soviet containment.

The Baltic question, like the German question, reappeared in 1989/90 on the international agenda as an unresolved post-war issue in the turmoil of the Cold War endgame. Unlike his dealings over German reunification, however, Gorbachev—a fierce defender of the USSR and its constitution—did not allow the Baltic states to *regain* their statehood.[17]

Independence declarations after the first free elections by the new People's Congresses in these SSRs in spring 1990 were followed by an energy boycott, and in early 1991, in Vilnius the Riga military force was used in a crackdown. In fact, Soviet tanks and special forces moved into Vilnius, while the West was focused on UN sanctioned military campaign to free Kuwait from Iraqi occupation.[18]

Gorbachev's inability, even unwillingness, to find a solution to the Baltic problem was one catalyst for the coup against him in August 1991, the failure of which, in turn, precipitated the disintegration of the Soviet Union at the end of 1991.

To be sure, the Soviet Union might well have survived without the three small Baltic republics, had Gorbachev let them break away earlier on the basis of their special (historic) position in the Union. But he did not; and he was certainly not pressured, because the West said fairly little until the bloodshed in Vilnius. Too great was the general fear of Soviet descent into anarchy and inter-ethnic strife, of a military-backed reactionary coup, or of uncontrolled total collapse in the USSR. The Western political focus on peace, stability, and territorial integrity—all embodied by the Soviet leader Gorbachev—then evidently trumped their legalistic rhetoric of upholding the non-recognition policies of

Baltic annexation and the UN and Commission on Security and Cooperation in Europe (CSCE), principle of self-determination.

As things played out, Gorbachev's problem was not only the loss of the Soviet periphery but, crucially, the danger of losing the heartland itself. There could be no Soviet entity without Russia (and Ukraine). Here, in its final consequence, the personal and systemic challenge posed by the separatist Russian Federation led by Boris Yeltsin (who in winter 1991 sided with the Balts), was of critical importance.[19]

* * *

After the surprisingly quiet crumbling of the Soviet empire in 1989/91, the European mosaic—as in the 1920s—had to be pieced together again. The Baltics now had to find their place in a post-Cold War Europe that was utterly different from the Europe seventy years earlier.

They initially flirted with the idea of neutrality, of becoming 'three little Finlands'. But then they made a firm decision to openly turn westward. Their goal: to join both the EU and NATO, committing themselves fully to the institutional West. This they were finally able to do so in 2004.[20]

It was later than they had hoped but they first had to undertake a major transformation—economically from economic plans and into the market, politically from the Soviet state structures and into the full panoply of parliamentary democracy. Alongside these changes, they also needed to manage currency reform and new social policies, as well as negotiating with Russia about borders and Red Army withdrawal. Particularly vexed was the issue of citizenship, of how to deal fairly with the large Russian minorities in their countries.

The Baltic turn west in the 1990s was part of a general integration of East and Central Europe into the post-Cold War 'West'. They steadily followed the pattern of contemporary politics in Germany and the Nordic States—in contrast to the eventual lurch to the populist right as witnessed in Hungary, Poland and Austria over the past decade.[21]

Often overlooked in the West, was the situation in Putin's Russia since 2000. Putin was no crypto-communist; but he had never accepted the loss of the Soviet 'Near Abroad.'[22] Indeed for him the fall of the Soviet Union was nothing less than the 'greatest geopolitical catastrophe of the twentieth century.'[23] With his hold on domestic power assured after 2012, Putin felt free to concentrate on foreign policy—annexing the Crimea, waging hybrid warfare in eastern Ukraine, intervening in Syria, and mounting cyber campaigns against Western elections. All the while, to justify his actions, he complained about NATO's betrayal of supposed promises never to enlarge NATO made in 1990 and of the Alliance's 'encirclement' of Russia. He even treated the EU as a challenge, if not an all-out adversary.[24]

Among the new NATO members, the Baltics always lay on the front line of Putin's aggressive security policy. They are plagued by perennial Russian airspace incursions and attempts to hack government networks. Military exercises along Russia's western border—such as *Zapad* ('The West')—are commonplace, and Russian propaganda on TV and social media seek to arouse disaffection among Russian minorities.[25]

To exacerbate the Baltics' sense of insecurity, Putin has been building up Russia's post-1945 enclave of Kaliningrad as a major military base and home to a new generation of short-range nuclear missiles that have been visibly transported down the Baltic. And to make his point about Russia's global reach and the Baltic Sea's strategic importance, in 2017 he invited the Chinese fleet to conduct joint naval exercises right outside Kaliningrad.[26]

Finally, history is a vital weapon in Putin's foreign policy.[27] Although he did not make much of the one-hundredth of the Bolshevik revolution in 2017, he used it to celebrate the grandeur of Russia back to Peter the Great with a huge naval parade in his hometown of St Petersburg.[28] And in February 2018 the Russian armed forces marked the centenary of the Red Army with a big display in Ivangorod, just across the bridge from the Estonian border city of Narva.

On the face of it, to many these aspects looked like posturing and sabre-rattling. But Putin—always the KGB man—showed he understood the power of history as intimidation. In 2016 he characterized the Bolsheviks' policy of nationalities' self-determination as a disaster: 'They planted an atomic bomb under the building that is called Russia.' In his view, Lenin got it totally wrong when he championed the independence of nations as part of his bigger scheme of spreading world revolution—because this allowed, amongst others, the Finns and the Balts to leave the Russian Empire.[29]

As he prepared for war, he rehashed this argument also in his address after Russia's Security Council meeting on 21 February 2022, where he extremely angrily and passionately argued Lenin was to blame for 'separating, severing what is historically Russian land.' And he described Gorbachev's decision to give Ukraine the right to become independent of the Soviet Union 'without any conditions', as just 'crazy.'[30]

For him, Gorbachev was neither a reformer nor a peacemaker or peace-preserver, but a traitor who lost Russia's historic empire. Because, in the 1991 'catastrophe', he had sold out the Soviet Union, which liberated Europe from the Nazis and for nearly half a century had stood as one of the two pillars of global power, leaving Russia as an international irrelevance.

None too subtly, Putin's words on Lenin's mistakes and Gorbachev's failures, as well as all his talk of Russia's 1,000-year history[31] then leave a question marks, too, over Baltic independence—especially when combined with his perennial attempts to rehabilitate the Hitler-Stalin Pact.[32]

What's more, Putin's most recent claim of supposedly 'repeat-ing'[33] Stalin's triumph over the Nazis as he urges victory in Ukraine[34] while justifying his territorial 'annexation' drive as a 'reclamation' or 'restoration' of what historically belongs to Russia—à la Tsar Peter the Great in the long Great Northern Wars—can leave us in no doubt as to his wider neo-imperial goals. Not least when we take note, that in almost the same breath, he suggested that through its actions, Russia was now taking its place in a 'new world order'—one whose rules would be set by 'strong and sovereign states.'[35]

* * *

With his act of aggression against a neighbouring country, Putin has lifted the curtain on a new era of uncertainty and instability. In this, power and the classic instruments of power politics will occupy a central position. Imperial thinking in Moscow is back not just in words but in deeds. And once again in European history, the continent's fate is being determined by a great power struggle for control of key strategic borderlands.

Putin's demands for security guarantees from the USA (over the heads of Europeans) and his choice for war in 2022 has already woken Germany from its thirty-year geopolitical slumber. For now, Germany's apparent awakening gives the whole of the EU greater unity and strength. Furthermore, the institutional 'West', which is deploying its economic and military power for a geopolitical purpose, does for the first time in history include the small countries to the east and north east of Germany.

Whether this institutional framework of EU and NATO will help secure the Baltics' existence remains to be seen. Also, whether these three small, but perennially strategic, states can help defend the normative European regime in which their statehood and the western order is anchored—though Finland's and Sweden's steps to become full Alliance members in the nearest future are bound to strengthen the region militarily as well as politically.[36]

For our generation, after what we have seen and heard in the last few weeks and months, Ukraine will never be 'a faraway country' inhabited by people 'of whom we know nothing.'

And now, with war ongoing and Russo-Western tensions worsening,[37] the Baltic States (and the Baltic Sea area at large) are moving from periphery to centre stage. So, we shall watch this space. Because it is a moving target.

4

ATTAINING BALTIC INDEPENDENCE

IN SEARCH OF A HELPING HAND

Professor Jonathan Haslam

The Baltic States emerged as independent states out of luck as much as good will on the part of the Great Powers assembled in Paris to make the peace early in 1919. The Royal Navy, as part of the allied war of intervention to overthrow the Bolsheviks, ensured that the Baltic did not fall to the enemy. And with his accustomed tactical agility their leader, Vladmir Il'yich (Lenin), decided in September 1919 to recognise the sovereignty of the three fledgling states as a means of disarming the bourgeois world in its hostility to the new régime in Russia.[1] This was the birth of a new foreign policy doctrine: that of 'peaceful co-existence' (*mirnoe sozhitel'stvo*)—dropping open inter-state warfare for class warfare conducted by the Communist International from Moscow. The Balts were thus the first unintended beneficiaries of rivals—Soviet Russia and Great Britain—in conflict.

Thereafter Latvia, Estonia and Lithuania were left to their own devices by the Great Powers until the 1930s, when, with the rise of Nazi Germany and the rearmament of the Soviet Union threw their continued existence into jeopardy. The Nazi-Soviet non-aggression pact of August 1939 contained within it a secret protocol allowing for Soviet predominance over Latvia and Estonia. The Friendship Pact in late September added Lithuania. After war broke out in Europe following Germany's invasion of Poland, the Russians had already negotiated their way into garrisoning the Baltic States. People's Commissar for Foreign Affairs Vyacheslav Molotov was dismissive of them: 'peas against a wall', he quipped in the course of negotiations. Only Finland had resisted and was attacked in late November. Meanwhile, Germany conquered most of Western Europe. Britain alone successfully held the Germans at bay. Alarmed at the speed and effectiveness of the German advance, and having made peace with Finland, in June 1940 the Red Army marched in to transform the Baltic States, at one time Tsarist provinces, into Soviet republics.[2]

Unlike neighbouring and neutral Sweden, for whom the Baltic Sea was not some distant expanse of water but their own sea-board—the *Ostsee*—the British and the Americans never saw any compelling need to recognise Soviet sovereignty over the Baltic States. But non-recognition was also convenient. After World War II the Northern Department of Britain's secret service, MI6, under Alexander McKibbin, recruited exiles from the Baltic with the promise of liberation as sources of secret intelligence and as a promising means of subverting Stalin's empire.

From 1947, MI6 ran operations from its residency in Stockholm, headed by a Lettish (Latvian) emigré; Sweden was rapidly filling up with refugees, mostly from Estonia. Soviet counter-intelligence forces were waiting for the boats as they motored in under cover of darkness, turned the occupants against their British sponsors and, where they resisted, wiped them out.[3] The 'operational games' played by the collaborationists to make MI6 believe they were still working against the Russians continued for a decade until the British realised what was going on and finally gave up.[4] At MI6, Daphne Park supervised operations from her diplomatic cover as second secretary at the British embassy in Moscow from 1954 to 1956.[5] What London eventually conceded, however, was that within the Soviet Union the issue of nationalities was dead in the water from political hypothermia. A reflection of this could be found within the US bureaucracy, where Paul Goble at the Bureau of Intelligence and Research (INR) and CIA was left in perfect peace to research the Soviet nationalities in as much depth as he liked but with blanket indifference to his findings from those who paid his salary.[6]

Only in 1988–9 did the issue burst into life again when the Soviet Union underwent upheaval. Those two years were not only the high point of Mikhail Gorbachev's perestroika, but 1989 was also the fiftieth anniversary of both Nazi-Soviet pacts; a sore point for the Baltic States, whose twenty-year history of independence ended abruptly with the arrival of the Red Army. November 1989 also saw the Berlin Wall collapse. The time had come to cleanse the past of its Stalinist stains.

In April of that year Anatoly Chernyaev, Gorbachev's foreign policy advisor, submitted to him a long memorandum written by an old friend, Vyacheslav Dashichev. Dashichev headed the international relations department of the Institute for the Economics of the World Socialist System, a closed think tank set up by Yuri Andropov in the early sixties to think the unthinkable. As a colonel in military intelligence, Dashichev, who edited the highly classified journal *Voennaya mysl'*, had been dismissed from the General Staff for supporting the historian Alexander Nekrich in exposing Stalin's failure to anticipate war in June 1941. He was rescued by Oleg Bogomolov who headed the Institute. The

Institute had top level clearance. Every embassy in the world socialist system has its institute man who reported both to Smolenskaya and to Dashichev's department. Few knew better how rotten the GDR was than he did. And not only did Dashichev argue the case for German reunification, he also advocated the liberation of the Baltic States. To long serving Germanists like Valentin Falin, who headed the International Department of the Central Committee and had the last word on the subject, Dashichev was a very dangerous heretic who should be silenced. What made him so infuriating was that he had top level access to classified material, was a veteran and also the son of one of Stalin's senior commanders and victims. The little-known point of all this is that Dashichev did not advocate merely German reunification, he also called for the liberation of the Baltic States.[7]

The Baltic housed the early warning systems principally guarding against lethal US forward based fighter bombers— F-111/F111A and from 1992 the F-15E—attacking from East Anglia, which, given the notorious inefficiency of Soviet air defences exposed by the arrival in Red Square by the plane of the young Mattias Rust in May 1987, presented an alarming threat against which there was minimal protection. To those charged with the defence of the Soviet Union, this must have seemed Dashichev's most irresponsible recommendation; particularly once the US war opposing Saddam Hussein's invasion of Kuwait (2 August 1990 to 28 February 1991) demonstrated on CNN the extraordinary effectiveness of US air power at low altitude; cruise missiles in particular. An official Swedish assessment written in mid-September 1991 noted that 'The experiences of the Iraq War last winter must have caused the Russian military to worry, increasing their concern from this perspective.'[8] According to other Swedish military experts, Russia 'would be particularly unwilling to give up the radar installations at Skrunda in Latvia, due to their military importance and the enormous investment.'[9] It had been built as a tiny self-contained secret base area in 1963, garrisoned by the 129th Radio Technical Unit and surrounded by 100 acres of woodland. Construction had been under way since 1985 for the Daryal UM Radar but was still incomplete when independence was achieved; though the Russians did not finally leave till 1995.[10] These installations were run with minimal personnel, so their protection in an independent country in the event of trouble would have required extensive military contingents of troops.

The issue of national self-determination was most certainly problematic, as always after colonisation, but especially so in the Baltic because of extensive Russian settlement following the Second World War. Whereas, in 1939, Estonia had an overwhelmingly native population at 92%, by 1989 it had fallen to 62%. Whereas Latvia had a native population in 1939 at 77%, by 1989 it had dropped to just over half at 52.5%. Only Lithuania actually increased its nationals: pre-war at 76% and post-war, 81%.[11] Resentment was thus easily turned against those who had decided to settle there. Gorbachev had already been told by his own specialists that the nationalities of the Soviet Union were anything but content with their lot. In the summer of 1985, he was briefed by the KGB—it had a thirty strong 2nd Department of the Fifth Directorate under Yuri Kobyakov—to that effect. Gorbachev confessed himself 'astonished' at what he heard.[12] But he had more important matters on his mind. It did not seem of great significance. And when the leading advocates of national liberation enthusiastically took up the issue of perestroika Gorbachev thought the problem solved. But there was a stone in this appetising fruit.

When the wall came tumbling down on 9 November 1989 and he was persuaded a couple of months later to support the right of nationalities to secede from the Union, Gorbachev never really expected the Balts, or, indeed anyone else, to run for the door or even edge their way in that direction. I well remember the delirious reception he received in Milan at the end of November when he went walkabout. It was shown live on Soviet television. Suddenly the mood changed. A Balt challenged him on the need for independence. 'Why?', Gorbachev demanded to know. Well, came the unanticipated answer, we do not even have enough *kolbasa*—garlic sausage—to eat (the lowest common denominator after bread and butter in the Soviet diet). Gorbachev fumed. 'You would break up the Union for sausage?', he scowled. It was, to say the least, an unhelpful retort.

But what was the attitude of the United States towards all this? As president, Ronald Reagan, had declared in favour of Baltic independence back in 1983. Inside the State Department the one man that held these states within his compass was upgraded in 1987. But more important issues necessarily took precedent: not least the thorny issue of German reunification. In the face of the meltdown of the Warsaw Pact alliance in Central/Eastern Europe, would Gorbachev even survive perestroika? Whereas Reagan was prepared to take inordinate risks, his successor, George Bush '41, had had enough of that, having been a war hero flying fighter planes from aircraft carriers in the Pacific. He subsequently forged an entire career out of playing safe. Moreover, his experience of being number two to Reagan had been so deeply humiliating that after inauguration, and with one exception, James Baker, he vengefully dismissed everyone who had served his predecessor so loyally in the White House.

As one might imagine, this had a deadening effect on the Washington bureaucracy. It followed the advice given in the event of a nuclear attack: 'duck and cover.' No one would take the slightest risk of being noticed, any controversial new information that could draw too much attention to its provenance was simply suppressed, and the taciturn national security adviser,

General Brent Scowcroft, whom Bush had befriended, was well matched: he too had made a successful career by not sticking his head above the parapet. Despite his height he too easily passed unnoticed in a room of smaller men. And as Secretary of State the hard-headed Baker took the narrowest view of what constituted the US national interest. So, this was not the time to air radical options for the White House to peruse. The fact that the CIA under Russianist Robert Gates took the most pessimistic view of Gorbachev's prospects meant that everything that happened came as a complete surprise.

Thus, in relation to the Baltic republics the initiative fell to neighbouring Sweden, whose diplomats later described their policy as 'ankpolitik'—like a duck, serene and unruffled on the surface but 'paddling like hell underneath' to keep afloat in face of the coming storm.[13] After the Berlin Wall fell, the Swedish General Consul in Leningrad was 'clear that the whole Baltic will attain independence.' 'For Sweden', Dag Sebastian Ahlander wrote, advocating extensive aid to the Baltic, 'it is nothing more or less than a political revolution that is taking place in the North—the first in our lifetime.' He compared it to the 1848 revolutions in Europe. This was an opportunity unique to Sweden, which took full advantage of it, short of confrontation with Moscow. Estonia and Latvia had historic ties that went as far back as the so-called 'good times'. Sweden had taken the greatest number of Estonian refugees in 1945, second only to Germany. Sweden was also non-aligned 'and thus less of a provocation [to the Soviet Union] than other countries like Germany and the United States.'[14] The outlook was, however, very uncertain. In a tour d'horizon the Swedes faced the alternative prospects of chaos, possible dictatorship in Russia leading to open conflict, muddling through, or co-operation with the emergent European Union—essentially Germany.[15]

Under Chancellor Helmut Kohl (Christian Democratic Union) and Foreign Minister Hans-Dietrich Genscher (Free

Democratic Party), a degree of caution was essential. Until German reunification had been secured and the Soviet Group of Forces in Germany had been withdrawn to the Soviet Union, it would not have been wise to bait the bear. The Baltic States had led the way in the movement for national independence from the Soviet Union; not surprisingly, perhaps, in view of the fact that they were the last addition to the long suite of republics. They were also the most respected as in many ways they were more advanced, more European if you like, than any of the others. If it was manufactured in the Baltic, it was taken to be a mark of quality. The power of example they set was therefore inflammatory, however they secured definitive independence.

From Moscow, Germany's ambassador Klaus Blech expressed a view commonly held among the reformers supporting Gorbachev: 'What is certain is that independence efforts in the Baltic States only have a chance of success if the extremely unstable process of democratization and liberalization within Russia can be consolidated.'[16] Kohl told Britain's Foreign Secretary Douglas Hurd: 'The problem is that the independence of the Baltic states would soon be followed by the Ukraine. The break-up of the Soviet Union cannot be in our interests...in that event we would only face more difficulties.'[17] So Germany effectively did nothing.

Of course, Germany was important, but the United States was the biggest player in the game and with the most to lose in relation to the future of the Soviet Union, whose thermonuclear capability matched that of the American equivalent. It had even greater cause to do nothing. To the Assistant to the President for National Security Affairs, General Brent Scowcroft, these were not just 'heroic little people.' 'The Baltic lobbies' were, in his words, 'very strong.' This 'put us in a box. We had very little freedom of action.' The dilemma was that 'We also saw that the Baltics were the possible occasion for an internal eruption inside the Soviet Union—if they were allowed to break free.' And the fate of the Gorbachev régime was in jeopardy. At the Malta summit on 2–3 December 1989 Bush had gently warned Gorbachev against the use of force, but, as Scowcroft recalled, 'We had no capability, in fact, to help the Baltics.' And Baker, an old-fashioned *étatiste*, had little time for what were to him a matter of only minor concern. When Bush, very much a consensus politician, gathered together senior members of the government, the heads of other departments, they 'were not at all interested...They all brushed aside the arguments in favour of the Baltics.' It did not help matters that the leader of the Lithuanian movement Sąjūdis, Vytautas Landsbergis, an outstanding national chess player, was, in respect of the Russians, 'throwing gasoline on a flame.'[18]

Lithuania was always the first and the boldest of the three Baltic States, the Sąjūdis movement having won the elections to the Supreme Soviet in March 1990. They announced the country's independence. The Kremlin responded with a blockade of petrol supplies, which lasted ten months. When the Lithuanian leaders were invited to Moscow to negotiate in August, they actually refused to leave the plane until Gorbachev arrived in case they were taken into custody; memories of how the Czech leaders were treated in 1968 could not have been far from their minds. In December, Vilnius radio and television ceased broadcasting in Russian. After all, 81% of the population were native to Lithuania.

On 10 January 1991, Gorbachev issued an ultimatum demanding that the authorities revert to the status quo. On the following day soldiers from the Vilnius garrison turned out to seize administrative buildings and communications hubs. In response to advanced warning from a source at the Central Committee building in Moscow, Landsbergis called the population out onto the streets to protect parliament and the telecommunications tower in the suburbs. The Vilnius motor-cycle division was called to arms. Gorbachev sent in 3,000 men from the 76th (Pskov) Guards Parachute division. Mikhail Golovanov, head of the anti-terrorist Alfa group of special forces, had come in three days before Gorbachev's ultimatum to reconnoitre the objectives they were to secure.

On 13 January, at a base to the north of the capital, Deputy Defence Minister Colonel General Vladislav Achalov explained that Defence Minister General Dmitrii Yazov had the go-ahead for the operation from Gorbachev. Achalov went on to brief commanders as to the mission. Inevitably shooting broke out once these forces advanced on their objectives. The young Alfa group officer, Lt. Shatskikh, who was shot in taking the tower, took a bullet from an AK-74 5.45mm rifle which was used by Vilnius special forces (OMON). From this alone it appears that at least some on the Soviet side wished to spill blood through provocation. More than 108 citizens were wounded and nine killed by the time the tower was taken; some crushed by tanks.[19]

The blow to the reputation of perestroika and the deep sense of shame was tangible. Moreover, the impact was long lasting as it was this overt display of force in Vilnius which galvanised the countries of Central and Eastern Europe into applying for NATO membership. The Swedish general consul in Russia's second city wrote that 'For natives of Leningrad this comes as an extra bitter blow. They know that they should really be able to become part of the West if it were not for the hateful Asians in Moscow.'[20] Evidently Gorbachev was persuaded that he could save the Soviet Union, instead this one intemperate act hastened its demise. Encouraged by their ability to rally their forces in time of need and despairing of Gorbachev's humane instincts, the deep state launched a coup d'état on 19 August that failed within a matter of days; symbolised by the spontaneous dismantling of the monument to Dzerzhinsky opposite the KGB headquarters in the very centre of Moscow. On 6 September, Moscow finally recognised the independence of all three Baltic States. This underlined the cruel fact that their standing was ultimately determined by the Russians.

The outstanding question that remained, therefore, was how long they could assure the sovereignty that had so easily been stripped from them half a century before. The deep-seated reluctance of any leading Power to stand by them in their hour of need, whether in 1940 or 1991, was not something anyone was likely to forget. Only Sweden could help them out in the practicalities of the Russian withdrawal. For Sweden, of course, the withdrawal of the Russians from the greater part of the Baltic coastline was of considerable strategic value. As for the Baltic States themselves, as in 1919–20, they always needed a bit of luck.

5

BALTIC LIBERATION, THE BALTIC SEA REGIONAL CONTEXT AND SWEDEN DURING THE END OF THE COLD WAR

Dr Mart Kuldkepp

Alongside Eastern Europe, the Baltic Sea Region was one of the focal points of international attention in the final years of the Cold War. As the Soviet Union seemed to be embarking on a new and radically different political path, states and international organisations around the world were keeping a close eye on its Baltic borderlands. At the time, they were widely regarded as a likely flashpoint where the tensions inherent in the process of the USSR's renewal or disintegration might come to a head. Not least, this concern was felt by the states in the immediate regional neighbourhood of the three Baltic republics. The Nordic countries, whether non-aligned or members of NATO, had a naturally strong interest in understanding the threats and opportunities inherent in the fast-changing international situation, and how these were likely to affect the parts of the USSR geographically closest to them.

At least in hindsight, we can say that from the Nordic point of view, the disintegration of the Soviet Union and the collapse of the bipolar, Cold War-dominated world order was a formative moment. As Finland and Norway were no longer frontier states on the boundary between capitalism and communism, and as neutral Sweden suddenly found that there was nothing left for it to be 'neutral about,' the participants in the so-called Nordic Balance security configuration had to fundamentally rethink the basic tenets of their foreign policy—a difficult process for states that had already settled into their essential policy positions by the late 1940s.

After World War II, the Nordic states' domestic focus was on building up their welfare states, which, together with steadfast cautiousness in relations with their superpower neighbour, had resulted in a kind of isolationism committed to not upsetting the regional *status quo*. This policy of careful balancing—facilitated by their fast-growing economies and a relatively stable security situation—was widely seen as an international success story. The Scandinavian states, and Sweden in particular, built up a reputation as a successful example of a Third, or the Middle Way between the two competing superpower blocs. But at the same time, the Nordics usually turned a blind eye to human rights abuses in the Soviet Union and in Eastern Europe.

Already before the onset of the economic recession in the early 1990s, however, a widespread domestic pessimism had set in regarding the sustainability of the so-called Nordic model. Starting in the early 1970s, changes in the world economy had been putting increasing pressure on the high-tax, high-spend Nordic economies, and thereby also on their welfare states. The process of European integration was becoming ever more important for economic success and resilience of European states, but the Nordics—except for Denmark—had participated in it only to a limited extent, and it was widely considered to be incompatible with their 'third way' ethos. The decline of Soviet isolationism towards the end of the Cold War also eroded the internationalist brand that Scandinavian neutrals had built up during their decades of activism as bridge-builders and mediators between the East and the West. Now, when the East and the West were able to negotiate arms reduction treaties with each other directly, the CSCE-style mediation by non-aligned states was no longer needed.

But there was light at the end of the tunnel for the Nordics. While the gradual lifting of the iron curtain reduced the predictability of the regional security environment, and stoked fears of a possible disorderly break-up of the Soviet Union, there was also a natural hopefulness about the future. The decline of traditional security concerns was opening new and exciting prospects for Western and Nordic values, democratisation, cultural exchange, expansion of markets and investments and environmental activism across the Iron Curtain. And the three re-emerging Baltic States on the other side of the Baltic Sea were more than willing and thankful recipients of these new Nordic ambitions at regional activism. It is fair to say that starting in the early 1990s, and continuing at least until 2004, the Nordic states played a crucial role in the Baltics' post-Soviet transition.

Why did they do it? It is possible to argue that there was some realist political calculation behind the Nordic willingness to support the Baltic States. Certain centre-right Scandinavian politicians, such as Uffe Ellemann-Jensen in Denmark and Carl Bildt in Sweden, seemingly thought that proactive engagement for Baltic independence was a way forward also for the Scandinavian states themselves, because it was more advantageous to be active, rather than passive in the new, complicated, and volatile international environment they now found themselves in. In a world that was leaving behind the bipolar order and entering an era of multipolarity based on networks of influence, it was the ability to create such networks—and to exercise one's soft power through them—that emerged as the crucial political asset. The days of isolationism were seemingly gone for good.

However, there might be reasons not to overemphasise the break with the previous policy tradition. International activism and norm entrepreneurship were, after all, not new for the Scandinavian countries. During the Cold War, they had often been the actors who had stepped up in the interests of peaceful conflict resolution, democratisation, and the rule of law. Their foreign aid budgets per capita had been the largest in the world, and their engagement for the benefit of the so-called Third World had earned them widespread admiration in left-wing circles around the globe.

But what was truly unprecedented was the fact that similar activities would now be directed towards the Baltic countries. Historically, Nordic attitudes towards Baltic independence had been characterised by a large degree of passivity and cautiousness. In the aftermath of World War I, the view that was quickly adopted by both the left and the right in Scandinavian politics was that the Nordics should remain devoted to its successful neutrality policy and not become entangled in the question of the future of Russia, since a future re-assertion of Russian territorial interests in the Eastern Baltic was thought to be almost inevitable. Despite all the efforts of Baltic politicians in the 1920s and 1930s to institute some form of closer political cooperation with the Nordics, this policy remained essentially unchanged and was subsequently—or at least that is how it appeared—proven to have been correct by the events that caused the loss of Baltic independence in 1939–1940.

Therefore, when considering the Scandinavian policy shift from Cold War-era passivism to post-Cold War era active engagement in favour of Baltic independence, it is not enough to base the narrative only on the realist aspirations of the new centre-right governments, seeking to retain status and influence in the rapidly changing world. We also need to consider the Nordics' feelings of guilt and shame over their past behaviour, which had not always been in line with their stated ideals, as well as optimism over future cooperation, which increasingly made inroads into public consciousness in the early 1990s. In this situation, Sweden is perhaps the most interesting Nordic country to consider, so in the following analysis, I will be focusing on Sweden in particular.

The enormous change in Sweden's security situation when the Soviet Union eventually collapsed in autumn 1991 was in some ways similar to that which had taken place at the end of World War I. Again, the developments were very favourable in principle—the implosion of the USSR and the end of bipolar superpower rivalry meant that Sweden's security situation had improved in sudden and unforeseen ways. Just as in 1918–20, a row of small independent nation states emerged on the other side of the Baltic Sea, further shielding Sweden from any remaining Russian threat. At the end of the Cold War, however, the Swedish response to these events ultimately proved to be different: active, rather than passive, and enthusiastic, rather than sceptical.[1]

To explain why this was the case, I will argue for the significance of three factors: firstly, the security–related concerns around the easing of superpower tensions and the future of the USSR; secondly, the move to the right in Swedish politics; and finally, the Swedish tradition of activist internationalism, which was now morphing into what has been called 'adjacent internationalism' (see below).

Going back to 1988, it is fair to say that already then, the looming changes in the international security situation were a cause for both optimism and concern for Sweden. The need to appease the USSR, which during the Cold War had made any close engagement with the Baltics impossible, had now the potential to become less relevant thanks to the apparently liberal policies of the new Soviet leader Mikhail Gorbachev, and the demonstrable unwillingness of the USSR to prevent the Communist regimes of its Eastern European satellite states from being toppled.

Nevertheless, this line of thought did not lead to immediate policy change for Sweden. In 1988, Sweden's Social Democratic government still felt that irrespective of the outcome of Gorbachev's reforms, the superpower confrontation would continue, making the Swedish neutrality policy a necessity for the foreseeable future. Any part that Sweden could play in furthering the détente was still thought to lie in its role as a neutral acting through international organisations.[2]

This assumption that the Cold War would go on made any rash political changes seem like threats to international stability. As later recalled by Örjan Berner, the Swedish Foreign Minister, Sten Andersson, had reacted to the 1989 events in Eastern Europe with much anxiety, rather than seeing them as a cause for celebration.[3] The Swedish Foreign Ministry's initial response to the Baltic developments must have been similar, since intensified instability so close to Swedish territory, not to speak of any 'disorderly' break-up of the Soviet Union, posed a considerable threat. The 1917–20 dissolution of the Russian Empire had shown that the war and violence, which had sparked in its former borderlands, were in many ways just as traumatic as the experiences of World War I, which had led to the Russian revolutions in the first place. In the age of nuclear weapons, a similar scenario would have been potentially very dangerous indeed.

At the same time, the potential magnitude of the crisis also meant that Sweden could not remain a complete bystander, however strong its passivist and neutralist inclinations. At the very least, it needed to be well–informed about the ongoing developments, which was most likely the reason why Swedish diplomatic presence in the Baltic States was prioritised early on. If Sweden wanted to ensure continuing regional stability and security, it obviously needed to know where this stability would be found— whether in the hands of Gorbachev or somewhere else—and what exactly could be done to promote it. For this reason, 'Swedish offices' were set up in Tallinn and Riga in December 1989 and May 1990, nominally as 'departments of the general consulate Leningrad'. In reality, however, they were a kind of proto–embassy, and Swedish diplomats became frequent visitors to the Baltic capitals.[4]

Secondly, the lead–up to the end of the USSR coincided with important domestic developments in Sweden, which created a space and expectation for new ideas and policy innovation. As noted above, the 'Nordic model' of the expansive and expensive Social Democratic welfare state, predicated on stable economic growth and high taxes, was, by the late 1980s, in increasingly deep crisis due to structural changes in the world economy (globalisation). By 1990, Sweden had fallen into its worst recession since 1929. At the same time, right-wing criticism of both domestic and foreign policy, paired with the legacy of having been the party responsible for Cold War era high-tax, high-spend policies, was making it difficult for the two consecutive Social Democratic cabinets of Ingvar Carlsson (1986–90 and 1990–1) to come up with effective and innovative political solutions. The subsequent electoral success of right-wing parties led to the new government of Carl Bildt (October 1991–October 1994), which, lacking such policy baggage, was in many ways better-situated to tackle these problems.

Nevertheless, the preparedness for fundamental policy change was more than just a matter of party politics. In fact, it was the incumbent Social Democratic government that took one of the most radical steps towards Swedish foreign policy renewal: the abandonment of old neutralist reservations about Sweden's participation in the process of European integration. This was first publicly demonstrated in August 1990 by Prime Minister Carlsson's statement of intent to apply for European Economic Community (EEC) membership, and, subsequently, by the actual lodging of the Swedish membership application on 1 July 1991. This step was in many ways a decisive break with the non-aligned foreign policy of the Cold War era and would have been completely impossible just a few years earlier—after all, from the Soviet point of view, the EEC/EU was nothing but an economic arm of NATO, i.e., a thoroughly partisan western alliance. Now, however, as Soviet policies changed and its power and influence waned, the pressure to follow the policy of neutrality decreased and more room for policy manoeuvre became available.

I would argue that Sweden's new interest in the Baltic States was yet another facet of this broader policy shift and shared some of its causes. The decisive move to the right in Swedish politics in autumn 1991 certainly had a pro-Baltic effect, since preference for regional (rather than global) international commitments had long been a typically right-wing policy stance, even if it originally only applied to Finland, not to the Baltic States. But in the longer run, the emerging Baltic States came to benefit even more from Sweden's new engagement with the process of European integration, and their willingness to lend the Baltic States a helping hand.

Thirdly, Swedish foreign policy and foreign service were politicised in a very particular way. From the 1960s onwards, as already noted, Sweden had developed a world-wide reputation for the promotion of internationalism, solidarity and global norm entrepreneurship in areas such as peaceful conflict resolution, democratisation, and redistributive justice. These values and activities, which by the 1980s had become an integral part of

Swedish liberal progressivist identity and a point of national pride, had primarily been directed at the developing world through international organisations, especially the United Nations. This tradition, Social Democratic in origin, probably did much to eventually bring the Swedish political left over to the side of the Eastern European and Baltic liberation movements. As pointed out by journalist Arne Ruth in 2009, even Sten Andersson himself had in the early 1980s argued that Sweden had a duty to facilitate Poland's transition to democracy 'when the time is ripe.'[5]

Now, when Cold War bipolarity was collapsing and third world Communist or neutralist regimes faltering, the groundwork was being laid for the idea of expanding Sweden's internationalist tradition to its own immediate geographical vicinity: the eastern part of the Baltic region, which, after decades of Soviet occupation, was in dire need of 'catching up' with democratic West. This partial rethinking of Swedish activist internationalism, which Annika Bergman has christened 'adjacent internationalism',[6] required Sweden to completely abandon its previous regional security policy that had been focused on its small-state security needs vis-à-vis the looming superpower threat.

Adjacent internationalism could therefore make a full breakthrough only after the collapse of the USSR, with Sweden and the other Nordic states taking on an active role in facilitating Baltic post-Soviet transition: they promoted democratisation, economic and social development, encouraged their participation in the process of European integration, and provided help with touchy issues such as the removal of Soviet troops and the rights of the Russian-speaking minorities. These initiatives brought Sweden's long-standing internationalist foreign policy in line with its stated goals in areas closer to home, and arguably realised an important identity function for a country that was looking for a new role in the world stage after the era of the 'Nordic model' and 'Nordic balance' seemed to be over.

Out of the three factors outlined above, it was certainly the first one—security concerns—that played the most important role in motivating Sweden's early engagement with the situation in the Baltic republics in 1989–91. However, this initial engagement for information-gathering purposes did not by itself cause the change in Swedish policy from Cold War-era cautiousness to post-Cold War enthusiasm. Reading the available primary sources, it is easy to see that the years 1989–91 were in many ways a period of doubt, indecision, and non-policy.[7] Indeed, it proved difficult for Sweden to let go of long-held convictions about Soviet prerogatives in the Baltics even in the aftermath of the failed *coup d'état* of August 1991, which was already at the time widely recognised to predict imminent Soviet collapse.

A decisive shift would therefore only take place when the other two above-mentioned factors rose to policy-shaping prominence in October 1991 with the assumption of office by Carl Bildt's centre-right cabinet. But by that time, this change had already been several years in the making.

To conclude, it took a convergence of a number of different factors to enable Sweden to take on an active role in Baltic Sea regional politics after the years 1988–91. This was, in fact, the first time in Sweden's modern history that it did so. In hindsight, the idea that an open and liberal Baltic Sea Region would be a viable replacement for the apparently obsolete Nordic model with its isolationist baggage, and a way forward not only for the post-Soviet Baltic States, but also the post-Nordic Scandinavian states, proved to be premature. The Nordic brand was stronger than many had feared. But nevertheless, the Baltic States clearly and crucially benefitted from the Scandinavian countries' willingness to extensively support their democratic, economic, and social development, later focusing their efforts on assisting the Baltics in their road to EU and NATO membership. We can now say with conviction that unlike in 1918–20, the Nordics placed their bets right in 1988–91. The Baltic States have prospered and once again reintegrated into the Western community of nations.

PART III

THE BALTIC INDEPENDENCE DIMENSION

6

THE MICE THAT ROARED[1]

Professor Stefan Hedlund

The collapse of the Soviet Union was the result of many coinciding forces, some internal and some external. Different experts have, over the years, liked to press home their own pet theories, from Ronald Reagan's Star Wars to low oil prices and a vendetta between Mikhail Gorbachev and Boris Yeltsin, not to mention sheer exhaustion brought on by an erosion of belief in the system as such. The sensible take is that these, and other related factors, all played their parts, and that it is futile to point at one as the truly decisive factor.

This noted, the following will present the struggle for freedom that was waged by brave activists in the three Baltic Soviet Republics as a significant, albeit perhaps not decisive, contribution to the collapse of Soviet power. Given that the three were not in any position to mount a challenge based on hard power, the story will be one of David rising to fight Goliath, with a shrewd deployment of soft power as the legendary sling stone.

The story will highlight the role that was played by interaction between forces in the periphery that were seeking to leave the union, and forces at the Moscow center that shied back from deploying sufficient violence to suppress those ambitions. The main feature is that Mikhail Gorbachev's ambition to seek friendly relations with the West (building a common European House) made it impossible for him to allow the hardliners to crack down on secessionists. Teddy bears do not, after all, drive tanks.

The latter was, arguably, also the reason why the challenge from the peaceful revolutions that unfolded in Central Europe during 1989 went unanswered. It is a striking fact that the Soviet armed forces had a garrison of some 380,000 frontline troops in the GDR, which theoretically would have been more than sufficient to clamp down hard. Yet, whether the Moscow hardliners really could have succeeded in preventing Poles, Czechs, Slovaks and Hungarians from exiting the camp of Soviet power is not at issue here.

What is important is that there emerged a powerful synergy between activism in Central Europe and in the Baltic region. The three Baltic Republics served as an important intermediary, between challenges issued by reformers in Central Europe and responses from hardline forces in Moscow. While activists in Central Europe could take heart from challenges that activists in the Baltics issued and got away with, the latter could in turn take heart from challenges that Central European activists issued and got away with.

The account of how the three Baltic States succeeded in reestablishing their sovereignty will begin with the early mobilization of discontent that focused on ecology and ethnicity. It then proceeds via tactics of subtle subversion that saw the formation of popular fronts, to open defiance in calling for independence and it rounds off with the final spasm of an attempted crackdown that could have ended very badly.

The account will feature Estonia as the main driver in the early stages, when activism was mainly about economic issues, and then show how the initiative was gradually taken over by Lithuania, as political issues of independence came to the fore.

Mobilization Against Soviet Power

It is not often that social science can point at a specific single event as the origin for a process of broad social and political change. The Estonian case is special in the sense of offering precisely such a rare case. On 25 February 1987, Estonian television's highly popular nature program, Panda, broadcast a story about a company called *Eesti fosforiit*. Located at Maardu, just east of the capital Tallinn, it had produced mineral fertilizer since 1920.[2]

Viewers knew that activity to be deeply disturbing. The mining itself had been associated with grave ecological damage, ranging from a drop in the ground water level to trench-like depressions on the surface that made rational agriculture impossible. Emission of pollutants from the enrichment plant had also resulted in negative health effects for the local population.

What made the television story so explosive was that Maardu accounted for only one percent of the total Estonian deposit, and mining covered only nine square kilometers. That was now to change. Large new fields would be opened at Toolse and Rakvere, implying that a total of 2,000 square kilometers of fine agricultural land, representing four percent of the country's total area, would be transformed into lifeless moonscapes.

The tragedy for Estonia was that it was estimated to hold about half of the total Soviet deposits of phosphorite ore. The implied message was that to compensate for the gross inefficiency of Soviet collectivized agriculture, a large part of Estonia would have to be devastated. The outrage felt by many Estonians was captured in a cartoon showing a Soviet peasant shoveling fertilizer onto his field in the shape of Estonia.

The potential disaster of phosphorite mining was not the only factor that mobilized Estonians into political activism. Associated bad news was spreading also about the production of oil shale. Mined at Kohtla-Järve, in the north-eastern part of the country, it was used to produce electricity, much of which was exported to other parts of the USSR.

In comparison, the environmental damage from oil shale was even more disturbing, ranging from the emission of pollutants to contamination of ground water and self-igniting slag heaps. The place already looked like something out of Dante's inferno. With a planned expansion of mining from 600 to 3,400 square kilometers, it was now set to get much worse.[3]

Although Estonians took the lead, they were not alone in experiencing outrage over ecological devastation, which mobilized anger against the Soviet Union. In Latvia, activists began protesting against a controversial hydropower project on the river Daugava, and in Lithuania activists mobilized against a planned expansion of the Ignalina nuclear power plant.

The key feature was that many who felt dissatisfaction with other aspects of living under Soviet rule found that ecology offered an area where voicing concern and even anger was suddenly permissible. Soon enough, however, mobilization was morphing into a nationalist cause that would prove to be considerably more threatening to the USSR.

Estonia again was an early driver. The opening of two new fields for phosphorite mining would not only lead to added ecological damage. It would also be associated with a new wave of labor immigration from other parts of the USSR. Some estimates suggested an influx of 10,000 workers. With dependents included, that would translate into a total of 30–40,000 new arrivals.[4] There were grounds for the local population to view this with concern.

During the 1970s, the Soviet policy of industrialization had led to a large influx of Russian-speaking workers into the newly incorporated Baltic region. Given that Lithuania played a marginal role in the program for industrialization, it had not experienced much of this immigration. But in Estonia and Latvia the inflow had been so large that nationalist circles had begun voicing fears of becoming minority populations in their own countries. If that had happened, it would have meant an end to any hope for restoration of independence.

As ethnic nationalism became more important, mobilization was increasingly focused on issues of language and of symbols like long-prohibited national flags. As this implied an open questioning of the fundamental Soviet policy of Russification, it served to raise the stakes in relation to Moscow.

Only days before the airing of the Estonian Panda program, Gorbachev had visited Riga and Tallinn, where he had blasted the negative influence of 'reactionary Baltic émigré circles,' and emphasized the importance of 'internationalist education.'[5] As the latter was a code word for enhanced Russification, his intervention met with an angry response. It would not be the last time that Moscow intervened in ways that galvanized the struggle for freedom.

In April, the old university town Tartu was home to a festival of Estonian cultural history. Organized by the Estonian Heritage Society, it attracted some 30,000 people. An important event was the unfurling of an old blue-white-black Estonian flag that had been found hidden in an attic.[6] That specific flag may presently be viewed on display at the beautiful Estonian museum of cultural history, erected on the site of the former Soviet air force base at Tartu.

Mobilization was now moving from ecology and ethnicity to the more challenging issue of independence. During the summer of 1987, much attention was focused on the Molotov-Ribbentrop Pact (MRP), the infamous agreement between Soviet Foreign Minister Vyacheslav Molotov and Nazi German Foreign Minister Joachim von Ribbentrop that was concluded on 23 August 1939, setting the stage for Germany and the Soviet Union to carve up and divide the countries between them.

On the 1987 anniversary, manifestations were held in all three capitals. Although the authorities still had sufficient clout to crack down hard, that was set to change. In the continued struggle for freedom, the MRP would serve as a main rallying point.

Subtle Subversion

As the process of mobilization for independence was gathering steam, leading reformers began developing tactics of subtle subversion that would prove to be highly successful. The main driver was to latch on to the flagship of Gorbachev's reforms, that of perestroika. The hope was that if Moscow could be convinced that the Baltic ambitions were fundamentally benign, it would agree to a long leash for the implementation of reforms. Again, it was Estonia that took the lead.

In September 1987, a group of reform-minded Estonian economists launched a project they called *Ise Majandav Eesti*, or 'self-managing Estonia.'[7] The idea was that in matters relating to budget decisions the Estonian Soviet Republic would be granted autonomy within the USSR. The proposal was sugarcoated in promises that the new arrangement would still be based on a common currency, and that Estonia would continue contributing to the common budget. These were important points, suggesting that success for the Estonian economy would bring in hard currency and perhaps also contribute towards achieving ruble convertibility.

Although nothing would come of this project in terms of actual changes in economic management, it did inject a sense of possibility that galvanized the reformers. It was probably no coincidence that in the Estonian language the acronym for the project—IME—means 'wonder.' It was a political rather than an economic project.

It was also symptomatic that the well-renowned Soviet philosopher Igor Klyamkin could publish an article that essentially rediscovered Maw Weber's thesis on a protestant work ethic. Protestantism had produced 'a new, responsible and disciplined laborer, who has given Western civilization almost everything.'[8] Protestant Estonians and Latvians were viewed as being in the vanguard of perestroika.

Moving beyond the ambition to seek greater economic autonomy, reformers deployed similarly subversive tactics in their parallel moves to seek greater political autonomy. Cloaking their rhetoric in traditional communist garb, they created 'popular fronts.'

On 13 April 1988, the prominent Estonian economist Edgar Savisaar appeared on Estonian television to suggest the formation of an Estonian popular front 'in support of perestroika.' His proposal received immediate approval from Estonian officialdom, and the *Eestimaa Rahvarinne* was born. This was the first time since the early 1920s that the sacrosanct prohibition on any form of factions within the Communist Party hierarchy was broken. It was a powerful indication that Moscow was indeed ready to allow Estonia a long leash for its reforms. The Rahvarinne would hold its founding congress on 1–2 October.

In Latvia, human rights activists had begun mobilizing already in 1986, by forming the Helsinki-86 monitoring group, and Latvian greens had responded to the controversial Daugava hydropower project by forming a Club for the Defense of the Environment, the *Vides Aizsardzības Klubs* (VAK). On 21 June 1988, an organizing committee was formed to create a popular front and a proclamation was issued that included the signatures of party moderates. On October 8–9, the *Latvijas Tautas Fronte* held its founding congress, one week after the Estonians. On the eve of its opening, hundreds of thousands of people rallied in support. Many long-prohibited red-white-red Latvian flags could be seen.

In Lithuania, mobilization was delayed by the absence of a sense of real urgency in matters of ecology and ethnicity, and by the presence of the conservative party chief Ringaudas Songalia, who was in firm opposition.

A watershed event was marked on 2 June 1988, when it transpired that plans were being made for a major expansion of the chemical industry. On the following day, some 500 prominent Lithuanians gathered in the grand hall of the Academy of Science, where they elected an 'initiative group' of scholars and intellectuals that were tasked with preparing the formation of a popular front in support of perestroika. The result was the *Lietuvos Persitvarkymo Sąjūdis* ('Lithuanian perestroika movement'), or simply Sąjūdis.[9]

Although the popular fronts pretended to work within the Communist Party system, they were becoming more and more focused on finding a way to escape. An important milestone was marked in the summer of 1988, when the Communist Party of the Soviet Union organized its nineteenth party conference in Moscow. The impact on the political scene in the Baltic republics was to be quite substantial, albeit indirect.

As the official directives had called for the nomination of multiple candidates, from which republican Communist Party Central Committees would choose their allotted numbers of delegates, the popular fronts had high hopes of being able to influence the selection of delegations. Those hopes were to be frustrated. The Baltic Communist Parties remained loyal to Moscow.

In the Estonian case, a total of 600 names were put forward for 32 slots. When the Central Committee met to make its selection, the Estonian Communist Party leader Karl Vaino simply tabled a list of 32 names that was submitted to a secret vote. In good Soviet tradition, the list was unanimously approved.

Having failed to influence the selection of delegates, the popular fronts instead turned to holding mass rallies to influence those candidates that were to be sent. At the beginning of June, around 100,000 Estonians gathered for a song festival on Tallinn's Singers' Field. This was when the Baltic struggle for freedom came to be known as the 'Singing Revolution.' Coined by the artist Heinz Valk, it was a moniker that went viral.[10]

The Communist Party of Estonia was now under serious pressure. On 13 June, an emergency meeting was called under the leadership of the Chairman of the Estonian Supreme Soviet, Arnold Rüütel. On the following day, media reported that Estonian would be made the official language and that the old flag would again be recognized as a national symbol. On 16 June, it was announced that Karl Vaino was ousted, having appealed to Moscow for military support. He was replaced by Vaino Väljas, a former Soviet ambassador to Nicaragua.

On 17 June, 150,000 people gathered on the Singers' Field, seeking to influence the selected delegates for the Party Conference. Estonian flags were everywhere. On 8–10 September, the Estonian Communist Party held a series of meetings to agree that the demands of the popular fronts would now also be the demands of the Party, and on 11 September, an unprecedented 300,000 Estonians, representing a third of the population, gathered in support.

Open Defiance

The third stage in the process would revolve around the Molotov-Ribbentrop Pact. Although the existence of the Pact had always been recognized, the Soviet authorities had been conspicuous in denying the existence of two secret protocols. In the first, which set the stage for carving up Poland, Lithuania was given to Germany. In the second, which was concluded in September, Stalin was given a free hand in all three Baltic States.

Under pressure from the popular fronts, in 1988 the USSR Supreme Soviet agreed to appoint a commission to investigate the existence of the protocols. The concession was a consequence of Gorbachev's parallel policy of glasnost, which called for openness. Although a copy of the MRP had long been available in the archives of the German Foreign Office, the Auswärtiges Amt, including maps showing the agreed partitioning, Moscow had refused to recognize its authenticity. That was set to change.

On the 1988 anniversary of the MRP, major rallies were held across the Baltic Republics. In Vilnius, it was estimated that between 150,000 and 200,000 people took part.[11] In October, party leader Songalia was ousted and replaced with Algirdas Brazauskas, who would play an important role.

By now, it was becoming obvious that Moscow had gone sour on the popular fronts. On 22 October, Gorbachev announced a proposal for amendments to the USSR constitution that entailed the formation of a Soviet Congress of People's Deputies and a new Supreme Soviet.[12] The reaction in the Baltics was outrage and despair. It was believed that the purpose was to dilute the role of republican representation and to make secession impossible.

On 8 November, representatives of the three popular fronts met in Riga, where a joint statement was issued demanding legal guarantees for economic autonomy. A total of 3.7 million people signed a petition in support. In response, Moscow opted to send senior Politburo members to the three Baltic capitals. But their intervention only made things worse.

In Lithuania, Sąjūdis took the lead in proposing amendments to the Lithuanian constitution. A draft was approved on 13 November, and a full package on republican sovereignty was to be adopted by the Lithuanian Supreme Soviet on 18 November.

THE MICE THAT ROARED

On 17 November 1988, the Estonian Supreme Soviet issued a declaration of sovereignty, stating that republican legislation would be placed above all-union legislation. Gorbachev was furious, and on 26 November the USSR Supreme Soviet ruled that the Estonian decision was null and void.

To prevent Lithuania from completing its proposed constitutional amendment, party secretary Brazauskas was called to Moscow for urgent consultations. Upon his return, he used all his influence to block the issue. On 20 November, Sąjūdis issued a declaration of 'moral independence.'

This was another case where intervention from Moscow backfired. The popular fronts were now gearing up to take over the local communist parties from within. Once that process had been completed, all leverage from Moscow would have been severed.

Elections to the first of Congress of People's Deputies were held in March 1989. As in the first semi-free elections that were held in Poland in 1988, the process was rigged to guarantee that the Communist Party would have a majority. When the Congress held its first session, in late May, it was obvious that Gorbachev would not yield. As the fiftieth anniversary of the MRP was approaching, the situation was becoming tense.

The point of no return was marked on 23 August 1989. At 7.00 pm, some two million people from Estonia, Latvia and Lithuania joined hands in what would come to be alternately known as the Baltic Way or the Human Chain. It stretched over 675 kilometers, from Tallinn via Riga to Vilnius. Barring a few spots in isolated areas, the chain was unbroken. Aside from Soviet fighter jets that made low passes, the authorities shied back from cracking down.

The official position on the MRP was now becoming untenable. On 23 December, a report was presented to the Congress of People's Deputies, and on the following day it was announced that a copy of the secret protocols had been found in the papers of

Molotov—only filed under 1946. It was an exact copy of the one held in the Auswärtiges Amt, including the controversial maps.

As the Congress proceeded to acknowledge the existence of the secret protocols, and to condemn them as illegal, the popular fronts believed that the annexation of the Baltic States would also be considered illegal. But Gorbachev would still not be moved. He maintained that their incorporation into the USSR had been legal and voluntary. The struggle for freedom was morphing into full confrontation.

During 1990, the USSR went into its death throes. In a reflection of how momentum was shifting towards Lithuania, it would be the first of the fifteen Soviet republics to attempt to break free. On 11 March, the Lithuanian Supreme Soviet issued a declaration of independence and elected Sąjūdis leader Vytautas Landsbergis as chairman, a post then known as President. The Communist Party of Lithuania had sided against the USSR.

On 14 March, the Congress of People's Deputies was to elect General Secretary Mikhail Gorbachev as President of the USSR. The Lithuanian move was made to preempt feared legal changes intended to curtail all openings for protest. Moscow's response was to impose a blockade that proved to be ineffectual.

The ensuing process came to be known as the 'sovereignty parade.' The USSR had fifteen republics, several of which in turn had autonomous republics. As the Soviet republics began proclaiming that their laws were above the laws of the USSR, lower entities followed by proclaiming that their laws were above republican laws. The nature of this 'war of laws' was reflected in a cartoon showing two peasants standing in front of their hut holding a banner stating that 'We hereby proclaim the independent republic of Ivan and Olga.'

By far the biggest challenge to the integrity of the USSR would emanate not from the Baltics but from the Russian republic, formally known as the Russian Socialist Federal Soviet

Republic (RSFSR). When the USSR was formed, as a union of ethnically defined republics, all but the RSFSR had been given formal institutions of governance. The fact that the RSFSR was excluded proves that it was all façade. Russia and the USSR were the same.

When Boris Yeltsin launched his campaign to unseat Gorbachev, his first move was to create his own machinery of power, in the form of RSFSR institutions of governance. In May, he succeeded in being elected Chairman of the Presidium of the RSFSR Supreme Soviet, a post then known as President.

In the following summer, Gorbachev made a valiant effort to turn the tide, by calling an extraordinary Party Congress. It was a success in the sense that he managed to keep the Party united and to stave off demands for multiparty elections. He also succeeded in being re-elected as General Secretary. But these were pyrrhic victories. The Congress would be marked by Yeltsin staging a dramatic walkout, proclaiming he could no longer work with the party.

During the subsequent fall, the political scene in Moscow was transformed. Liberals were replaced by hardliners and Gorbachev was granted a right to rule the country by decree. At a December session of the USSR Supreme Soviet, Eduard Shevardnadze announced his resignation as Soviet Minister of Foreign Affairs. And he used the opportunity to warn of 'dark forces' lurking behind the President.

The Final Spasm

The final spasm of Soviet power over the Baltic States was marked at the outset of 1991. Two factors combined to convince the hardliners in Moscow that the time was ripe to put an end to attempted secessions. One was that the United States was presumed to be so busy with its war to liberate Kuwait that it would not be ready to mount a response of any consequence. The other was the increasing weakness of Gorbachev, who was under pressure from both liberals and hardliners.

A first sign of what Shevardnadze had warned about was seen on 2 January, when Soviet OMON special forces occupied the press building in Riga, claiming it was Communist Party property. Rumors held they were also planning to take the television tower, but that never materialized.

In a surprise move, President Landsbergis dismissed the government in Lithuania, thus forcing the hand of the Russian hardliners. On 13 January, Soviet troops surrounded the television tower in Vilnius. The plan had been to have pro-Moscow demonstrators occupy it and then send in troops to protect them. But when the troops arrived there was already a large crowd of Lithuanians on site. In the ensuing melee, 14 civilians were killed.

President Landsbergis tried repeatedly to get in contact with Gorbachev on the phone but failed, being informed that the Soviet President was out to lunch. It would come to be known as the longest lunch break in history. In Latvia, the crackdown was limited to some random shooting by OMON special forces in the center of Riga, and in Estonia the Soviet forces did not leave their barracks.

The January crisis was a watershed event that could have gone horribly wrong. Allegations have been made that the hardliners had prepared lists of people who were to be arrested and deported, in a repeat performance of the Soviet annexation. What likely saved the day was that Boris Yeltsin intervened.

In a characteristic move, he travelled to Tallinn. There he met with the leaders of the three Baltic Republics, to sign a joint statement of mutual support. Upping the ante, he called on the United Nations to intervene and on Soviet troops stationed in the region not to intervene. Rounding off, he even suggested that it might be necessary to form a Russian army, to protect Russia against Soviet troops. Allegedly fearing KGB assassination, Yeltsin opted to return to Moscow by car.

In the spring, Gorbachev tried to shore up support by organizing a referendum on the future of the USSR. Held on 17 March, Soviet citizens were asked if they were in favor of the preservation of a 'renewed federation.' It was a shambles, with even senior Soviet officials shaking their heads at the absurdity of the wording of the question.[13] Even more troubling was that six of the fifteen Soviet republics refused to participate.

The three Baltic Republics decided to organize referendums on their own, and to move first. On 9 February, a full 90 percent of voters in Lithuania voted in favor of independence, with an 85 percent turnout. This result reflected the small size of the Russian minority. The other two held their referendums on 3 March. In Estonia, 78 percent voted in favor of independence, with an 83 percent turnout, and in Latvia the numbers were 74 and 88 percent. A substantial part of the Russian minority had voted in favor of independence.

While Ukraine compounded the fiasco for Moscow by adding a question on sovereignty, the most important challenge emanated from the RSFSR. Banking on the fact that Gorbachev had merely been 'selected' as president by the Congress of People's Deputies, Yeltsin upped the ante by adding a question on whether Russians were in favor of a popularly elected presidency. The result was affirmative and fierce campaigning began.

During March, Yeltsin first called on Gorbachev to resign, then narrowly survived a vote of no confidence in the Russian Supreme Soviet and finally saw a crowd of around 300,000 turning out on Moscow's centrally located Manezh Square to express their support for his campaign. On 12 June, he became the first democratically elected President of Russia ever, and on 10 July he took the oath and received a blessing from Patriarch Aleksii.

One of his first moves following this triumph was to issue a prohibition against Communist Party activity in workplaces in

Russia. Given that the workplace cells formed the very backbone of the Party organization, this was tantamount to a prohibition against the party itself. By then, the game was essentially over.

On 19 August, the hardliners made a botched attempt at a coup, which folded after three days. Those three days also decided the struggle for power between the two Russian presidents. During the coup, Yeltsin made his classic stand against the coupsters from atop a tank parked outside the Moscow White House. Gorbachev in contrast would show himself to be totally out of touch with the fast-moving reality. Upon his return to Moscow, having been freed from captivity in Crimea, he told waiting representatives of the world's press that the failure of the coup was a victory for perestroika.

The outcome was a rather bizarre situation where it was basically up to the leaders of the major Western powers to decide who was president in Moscow, and they decided overwhelmingly to hold on to Gorbachev.

On 8 December, the leaders of the three Slavic republics—Boris Yeltsin from Russia, Leonid Kravchuk from Ukraine and Stanislav Shushkevich from Belarus—met at a small town just outside Minsk called Belovezh. There they agreed on the formation of a new Commonwealth of Independent States. When Gorbachev was informed of the fact that the USSR had ceased to exist and that he was out of a job, he at first refused to accept it. But on 25 December, he finally got the message and announced his resignation.

The red flag with the hammer and sickle of the Soviet Union was lowered over the Kremlin, and the Russian tricolor was hoisted. Out of the ashes of the USSR emerged fifteen sovereign nations, three of which were Estonia, Latvia and Lithuania. David may not have beaten Goliath singlehandedly, but the sling stone that was sent by the Baltic popular fronts had surely made a big difference.

7

CONTRIBUTIONS OF THE BALTIC INDEPENDENCE CAMPAIGNS TO SOVIET COLLAPSE*

Professor Kaarel Piirimäe

Measuring the importance of the Baltic independence campaigns in the collapse of the Soviet Union would be a most daunting task, to say the least. The Soviet dissolution crisis can be seen as a complex social process par excellence.[1] Jack Matlock, the United States ambassador to Moscow in 1987–91, who was a perceptive observer and chronicler of events, identified three parallel but not entirely synchronic deep processes within the collapse: the end of the Cold War, the end of communism as a

* Research for this chapter has been supported by the Academy of Finland (project BALTRANS) and the Estonian Science Foundation ('Self-Determination of Peoples in Historical Perspective', PRG942).

system of rule in the USSR, and the end of the Soviet Union itself.[2] Archie Brown has added one process and enlarged on others: the end of the Cold War, the transformation of the Soviet system, the transition from Communism in Eastern Europe, and the break-up not only of the Soviet Union but also of the two other federal states, Czechoslovakia and Yugoslavia. All these events should be kept analytically apart, Brown argues.[3]

With the benefit of hindsight one can add still more macro-processes that shaped the context of the Soviet crisis, such as the surge in the 1980s in the economic and political integration of Western Europe that acted as a magnet for the stagnating economic system of the COMECON in Eastern Europe in the context of deepening globalization,[4] the sovereign debt crisis affecting many developing countries,[5] or even the communication revolution that washed away the remnants of the Iron Curtain and dramatically increased the openness of the Soviet system to outside influence and interference, which one could see, for example, in the way Western diplomats, journalists and activists monitored the situation in the Baltic republics almost in real time.[6]

This did not mean that Soviet collapse was inevitable, as there were also tendencies that worked against the dissolution process. One of the other sides of the speeding up of globalization and the deepening integration was that nationalism as a social force seemed to be beyond its expiry date. After 1978–9, national separatism was quashed under the carpet in Spain after Franco's death as well as in the United Kingdom after the coming to power of the Conservatives and Margaret Thatcher (ironically, with help from the Scottish National Party). In a Europe seeking stability through integration and cooperation across ideological divides, national self-determination as a right to secede from empire had patently been banished into the postcolonial world. For most Western intellectuals, nationalism appeared a phenomenon needing to be historicized and overcome, representing uglier times in

European history. Since Western antinationalist thought was directed in practice against smaller nations in Eastern Europe that still aspired toward self-determination, it was clearly also a continuation of the historic Western colonialism vis-à-vis Eastern Europe.[7] This was a major obstacle to the independence of the Eastern Europeans and their 'return to Europe' in the 1990s.

Leaders of the Baltic national movements knew that the banner of self-determination would not get them far. Activists of the Baltic diaspora had tried for several decades to link the Baltic question to the norms of anti-colonialism and self-determination, with little success. The ideas of historic justice and rights guaranteed by international law proved more compelling. The Baltic Appeal of 1979, in which Baltic dissidents framed the independence struggle primarily as the undoing of the injustice of the Molotov-Ribbentrop Pact of 1939 (and as living up to the ideals of the Atlantic Charter), was published by *The New York Times* and inspired the 1983 resolution of the European Parliament condemning Soviet occupation and annexation.[8] History proved a robust weapon of the weak, as we will see below.

In addition to transformative social processes that can to some extent be delineated, there was, as always in history, the factor of contingency, which in the case of the Soviet collapse seemed to be especially pronounced and usually associated with important individuals, like Mikhail Gorbachev or Boris Yeltsin.[9] That transformative times witness the rise of strong leaders is predicted by social theory,[10] however it is less clear if those individuals are producers or merely the products of those 'critical junctures'. Either way, the human factor makes the tracing of causalities even more difficult in complex processes, such as the Baltic independence movement and the Soviet collapse.

This chapter discusses some of the recent scholarship on the topic and brings out the importance of two factors: first, the importance of innovative *ideas* emerging from the Baltic republics and helping to mobilize social forces not only in the Baltics but also in other parts of the Soviet Union, and second, the special urgency of Baltic actors in putting those ideas into *action*. It is the latter aspect that I think is the most original contribution of this chapter to scholarship.

* * *

Some of the discussion in scholarship has centred around the question whether internal or external factors were crucial in Soviet collapse. Much of the literature on the end of the Cold War has emphasized international forces, many American historians highlighting the clever dozing of pressure and diplomacy by US leaders that ostensibly led to Gorbachev's decisions for change.[11] Mark Kramer has demonstrated the centrifugal effects of the loss of the outer empire in east-central Europe on the internal crisis in the Soviet Union.[12] Alex Pravda, who emphasises the overwhelming importance of domestic factors, has noted in this connection how Gorbachev's decision to accept a unified Germany as member of NATO represented the final straw for some of the instigators of the Putsch of August 1991.[13]

In recent years there has been a swing toward emphasising internal rather than external factors. Serhii Plokhy shifted the focus on developments *after* the attempted coup in August, particularly on the counter-coup of Boris Yeltsin and processes in Ukraine, insisting that theoretically the empire could have been saved in some form even after the Balts had left.[14] Recently, Vladislav Zubok has shed new light on Gorbachev's utterly misguided economic reform policies as an important conditioning factor but concluded that the 'exit of Russia' from the Soviet empire was the crucial blow, overshadowing decisions made in and over Ukraine.[15]

Where does this leave the Baltic States? In Russia, some authors have placed part of the blame for the collapse on the

Baltic states,[16] while others dismiss this as a popular myth. Renald Simonian stresses that national unrest did not start in the Baltic republics and that the demands of Baltic nationalists were initially modest, radicalizing only after Gorbachev's reform movement fizzled out around 1989.[17] Baltic historians have focused mostly on developments inside one republic—Lithuania, Latvia or Estonia—which is a valuable addition to the historiography, but taken in isolation tends to suggest that the Baltic independence movements were central to the story of Soviet collapse.[18]

This is the trap that I would like to avoid. The Baltic independence movements did not decide the fate of the Soviet Union. Nevertheless, there is also no need to discard the notion of the Baltic States occupying, in Alex Pravda's words, a 'special place' in the Soviet endgame.[19] According to Pravda, the Baltic republics had always been uniquely open to external influences but not only that, they also mediated foreign influences to other parts of the USSR. They were not only the most East European of the union republics, as Pravda observes,[20] but through their historic connections, for example via the large and active Estonian diaspora in Sweden, continued to belong, despite limits imposed by the Cold War divisions, to the Baltic Sea Region.[21]

A British consul visiting Tallinn, the Estonian capital, in 1981 with other members of the Helsinki diplomatic corps described Estonia as a 'shop window' to the USSR: 'It is evident, from its geographical proximity to Finland, the history of its people, and not least the pervading influence of Finnish television, which purveys western values, that Tallinn is in a special position within the Soviet Union'.[22]

Because of Baltic peoples' recent memories of the years of independence before WWII, of armed resistance in the era of Stalin, limited contacts with the West and cultural differences vis-à-vis the rest of the Soviet Union, the Baltic republics were regarded as the 'Soviet West' or 'Soviet abroad' both outside and inside the USSR.[23] The proximity to Finland and Helsinki's special relations with Moscow allowed the development of tourism between Finland and Estonia since the 1960s. The state tried to control the flow of visitors and goods both ways, but not always successfully,[24] not to speak of the waves of radio and TV that easily crossed the Gulf of Finland and the Iron Curtain.[25]

In addition to their different histories as independent countries from WWI to WWII, the Baltic republics were different from the rest of the Soviet Union because of their relative prosperity. The living standards of Estonia and Latvia were the highest of all the union republics from the end of Second World War until the collapse of the Soviet Union; Lithuania lagged behind but closed the gap in the 1970s and the 1980s.[26] The ideological conformity and allegiance of the Baltic republics to Moscow remained questionable but was not readily apparent until Gorbachev's policy of glasnost reached the Baltic States around 1987.

Mark Beissinger, who has presented probably the most comprehensive analysis of the various nationalist protest groups emerging in the Soviet Union in the latter half of the 1980s and assessed their cumulative effect on the Soviet disintegration crisis, has concluded: 'In the end, it was not the Baltic, Transcaucasian, or Moldovan governments [...] that took the final decision to abolish the Soviet state [...] Rather, the decision was adopted by the Russian, Ukrainian, and Belorussian governments—governments of cultural groups traditionally closely associated with Soviet power'.[27] Many other historians have agreed that it was the traditional core of the empire that suddenly and for a relatively brief moment threw away the imperial legacy, or the imperial mission. It was particularly surprising that Russia seemed to turn against the very empire it had created.[28]

However, Beissinger also notes that those decisions in the Belovezh forests in December 1991, and the many smaller decisions leading to that, were not taken in a vacuum but in the context that he characterizes as a widespread sense of inevitability about Soviet disintegration. Independence of the union republics, which had seemed unthinkable only two years before, and for which popular support was quite modest even in March 1991 during Gorbachev's referendum about the future of the Union, seemed in late 1991 the most sensible way out of the crisis.[29]

In the creating of that sense of inevitability about the dissolution of the unitary state along the borders of union republics, the Baltic States played a significant role. Beissinger, who has studied the rise of Russian nationalism, has come to the conclusion that it was the Baltic independence movement that inspired mass mobilization also of the Russians. He has detected three waves of mobilization. First, Russian-speaking minorities in the Baltic republics mobilized in reaction to Baltic separatism in the Baltic republics. These groups could be characterized as conservative and nationalist. In the Baltic States, they are referred to as the interfronts.[30] Second, in spring 1989 that wave of mobilization spread to Russia proper but not as a conservative movement but as a liberal and democratic movement supporting the Baltic freedom struggle rather than fighting against it. It was this movement that in January and February 1991 organized mass protest demonstrations against the use of force in Lithuania and Latvia earlier in January. This was important not only to avoid further violence in the Baltic republics but also to signal the opposition of the Russian people to the use of force in politics in general, and may have helped deter the Soviet military from going along with coup d'état later in August.[31]

Moreover, the Balts presented not only an example to follow, but were actively spreading the form of mobilization and resistance, which had proved its worth in the Baltic, to other republics, in order to build a broad coalition of union republics against Gorbachev's centre. In this regard, nationalism in the Soviet Union was not a parochial movement, as many scholars would want to think, but could be seen as an open, transnational move-ment.[32] The main organizational form that the Balts exported to other republics was the popular front, first established in summer 1988 in Estonia. It allowed for the mobilization of broad sections of the public for what was seemingly a program supporting per-estroika—and Gorbachev and his closest advisers surprisingly bought the notion that they were supporting perestroika—but in actual fact included the objectives of the Estonian national movement. It was a pragmatic program avoiding the radical demands of the dissidents and therefore obvious risks for people becoming involved.[33]

The popular front is only one example of innovative political, social and economic thinking that originated from the Baltic republics and most often from Estonia. There was also politics of history and the condemning of the Molotov-Ribbentrop Pact, which originated from the Baltics.[34] As Jaak Rakfeldt has noted, Baltic nationalism gained much of its strength from collective memory—the 'memory of memories'—that was in direct oppo-sition to the officially sanctioned histories and created a sort of parallel universe of social meaning.[35] The post-glasnost indepen-dence movement sought the aligning of public narratives to indi-vidual, familial and communal memories of memories, which of course meant that the myths representing the core of state and imperial identity of the Soviet Union were challenged. Boris Pugo, a leading Latvian communist and would-be instigator of the Coup of August 1991, complained in 1988 that the publish-ing of the MRP secret documents in a Latvian newspaper 'destroyed the Soviet Union'.[36] Indeed, the Baltic 'memory struggle' focused on the MRP and in December 1989 ended in a hard-won compromise: the Congress of People's Deputies con-demned the MRP but denied any linkage between the pact and the Soviet annexation of the Baltic States in 1940.[37] Gorbachev had saved the core of the imperial narrative vis-à-vis the Baltic states for his political successors in the Russian Federation but the lesson that the Balts drew was different: history could be used as a powerful weapon.[38]

Several other ideas spread in the economic field but also spilled over into politics, including contractual work and the self-accounting of enterprises. According to Juhan Saharov, the former may have developed into the idea of basing the union on a contractual basis between the republics and the centre (union treaty), the latter may have resulted in the notion of the self-accounting and eventually of sovereignty of republics, leading to the landmark decision of the Estonian SSR on sovereignty in November 1988.[39] These ideas challenged Gorbachev to speed up his reform program, which he was reluctant to do. He agreed to the idea of the economic self-accounting of the Baltic republics in 1989 (though never implemented in fact) but opposed the concept of sovereignty and, indeed, essentially pretended that the sovereignty laws did not exist.[40] However, he went along the path of devolving power from the centre to the republics and even took the course of negotiating a union treaty with the republics, but too late to appease the Balts and too soon to placate his own entourage, which began to plot his removal.

The Balts were in the forefront of innovative social and political reform. Baltic delegates to the Congress of Peoples' Deputies joined Russian democrats and liberals to form the Interregional Deputies Group. They were among its most active members. Yeltsin, a rising star of the opposition against Gorbachev, is said to have listened most carefully to what the Baltic deputies had to say.[41]

* * *

Ideas alone cannot explain the importance of the Baltic republics, however. Two things stand out. First, in the Baltics there was broad societal support for change and, second, there seemed to be special urgency about turning the ideas into practice, which was not visible in other republics, at least not too the same degree. Why did the Balts push ahead of everyone else?

The most common answer would be that Estonians, Latvians and Lithuanians were simply the more developed parts of the Soviet Union, their experience of communism was shorter, as a lot of people still remembered and had first-hand experience of pre-war republics. For the Balts, certainly for the generation born before the war, Soviet life was never the normality as it appeared for the 'last Soviet generation'.[42] In 1981 a British diplomat, John K. Gordon, who was the first secretary and cultural attaché of the Moscow embassy, met the Estonian writer and future foreign minister and president, Lennart Meri, and his father Georg (who had been an Estonian diplomat before the war), during a visit to Tallinn and reported back to London:

> His own views were strongly anti-Soviet, and pro-British; his last gesture of the evening was to play me a recording from "Voice of America" of Churchill's funeral ceremony [in 1965]. The strong impression I received was of a determined and talented family who have occupied a pre-eminent intellectual position under both pre-communist and communist regimes and who are waiting for (as they see it) the tide of history to restore independence to their country. In my experience this type of intellectual is not uncommon in Hungary (and I would assume also in Poland and Czechoslovakia); but is probably a rare animal—at least outside the Baltic area—in the USSR?[43]

People like Meri were waiting, as Gordon noted, for 'the tide of history' to turn when restoring pre-war republics would become a possibility. Such kind of temporal thinking was impossible to imagine in other parts of the Soviet Union. That men like Lennart Meri were perceived as 'un-Soviet' opened doors, literally and figuratively, in the West then and later. When Meri became the foreign minister of the popular front government in

1990, he asked for an audience with the British Secretary of State Douglas Hurd. The Foreign Office decided to make an exception and arrange the meeting despite the long-standing policy of non-recognition of Baltic annexation and not meeting with officials of union republics. It was expected that due to his background Meri would have valuable information and insights useful for the British government.[44]

That Baltic people were more Western in their outlook is only part of the answer why the Baltic States were in the forefront of change, however. It is true that technocrats in the Baltic republics were known for their innovative thinking, that Baltikum was prized as the laboratory of reform long before Gorbachev imagined it a testing ground for perestroika, before Yakovlev, who inspected the situation in Riga and Vilnius in August 1988, came to the conclusion that the popular mass movements were all in support of perestroika.[45] Baltic leaders were not only men of ideas but also, or even more importantly, *men of action*. Ideas could be borrowed from elsewhere, and usually they were,[46] but the Balts excelled in putting those ideas into action.

Again, we can take the testimony of a British diplomat as evidence. David Manning, who observed Baltic affairs from the British embassy in Moscow, noted: 'Estonia, Latvia and Lithuania had outstanding leaders, whose bravery was combined with a great sense of time. (The role of individuals in history is important, indeed)'. The most important lesson that Manning drew, looking back at the Soviet collapse from his vantage point of 2009, was that the Baltic States did not postpone decisions, they did things that were politically possible immediately. Manning referred not only to the independence struggle but also to the Baltic return to Europe, including the joining of NATO and the EU, in the 1990 and the 2000s.[47] The Balts remain the only former Soviet republics to join these institutions to this day.

Why were the Baltic leaders brave and why were they trying to grasp the moment, sometimes even desperately so? It was because they believed Gorbachev perestroika presented a unique window of opportunity to break free of the empire. But why was it so urgent?

I will base the following interpretation on research done on the Estonian national movement, acknowledging differences with Latvia and particularly with Lithuania (where the demographic situation was different). One can see that nationalists in the Baltic republics feared for the survival of their nations in the context of mass immigration and Russification. In Estonia, the first instance when Estonian intelligentsia challenged the regime directly happened in 1980, when forty intellectuals sent a letter to four Soviet newspapers. It was not published but spread as samizdat. In that letter, it was stated that the Estonian nation was becoming 'a minority ethnic group' in the near future and this was the main reason for social unrest. Authorities dismissed the existential anxiety as a capitalist propaganda ploy and suppressed all opposition.

It was only in 1988, with glasnost in full swing, that the Estonian intelligentsia could again raise the nationalities question in public. In April 1988 there was a plenum of Cultural Associations, which became the forum for the Estonian intellectual elites to present their concerns and claims. Lennart Meri probably expressed the feeling of everyone present: 'For the Estonian nation the situation is critical. Our first duty is to free the nation from the fear of biological and social extinction'. 'Biological' referred to the mass immigration of Russian-speakers and 'social extinction' to the policies of cultural Russification.

There is no space here to discuss whether the perception of the Estonian national movement that Estonians were facing an existential threat reflected demographic and social realities or not. What mattered was perception: existential fear was a social fact having an effect on people's expectations and their willingness to take risks in the present to change the situation. That entailed the challenging of the full force of the Soviet state with all the risks involved for individuals concerned. It was also important that this threat perception was shared by a large coalition of Estonians from Communist Party members to dissidents. For example, Vaino Väljas, who in 1988 became the First Secretary of the Estonian Communist Party as Gorbachev's close ally, shared the concern and bandwagoned onto the nationalist cause, all the time assuring Gorbachev that what was happening was in the plans of perestroika. Under the direct supervision of Väljas, in November 1988 the Estonian republic declared sovereignty—an innovative move that led to the parade of sovereignties by all the other republics within the next two years.

This story is well known but it is less understood why sovereignty was needed. It was a tool for the Estonian reform-communist government to prevent 'social and biological extinction' by closing Estonian borders to mass immigration and protecting the Estonian language and culture against Russification. The Estonian national movement did not want to stop there. As Trivimi Velliste, a leader of the radical wing of the national movement, said in one of the most memorable speeches of the time: 'the main political problem is the question of our survival. The continued existence of the Estonian nation is impossible without independent statehood.'[48] Baltic nationalists were determined to press ahead as long as and as much as Gorbachev was allowing. With time, the façade of perestroika fell away giving way to open confrontation between the Balts and Gorbachev. Lithuanians led the way with their March 1990 declaration of independence, Latvians and Estonians tried to be more tactical, but the aim was the same.

As a writer and filmmaker with an acute sense of time, Lennart Meri best expressed the Estonian concept of time. In an internal Foreign Ministry memo of autumn 1990 Meri said: 'Estonian foreign policy has less time than the other European nations, because in Estonia, time determines whether the nation will survive or perish'. The next year, in autumn 1991 Meri wrote: 'Fifty years of hard times have brought us to the situation where we must admit: time is working against us. The destructive processes are intensifying and turning those processes around will take immense efforts.' Incredibly, he wrote this in a government white paper immediately after the August 1991 declaration of independence in August 1991, demonstrating that the Estonian national movement did not consider independence as an end point but just a beginning in the long and hazardous road toward securing independence in a Western-centric international order.

The government white paper of August 1991 suggested that Estonians work even harder despite having made superhuman efforts in the previous two and more years. In late August 1991, Meri established a seven-day working week for all employees in his ministry; by and large this only formalized existing practices. As Meri's officials reported, the chief himself had been working almost 24 hours a day and expected his staff to do the same.[49] Following Meri's example, people had been working at the limits of their capabilities since the Popular Front government had taken office in spring 1990. Prime Minister Savisaar had been legendary for his exceptionally long working hours already before 1990.[50] Raivo Vare, who as 'minister of state' was responsible for the running of the government offices, recalled that staff meetings began at midnight because no one had time for reflections and policy planning during the day. Meetings lasted into the early morning. At Meri's home, they would often start at three a.m. and later.[51]

For Estonian leaders, the end point of the struggle was the return to Europe and the securing of the nation against biological and cultural extinction, which the Estonian elites thought was accomplished only after the joining of NATO and the EU.[52]

The same urgency probably characterized Latvia and Lithuania at least up to 2004.

* * *

To conclude, it will always be a matter of debate whether the use of mass violence would have prevented the separation of the republics and the collapse of the unitary state. The exact part played by the Baltic States in the Soviet collapse will remain hard to calibrate.

There is also the interesting question whether allowing the Baltic republics to leave earlier through a peaceful process of divorce would have strengthened Gorbachev's hand in dealing with more important issues and thus helped save the rest of the empire. The Baltic leaders argued for this point of view, but Gorbachev thought, perhaps thinking as a lawyer, that Baltic independence would set a dangerous precedent for others. Thus, he insisted that all solutions should remain within the confines of the Soviet constitution and law, which was unacceptable for the Balts. Moreover, Baltic independence appeared not to suit the general secretary's timetable: he assumed that questions concerning the centre-periphery relations would be solved in the second stage of perestroika when the reform of central institutions had succeeded.[53] Anyway, differently from some of his closest advisers, like Anatoly Chernyaev, he lacked the sense of the acuteness of 'nationalities problem', until it was too late.[54] Eventually, the divorce came in an haphazard way—as a result of the Putsch—which combined with other factors contributed a mix of circumstances that made the development of constructive relations between the Baltic States and Russia after 1991 nearly impossible.

It is also important to stress that more than any other region in the Soviet Union, the Baltic States were susceptible to outside influences. In fact, in large part due to the non-recognition policy, the Baltic republics became pawns if not players in the international politics of the Cold War endgame. Superpower diplomacy helps explain, partly, why Gorbachev failed to apply force consistently and to a sufficient degree to suppress Baltic nationalism, for Gorbachev had promised to avoid the use of force, or so at least his Western partners believed.[55] Given their special status as unrecognized annexed territories of the USSR, Western reactions to the violent crackdown in Vilnius and Riga in January 1991 were so strong that for Gorbachev these appeared as the revival of 'the worst moments of the Cold War'.[56] Note that he wrote about the Cold War as a thing of the past.

Western non-recognition policies and the special care with which the Western powers seemingly treated the Balts can be characterized as an example of 'organized hypocrisy'.[57] After all, the Western policy of ending the Cold War was premised on the assumption that the Soviet Union would remain intact, that the future of the empire was not a fundamental question of the Cold War. It had been the policy of Reagan's administration since 1984 that America would not seek the destruction of the Soviet Union; the line was accepted by Bush.[58] As long as the Soviet Union was peaceful, co-operative and did not threaten the rest of the world with nuclear Armageddon, it could retain its vast territories in the Baltic and elsewhere. This was the gist of the message of President George H.W. Bush about 'suicidal nationalism' in Kiev on 1 August 1991 just weeks before the Ukrainian declaration of independence. Again, one can argue that the Baltics was a special case, the US was already contemplating the setting up of direct diplomatic relations,[59] etc., but the basic policy line had not changed. The US, or other Western powers, would not intervene directly in the 'internal' affairs of the Soviet Union and the outcome of the dissolution crisis depended on the relative weight of the social forces, ideas and actions of people interacting with each other in the last European empire. That the struggle to end the empire would remain largely inconclusive was taken for granted at the time, and indeed confirmed by developments later in the next millennium, especially in events related to Russia and Ukraine.

8

BALTIC EXCEPTIONALISM FROM VERSAILLES TO BELOVEZHSKAYA PUSCHA

Dr Donatas Kupčiūnas

Exceptionalism, defined as substantial difference, or even unique-ness, of an ethnicity, state or region vis-a-vis their peer group, is a term that has been widely used in both academic and practical realms of international relations. Claims of exceptionalism, imbued with forgetting, historical error or pure fantasy, have been at the heart of the ideology of nationalism ever since its rise in the late eighteenth century.[1] Recently, claims of national exceptionalism were at the heart of Brexit, while some European states invoked it as an excuse for slow or inadequate response to the Covid-19 pandemic.[2]

The discipline of geopolitics, from its very beginnings, had a strong flavour of national exceptionalism, with authors making expansionist or containment claims on the basis of unique characteristics of their own states. In this connection, the most cli-chéd expression is 'American exceptionalism', used not only to explain, but also to justify American foreign policy.[3] 'Baltic exceptionalism', or the idea that the Baltic states of Estonia, Latvia and Lithuania were in another league compared to their neighbours or peers, has been mostly associated with the progress that the former made in the last two decades. Indeed, the Baltic States look much better than other former republics of the Soviet Union in different indexes of prosperity, development and human rights. In the wake of the 2008 financial crisis, the Baltic States were deemed exceptional for their austerity policies, also called 'fiscal discipline' by its proponents, or simply for the humiliation they caused for Paul Krugman.[4] More lately, revolt against liberalism in Poland and Hungary highlighted Baltic resilience against populism and political polarization.[5] In the corridors of Brussels, the Baltic States have been known as one-issue republics, owing to their exceptionally hawkish stance towards Russia. On the front of historical memory, harsh condemnation and denouncement of Gorbachev on the day of his funeral by the top officials of the Lithuanian government sat in stark contrast to eulogies coming from the world outside the Baltics.[6]

In hindsight, one of the more interesting aspects of Baltic exceptionalism has to do with geopolitics: why and how the Baltic States managed to escape the Russian (or Soviet) orbit and entrench themselves as part of the West, while others, such as Belarus, Ukraine, or Georgia, did not. In the long twentieth century, the Baltic States escaped Russian/Soviet jurisdiction two times: first—after reorganization of Europe that came with the Treaty of Versailles in 1919, and second—after the Belovezha Accords of 1991 that formally dissolved the Soviet Union. This second escape was followed by the peaceful slipping away of the Baltic States into the EU and NATO in 2004, marking their total exit from the Russian economic and security orbit.

BALTIC EXCEPTIONALISM

Of course, to some degree, Baltic geopolitical exceptionalism had nothing to do with the Baltic States themselves but depended on the choices and circumstances of their neighbors and peers against which they are favourably compared. There was also geographical determinism at play, the Baltic States having been the westernmost provinces/republics of the Russian Empire/Soviet Union that also enjoyed access to the sea. Unnatural barriers, whether the Russian-East Prussian border in the nineteenth century, or the iron curtain in the twentieth, were porous enough to allow for exchange of people and ideas with the West, while proximity to Poland or Finland in the age of radio transmission made it possible to catch some forbidden waves that those situated deeper in the hinterland could not. Finally, the Baltic States were dinghies in the larger and hardly predictable sea of geopolitics, where keeping afloat was often coincidental. Had not Poland pushed the Red Army eastwards during the Russo-Polish War of 1920, the Baltics would have most likely followed the fate of the interwar Belarus and eastern Ukraine. Had Gorbachev been just a younger Brezhnev, this article on Baltic exceptionalism would have to be much shorter.

Leaving all those considerations aside, Baltic geopolitical exceptionalism, or why the Baltic States managed to escape the Russian orbit while others could not, involves three important dimensions. First, the agency of the Baltic States themselves. Second, how they and their aspirations were seen and treated by the West, and third, were they exceptional in the eyes of Russia/Soviet Union, what might have helped the latter acquiesce to the loss of its former Baltic provinces/republics. It is the second and third dimensions that this paper will try to address, contrasting both episodes of the Baltic States leaving the Russian orbit: the first, which came with the breakup of the Russian Empire, and the second, which followed the dissolution of the Soviet Union in 1991 and culminated in the accession of the three states into EU and NATO in 2004.

* * *

In 1919, it was the winners of the war—Britain, France, and the US—that independence-seeking Balts had to charm. Baltic surnames, however, were not to be found on the seating plan at the majestic Hall of Mirrors, where the Paris Peace Conference (PPC) opened, and where Poland, Czechoslovakia and Romania were represented. Baltic delegations came to Paris uninvited and joined a whole host of other conference underdogs. Among them were not only delegations of many other nationalities of the Russian Empire, including Belarussians, Ukrainians and Georgians, but also (ex)statesmen of both imperial and republican Russia itself, now disbanded by the Bolshevik revolution.

Western slogans of wartime propaganda were not of much help to the Baltic States. The biggest point in Wilson's famous 'fourteen points', for instance, was about keeping Russia 'unembarrassed', and this meant that there was no mention of the Baltics. By 1919, however, the volatile situation on the eastern Baltic coast, the fog of Russian civil war, as well as increasingly bold demands of Baltic nationalists could not but put the Baltic question on the agenda. On this issue, like on a myriad of others, British, French and American delegations came to Paris prepared and brought with them country reports, written by their governmental think tanks, which enlightened the 'peacemakers' about this little-known region and informed Allied Baltic policy.

Baltic reports of the French *Comité d'études* only covered Lithuania and Latvia, but their conclusions also applied to Estonia. On the one hand, French analysts recognized Baltic civilizational exceptionalism in the Russian Empire. 'The Lettish people are not an ignorant and disorderly mass', read the report on Latvia, 'it is a nation of educated cultivators, industrious, tidy, thrifty, comparable to wealthy peasants of western Europe in their low birth rate, a people with an active and influential middle class, used to administering its own affairs, to forming associations, raising its delegates, capable of forming a state and to rule themselves, just as much as Danes or Norwegians.'[7] It was acknowledged, however, that complete independence of the Baltic States was not possible. In the French view, the three nationalities were too small to exist without foreign help, and withdrawal of Russian rule would eventually be substituted by German domination, which Paris, unsurprisingly, thought undesirable. On top of that, it was observed that Baltic ports were too important for Russia, while Russian hinterland was no less important for the prosperity of the Baltic provinces. Autonomy or federation with Russia was thus the optimal way forward for Latvia and Estonia, while agrarian Lithuania also had an option of joining Poland.[8]

In the same vein, the US Inquiry report, prepared for the US peace delegation, recommended reunion with the future democratic Russia of most breakaway provinces, except Finland, Poland, the Armenians in Transcaucasia, 'and probably Lithuania'. The latter, though, would not be able to stand alone and, in the view of American experts, had only two options—reabsorption into Russia, or a union with Poland, which Americans preferred.[9] Of more than 160 area studies that the British prepared for the PPC, two dealt with the Baltic provinces. British analysts did not even consider statehood for Courland, Livonia and Estonia, and stressed that the latter had 'never been regarded internationally as in any way distinct from the mass of the Russian Empire.'[10] While a separate report on Lithuania included extensive analysis of the development of Lithuanian nationalism, it refrained from suggestions on the country's future and predicted its conflict with Poland.[11]

Allied Baltic policy in the PPC did not differ from expert recommendations and was equally unenthusiastic about Baltic statehood. The main obstacle was, of course, Russia. It was a former ally of the West and a great power whose resources were vital for postwar reconstruction, and whose weight was desired for balancing Germany. The French missed non-Bolshevik Russia most of all, as they held eighty percent of the Russian government debt and owned petroleum fields, mines and industries, all of which was gone with the Bolshevik revolution. The Allies thus hoped for the Bolshevik demise and even tried to help bring it about by supplying the Russian Whites and by conducting a half-hearted military intervention in Russia.

Consequently, while the Allies supported the Baltic States against the Bolsheviks, at the same time they were extremely wary to annoy the 'future democratic Russia' and Russian Whites by supporting aspirations of Baltic independence. 'If Russia recovers, she with her 160 million inhabitants, will have to be reckoned with in Europe', British premier Lloyd George scaremongered his peers.[12] 'We will then be able to turn to the Russians and say: "Here is what we have done for you"', Clemenceau hoped.[13]

The lukewarm reception of Baltic independence aspirations in Paris was further complicated by frictions between the Baltic states, with Lithuanians trying to jump in front of the queue, claiming exceptionalism at the expense of their Baltic neighbours. Witnessing that the Allies regarded possession of ports of Riga and Tallinn as vital interests of Russia, the Lithuanians were avoiding associating themselves with Latvians and Estonians and argued that the case of Lithuania was exceptional due to its relative unimportance for Russia.[14] Lithuanian foreign minister Augustinas Voldemaras did not hesitate to stress that Lithuania, unlike Latvia and Estonia, was a historical nation, which should accord it the same status as enjoyed by Poland and other conference invitees. In the common meetings of uninvited Conference delegations, Estonians and Latvians complained about the lack of cooperation coming from Lithuanians, and it was not long before Lithuanians stopped attending these meetings altogether. It also did not help that the Lithuanians were currying favour with the Russians in Paris in their attempt to counteract Polish claims to Lithuania, while Russian statesmen were stoking Lithuanians against their southern and northern neighbours.

As for the Russians of all flavours and colours, none of the factions were prepared to let the Baltic provinces go in 1919. White Russian strongmen, such as generals Kolchak and Denikin, swore by the idea of a united and indivisible Russia. Liberals were not far behind. According to the Russian envoy in London Konstantin Nabokov, 'Estonian and Latvian aspirations of statehood can be justified as much as an attempt of negroes in America to declare an independent negro republic.'[15] The Bolsheviks, on their part, approached the embryonic Baltic governments with peace proposals in the end of 1919, but this decision was merely tactical. Baltic nationalisms were only useful in so far as they helped to destroy tsarism in Russia. Once that happened, the Bolsheviks expected the Baltics to join the family of communist nations. Baltic statehood after the Great War therefore happened not because of, but largely against, the wishes, expectations and policies of both East and West.

* * *

The Baltic States arrived at the dissolution of the Soviet Union in 1991 in a much better position than they were in 1919. After the First World War, only Lithuania of the three could boast about being a 'historical nation', and even that historicity was separated by nearly two centuries of contested history. In 1991, the relatively recent statehood of all three Baltic States, as well as their annexation by the Soviet Union in 1940, which was proclaimed null and void by the Congress of People's Deputies of the Soviet Union in 1989, was public knowledge in both East and West. US policy of non-recognition had been annoying Gorbachev up until he left the Kremlin. While repressions of the that period had left an indelible record in the Baltic historical memory, Soviet period also served as a laboratory of Baltic nationalism, where cultural nationalism, in areas such as linguistics or folklore, was allowed, or even officially encouraged. It was thus unsurprising that Baltic nationalisms sprung back to life as soon as Gorbachev began liberalising the Soviet empire, and had the best chance of establizhing their own states among all Soviet republics.

Western attitudes toward Baltic demands for independence during the last years of the Soviet Union are discussed in greater detail elsewhere in this volume. In short, just as in 1919, when it came to the Baltic question, the West avoided commitment and waited for the outcome of developments in Russia. Unification of Germany, as well as independence of Soviet satellites in central Europe, was considered good enough. No Western power wanted to rock the boat by supporting secession of the Baltic States and risking reactionary reversal of the 'Gorbachevian moment', which was seen as nothing short of miraculous. Consequently, Western recognitions of Baltic statehood only started pouring in after Russia recognized them itself in the end of 1991.

Escape of the Baltic States from the *post*-Soviet orbit, however, has received much less scholarly attention, especially when seen from the Russian perspective. Why did Russia, with Putin at the helm, let them slip into NATO peacefully in 2004, while it drew a line in the sand over Georgia and Ukraine just four years later? Was it because of Russia's moment of weakness, its temporary romance with the West, or the much greater strategic importance of the Black Sea region? Or was it also because Russia saw '*Pribaltika*' as a special case and considered its Western orientation uncomfortable, but still legitimate? What follows is an attempt to sketch, *prima facie*, the outlines of Baltic exceptionalism in the 'Russian mind'—a set of historical circumstances, perceptions, stereotypes and cleavages, deeply embedded in the official historical narrative and political discourse of modern Russia, elements which remained after the Russian democratic moment subsided.

In the 'Russian mind', the 'Baltics' incontestably belong to the non-Slavic and Western-Christian civilization. As a consequence, post-1991 Russia has seen its minorities in the Baltic States in the ordinary sense of this word, and not as competing with the titular nationality for dominance in the host country. There also exists institutional memory of the blatant failure of Russification, attempted, in different ways, by both Russian and Soviet empires in the last two centuries. Characteristically, a recent history textbook for higher education sighs at the 'cultural insularity' of 'absurd proportions' of the Baltic governorates in the nineteenth century: 'on the territory of Russian empire, state institutions were not accepting documents, written in Russian, while in order to bury an Orthodox citizen one had to get permission from a Lutheran pastor!'[16]

Such clear perceptions of civilizational divide or affinity had geopolitical significance at the time of the dissolution of the Soviet Union. From the outset, the new Russia expected a tight alliance with Belarus and Ukraine on confederation, commonwealth, or at least a close cooperation basis. Just before signing the Belovezha Accords with Belarussians and Ukrainians, at the Belarussian Parliament in Minsk, Yeltsin read aloud, in the Old Slavonic language, a decree of one of the Russian tsars that celebrated the Russian victory over the Polish-Lithuanian Commonwealth, and that promised Belarus Russian protection. While such a shtick was supposed to show brotherly Russian attitude towards Belarus, it caused an uproar among Belarussian MPs. In a more informal setting, Genady Burbulis, the first and last Secretary of State of the Russian SFSR who accompanied Yeltsin to Minsk, quoted Rudyard Kipling about Russians, Belarussians and Ukrainians 'being of the same blood.'[17] The latter idea was echoed in the preamble of the Belovezha agreement of 8 December 1991 which dissolved the Soviet Union and created the Commonwealth of Independent States (CIS). There was, however, no talk of the 'same blood' when referring to the Baltic States. The latter did not join CIS, and were not expected to.

A closely related element of Baltic exceptionalism in the eyes of Russia is civilization as such, as opposed to non-civilization. The Baltics were exceptional in both Russian and Soviet empires for their higher level of development, compared to other regions. In the Soviet Union, the Baltic States were called 'the Soviet west'. Baltic nationalists also used this argument themselves in the nineteenth century, arguing that they were hostages to the backwardness of the Russian empire. Consequently, imperialism based on the rule of civilized over uncivilized, or any variation on the *Kulturträger*, is rarely invoked when referring to the Baltic, with the exception of emphasis on industrialization and investment that the Soviet Union brought into the Baltic States. Moreover, wars between Russia and the Grand Duchy of Lithuania, and between the latter and the Polish-Lithuanian Commonwealth, are taught extensively in Russian schools, which reinforces the image of the Baltics as historically hostile, but legitimate peers rather than subjects.

The 'fascist connection' forms a separate and very important category of elements of Baltic exceptionalism in the eyes of Russia. It is widely believed that the Soviet Union, or Russia, not only liberated the Baltics from the German Nazis, but that it also fought fascism native to the Baltics. Episodes of Baltic collaboration with Nazi Germany, including the existence of Latvian and Estonian SS legions, is often seen not as an exception, but as proof of the inherently fascist nature of Baltic nationalities. A good illustration of this is the fact that in the Soviet Army, until the last days of the Soviet Union, conscripts from the Baltic were often mocked by calling them 'Germans' (*nemtsy*).

'Liberation of the Baltics' was also an issue that clashed with the US official policy of non-recognition of Baltic occupation in otherwise cordial Soviet-Russian talks at the time of the dissolution of the Soviet Union. Characteristically, Mikhail Moiseyev, chief of the Soviet general staff, in informal talks with his American counterpart did not hide his outrage at the Baltic States' hatred of the Soviet Union, while seven of his uncles died liberating them from the Nazis.[18] In this connection, the proof of Baltic ungratefulness, as well as its civilizational otherness in general for Russia is the Baltic boycott and even denouncement of the Victory Day parades of 9 May. In contrast to ex-Soviet republics of Belarus, Georgia and, until recently, Ukraine, the Baltics have not been celebrating the 9 May from 1991, and any manifestations on that day have been almost exclusively limited to the Baltic Russian minorities.

The Baltics in the official 'Russian mind' thus are alien, unfriendly, fascist-leaning, history-distorting countries who do not even need 'colour revolutions' in order to be pro-Western and anti-Russian, and who even have the audacity to compete for dominance in what Russia considers to be its 'near abroad'. It is thus unsurprising that even Vladimir Zhirinovsky, the late court jester of Putin's regime and a caricature arch-chauvinist, acknowledged Baltic exceptionalism. According to him, Lithuania, Latvia and Estonia were 'different nations, different language groups, different culture', and Moscow should have given them more autonomy within the USSR, in order to avoid trouble in the future.[19]

* * *

Baltic geopolitical exceptionalism was made possible not only by tectonic shifts in world order, such as those 1919 or 1991, but also by fundamental shifts in perceptions. Neither in 1919, nor in 1991 did Western powers commit themselves themselves to the independence of the Baltic States in the absence of Russian acquiescence. Similarly, both in 1919 and in 1991 Russia/Soviet Union did not want to hear about their secession. The main difference was that in 1991, Moscow saw the largest demonstrations since the Bolshevik revolution in support of Baltic independence. In 2004, the Baltic States escaped to the Western orbit unscathed. While favorable balance of power was undoubtedly important, it was also significant that Russia saw '*Pribaltika*' as a special case and considered its Western orientation uncomfortable, but tolerable or even legitimate. In the *Russian mind*, the Baltic States had more in common with Poland and Czechoslovakia than they had with other former republics of the USSR. This view might help explain why Russian Baltic policy so far has been bark but no bite.[20] Further analysis of Russian attitudes towards Baltic exceptionalism could shed light on more speculative questions of security in the Baltic: did Russia really acquiesce to the loss of the Baltic States, or are the 'Baltic States next', as is often repeated in the fog of Russian war of aggression against Ukraine? Analysis in this chapter supports the optimistic conclusion.

PART IV

THE RESPONSES FROM MOSCOW

9

CONTEXT, CROSS-PRESSURES AND COMPROMISE

THE ROLES OF GORBACHEV AND YELTSIN

Professor Archie Brown

At some point in the 1990s I found myself sitting next to President Lennart Meri of Estonia at a dinner in my Oxford college. He did not agree with my suggestion that, if Mikhail Gorbachev had not become General Secretary of the Soviet Communist Party in 1985, he would not be holding his high office in an independent Estonia but would still be living in the Soviet Union. Yet, there was nothing preordained about a Soviet leadership refraining from using the force that was at their disposal to stop the separatist tendencies. Indeed, had any other member of Konstantin Chernenko's Politburo succeeded that colourless apparatchik, expectations would not have been aroused in the first place, and the everyday levels of coercion of the post-

Stalin era would have sufficed to keep all fifteen republics within the USSR.

Nevertheless, the three Baltic States were always potential flashpoints in the Soviet Union and important for the breakup of the Soviet state. Indeed, a different way of looking at it is to say that the Soviet Union would not have disintegrated had not Estonia, Latvia and Lithuania—plus Western Ukraine—been forcibly incorporated in the Soviet Union, following the Hitler-Stalin Pact. The Ukrainian-American historian Serhii Plokhy is among those who makes the point that, however paradoxical it appears, the person ultimately responsible for the dissolution of the USSR was none other than Josef Stalin. Plokhy rightly observes that there could still have been a Soviet Union without Estonia, Latvia and Lithuania, but his emphasis is on Ukraine, which was more integral to the survival of the Union. Lviv in the late 1980s, Plokhy notes, 'became the centre of nationalist mobilization for Ukrainian independence', to which he adds: 'It was as difficult to imagine Ukrainian independence without Lviv as to imagine the Soviet Union without Ukraine in the fall and winter of 1991.'[1]

Ultimately, though, what made the breakup of the Soviet Union certain was not national-separatism in the Baltic republics of the Soviet Union or, indeed, pressure from Ukraine, for as late as the Soviet referendum of March 1991 more than seventy percent of Ukrainians voted to remain within a 'renewed Union', one with competitive elections and a lot of power devolved to the republics.[2] What was decisive for the breakup of the Soviet state was Boris Yeltsin's assertion of *Russian* independence from the Union. It was a curious position for a Russian leader to take, since Russia had been the dominant partner in that Union, and many Russians took pride in the Soviet Union's superpower status and its international significance. For the leadership of the Russian republic to refuse to accept Soviet jurisdiction had far more to do with Yeltsin's ambition to be the supreme ruler in the Kremlin than with concern for Russia's national interest.

However, that is not to deny a crucial role also to Lithuania (the most vociferous), Estonia and Latvia. Without the campaign, first, for far greater devolution of power, and later, for full national independence, from the Baltic republics, Georgia and Western Ukraine, it would have been unthinkable for Yeltsin and his advisers to demand Russian independence from the Union. For opportunistic reasons, they mounted a bandwagon that had been set rolling in the Baltic republics, where there were long-held, legitimate—though hitherto repressed and unrealisable—desires for independent statehood. So far as the fate of the Union is concerned, there was, however, simply no comparison between the Baltic republics attempting to leave the USSR and Russia opting out. There had been a Soviet state before Estonia, Latvia and Lithuania were forcibly incorporated in 1940 as Union Republics of the USSR, and the latter's viability did not depend on them. The Russian republic was in a totally different category. It occupied three-quarters of the territory of the Union and contained half its population.

When Yeltsin supported the Baltic republics in their demand for national sovereignty in early 1991, it was not because he cared deeply about them, but rather, part of his struggle for power with Gorbachev and the central Soviet authorities. That support, nevertheless, was important, for by this time Yeltsin was the most popular politician in Russia and the USSR. Contrary to post-Soviet Russian propaganda and conventional wisdom, it is not true that Gorbachev was popular only in the West, never in Russia. During his first five years in power, he was—according to the best survey research of the time, that conducted by the All-Union Public Opinion Research Centre (VTsIOM) under the leadership of Tatiana Zaslavskaya and Yuriy Levada—the most popular politician in the country. In a survey conducted in late

1989 and published by the Levada team in January 1990, in which citizens were asked to name the most outstanding individuals of all times and all peoples, Gorbachev was the only living person to appear in the top ten.[3] It was in May–June 1990 that Yeltsin overtook Gorbachev as the most popular politician in Russia and the USSR.[4] In 1990–1 the economy was going from bad to worse and that, together with nationalist unrest and the fissiparous tendencies, produced a steep decline in Gorbachev's standing—to the benefit of Yeltsin who, by early 1991, represented a political force to be reckoned with, capable of bringing 100,000 people on to the streets of Moscow to demonstrate against the all-Union authorities.

A great many educated Russians, especially those who self-identified as belonging to the liberal or democratic intelligentsia, shifted their support in the last two years of the Soviet Union from Gorbachev to Yeltsin. And many, though far from all of them, followed Yeltsin in opposing any violent crackdown on the pro-independence movements in the Baltic States. That was a significant source of encouragement for people in Estonia, Latvia and Lithuania.

A hugely important part of the context both for Moscow and for the peoples of the Baltic republics in 1990–1 was what happened, and did not happen, in 1989. By that I mean the East-Central European countries becoming independent and non-communist, and the Berlin Wall coming down, without a single shot being fired by a Soviet soldier. Seeing Hungarians, Poles and Czechs getting away with it, Estonians, Latvians and Lithuanians sensed the possibility of long-held dreams becoming political reality. Gorbachev in 1988, especially in his United Nations speech in December of that year (when international attention was paid to his words), declared that the people of every country had the right to decide for themselves what kind of political and economic system they wished to live in.[5] He did not at that time think this applied within the multinational Soviet state, for he believed (wrongly, as it turned out) that even the most disaffected nationalities within the USSR would see the advantages of remaining within a democratizing Soviet Union and one in which federal forms were being given federal substance.

Gorbachev did, however, have the countries of East and Central Europe in mind, though events there moved faster than either he or Western leaders expected. In January 1989, Vadim Medvedev, a Gorbachev ally within the Politburo, warned the Soviet leader that there would be what he called 'a crisis in Eastern Europe.' Gorbachev's response was to say, 'Whatever it is, they will have to decide themselves how they will live.'[6] His actions—and crucial inactions—remained true to those words throughout a year in which the geopolitical map of Europe changed dramatically. What made the biggest impact on people in the Baltic republics in 1989 was that Soviet troops were kept in their barracks while those momentous events took their course.

Gorbachev, however, in the winter of 1990–1, displeased almost everyone. The new tolerance and new political pluralism had provided the facilitating conditions for the growth of national independence movements, although the breakup of the USSR was very much an unintended consequence of perestroika. But forcible repression remained an option for the central authorities, and it would have taken much less bloodshed and destruction than the Putin government is, at the time of writing, inflicting on Ukraine to restore the status quo ante. I am at one with my fellow contributor to this volume, Vladislav Zubok, in attributing to Gorbachev a hatred of bloodshed, but our evaluation of that disposition of the last Soviet leader differs greatly. Zubok, commenting on Gorbachev's 'visceral aversion to the use of force', has written, 'An admirable moral quality in an individual, this was a huge political flaw in the leader of a country with a tragic history and facing a rising wave of toxic nationalism.'[7] The majority of Russians, Zubok contends, 'wanted Gorbachev to use his power, not to devolve it.'[8]

When earlier demands from the Baltic republics for greater devolution of power were further emboldened and turned into campaigns for outright independence, opinion in Moscow was deeply divided. Gorbachev was caught in political crossfire and, though his authority was on the wane, how he reacted was still crucial. On the one side, nationalists in non-Russian republics became temporary allies of Russians who purported to be more radical democrats than Gorbachev, joining them in harsh criticism of the Soviet leader. On the other side, Gorbachev was coming under intense pressure from senior party and state officials, the security organs, and the military-industrial complex, to impose 'presidential rule'—a euphemism for martial law—to ensure that the Soviet Union was preserved intact. Such a crackdown would have come with a high cost for Soviet citizens, and not only those in the Baltic republics. Now that expectations had been aroused, a still more oppressive regime would have been needed (if it was to be effective) than that which had prevailed during the post-Stalin but pre-perestroika years.

The part played by Gorbachev and his most like-minded allies in the Soviet leadership in preventing the comprehensive crackdown on separatist movements is insufficiently appreciated in the Baltic States even today. A reluctance to give credit to a General Secretary of the Central Committee of the Communist Party was, of course, understandable for historical reasons.[9] Nevertheless, giving, as is often the case, greater credit for Baltic independence to American President George H.W. Bush and British Prime Minister Margaret Thatcher ignores the serious limitations on their ability to influence decisions on the use of force taken in Moscow; it also plays down their concern not to undermine Gorbachev. Bush and Thatcher played significant parts in the ending of the Cold War (as did Ronald Reagan, who held annual summit meetings with Gorbachev between 1985 and 1988), but they regarded Gorbachev's continuation in office as by far the best guarantee that there would not be a reversal of the transformation of Soviet foreign policy that occurred between 1985 and 1990.

They feared that were Gorbachev to lose parts of the Soviet Union, following 'the loss', as it was perceived by the Soviet military-industrial complex, of Eastern Europe, that was liable to end with his ousting. Therefore, far from actively encouraging independence movements in the Baltic republics (even though they had never accepted their incorporation in the USSR as legitimate in the first place) and Ukraine, they urged restraint. Bush told Gorbachev in 1990 that he was 'being hit both on my left and my right' by those who said he was not pushing hard enough on the issue of self-determination for the Baltic States, but, he added, 'I've tried to conduct myself in a constrained way because I know you have big problems.'[10] Margaret Thatcher was even more anxious than Bush not to damage Gorbachev. In a lengthy May 1990 meeting with the de facto Prime Minister of Lithuania, Kazimira Prunskienė, Thatcher, as her official biographer puts it, 'successfully walked the tightrope—supporting the aspirations of the Lithuanians for self-determination, while urging Mrs Prunskienė to help Gorbachev in his handling of the situation.'[11]

To realise what Gorbachev was up against from the opposite side to that of nationalist separatists and radical democrats, it is salutary to note the institutional positions held by those who tried to take power from Gorbachev in August 1991. They were the KGB Chairman, Vladimir Kruychkov; the overseer of the military-industrial complex, Oleg Baklanov; the head of the government (as distinct from party), Prime Minister Valentin Pavlov; Minister of Defence, Dmitriy Yazov; the Minister of Interior, Boris Pugo; the Politburo member who supervised the party apparatus, Oleg Shenin; and the Vice-President Gennadiy Yanaev. They were supported, more tacitly, by the Chairman of the Supreme Soviet of the USSR, Anatoliy Lukyanov. The institutions these people represented are more important than their names. They were (Vice-Presidency excepted) vast organisations wielding great coercive and political power.

Although every such institution contained people of different mindsets, the predominant view within the party-state apparatus was clear. They wanted a return to strict central control over the whole of the USSR, with the immediate aim of preserving intact the entire Soviet state. The leading August 1991 putschists had claimed in earlier years to be firm supporters of perestroika, but 'perestroika' not only meant different things to different people, it also meant different things to the same people at different times—from one year to the next (and, in the last two years of the Soviet state, sometimes from one month to the next). Insofar as their earlier professed support for perestroika was genuine, none of the senior party and state officials who attempted to seize full power in 1991 had contemplated a few years earlier the possibility of it leading to the disintegration of the Soviet state. Watching in horror as separatist movements gained ground, they found their attachment to traditional communist 'democratic centralism' and nostalgia for the old strictly hierarchical power structure returning reinforced.

Gorbachev's political views evolved in a different direction—to the point at which his understanding of democracy had far more in common with his Western counterparts than with that of a typical Communist Party secretary. He felt especially close to social democratic leaders, notwithstanding the history of hostility between communist parties and socialist parties of a social democratic type. Gorbachev's favourite foreign interlocutors were Spanish socialist Prime Minister Felipe González and former West German Chancellor Willy Brandt. It is hardly surprising, then, that he lost the support of the heads of Soviet party-state institutions whose stability and very existence were threatened by the transformative change of the political system that was well underway.

It was only after they had failed to persuade or coerce Gorbachev into giving his imprimatur to ruthless coercive force that the top leaders of those state institutions mounted the putsch against him. Even then they sought the greater legitimacy that might have accrued to their action if it could gain presidential blessing. One member of the putchist delegation who tried to pressurize Gorbachev into supporting 'the state of emergency', General Valentin Varennikov, later complained that Gorbachev used 'unparliamentary expressions' in telling them where to go.[12] Of course, Gorbachev himself did not wish to lose any component parts of the Soviet state, but it was to be a different kind of Union—genuinely federal and with a great deal of power devolved to the republics—and to be achieved through compromise and persuasion, and then constitutionally ratified with the signing of a new and voluntary Union Treaty. The breakup of the Union was *almost* the last thing Gorbachev wanted. A prospect he abhorred even more was that of preserving the Union through martial law and wide-ranging, violent repression. A leading reformist ally who was given fast promotion by Gorbachev after 1985, Aleksandr Nikolaevich Yakovlev, became critical of his patron in many respects. Yet Yakovlev noted that those who later mounted the coup against Gorbachev and who, earlier in 1991, tried hard to link him with the killings they perpetrated in Vilnius and Riga, failed in that endeavour. Gorbachev, as Yakovlev put it in his memoirs, had gone into history 'without blood on his hands.'[13]

The violence—except in Baku where Gorbachev did authorize the use of lethal force to end a pogrom of Armenians, though not the indiscriminate killing of Azeris which followed—was halted each time by Gorbachev after one night. He lost many of his liberal supporters because he failed to remove from office those responsible for the violence and for not instantly condemning it. But he may well thereby have bought himself some time by postponing the hardliners' attempt to replace him that was eventually made in August 1991. The British Ambassador to Moscow, 1988–92, Sir Rodric Braithwaite, learned of a handwritten ultimatum to Gorbachev, apparently delivered in January 1991, signed by twenty Soviet marshals and generals, including the formidable and respected former Chief of the General Staff, Marshal Sergey Akhromeyev, warning him against tolerating the loss of any part of the Soviet Union.[14] If such an ultimatum (which has not, so far as I am aware, yet surfaced in the state archives) was indeed delivered to Gorbachev, it makes his temporary fence-sitting the more understandable. Ultimately, though, his tactical retreat, in the winter of 1990–1, satisfied neither side in an increasingly polarised society—even if we speak only of Moscow.

A long meeting took place between Gorbachev and the American ambassador to Moscow, Jack Matlock, in the Kremlin on 24 January 1991. Matlock came with a letter from President Bush, expressing concern about what was happening in the Baltic republics. Bush said he'd been very restrained when speaking about the Baltics, but that he was coming under increasing pressure (incomparably less ferocious, it should be added, than the cross-pressures Gorbachev was under). Gorbachev told Matlock that Russia suffered from what he called a 'low political culture' and the absence of a tradition of compromise. His task, in a time of high tension, was to prevent civil war, and there would be 'zigs and zags.' For Matlock, it was important that Gorbachev was confirming, in effect, that this was a tactical retreat, not a change of course, though he believed that Gorbachev was being 'blind to the dangers of encouraging and cooperating with the hard-liners.' Gorbachev himself was over-confident in his conviction that he could make enough concessions to keep them on board and ultimately outwit them. But his explanation to Matlock was enough for the US administration not to deploy the sanctions they were being urged to apply.

Crucially, Gorbachev did not impose the so-called 'presidential rule' (or martial law) senior party-state officials were urging him to deploy. For a majority of members of the Politburo (no longer the highest executive body in the land) and the Cabinet of Ministers, the time was long past to reimpose order. Within the ranks of the *siloviki*—the army, the KGB, and the Ministry of Internal Affairs—there was especially fierce opposition to losing any part of the Soviet Union, following the loss of Eastern Europe which had been a bitter enough pill for them to swallow. Western journalists and politicians focused more on the demands of the separatists and political activists who presented themselves as radical democrats than on the people and the institutional resources on the other side. Gorbachev had to take account of both sides. And it was not independence-seekers in the Baltic republics, or the movement called 'Democratic Russia' that contained the big battalions in the most literal power-wielding sense. That power belonged to the KGB, the troops of the Ministry of Internal Affairs, and the army.

If any confirmation is needed that Gorbachev was at risk of being overthrown, the events of August 1991 confirmed it. It was on the late afternoon of the eighteenth of that month that Gorbachev's telephones in the presidential holiday home at Foros, on the Crimean coast, were disconnected and he and his family were prevented from leaving the complex. It was only the following day that Soviet TV conveyed to the people of their own country and the outside world the pack of lies about Gorbachev being too ill to perform his duties, as the reins of power were seized by a self-appointed 'State Committee for the State of Emergency.'[15] By 22 August the attempted coup had collapsed.

A coup mounted against Gorbachev in early 1991 would have had far greater chances of success than in August. In January, Yeltsin had not yet been elected President of Russia in a free election by universal suffrage. That election took place in June. Yeltsin's landslide victory made especially hollow the putschists' claim two months later to be speaking in the name of the people. A coup on a cold January night before Yeltsin had achieved that electoral legitimacy, and before Gorbachev had renewed, as he did in April, his attempts to hold the Union together through negotiation and voluntary agreement, would most likely have succeeded in preventing the independence of the Baltic States and of any other Soviet republics. The idea that there was some-thing inevitable about the breakup of the Soviet Union, and if it had not been Gorbachev who presided over its dissolution around that time, it would have been someone else, is, in my view, the sheerest nonsense, though it is a nonsense that was widely believed. It may have taken Putin's brutality in Ukraine to bring about a realization that the Soviet leadership still had the coer-cive force at their disposal to suppress national separatism, had they possessed the political will to use it.

Gorbachev's power by 1991 was on the wane. Transformative change in the Soviet political system included a conscious aban-donment of 'democratic centralism.' This relaxation of the tradi-tional intraparty iron discipline enabled Communist Party mem-bers to compete against one another in elections—on radically different political platforms—and to differ fundamentally on policy in the new legislature. The change was endorsed by Gorbachev, in spite of the fact that it undermined the top-down power of the General Secretary.

Yet, even in 1991, Gorbachev still mattered. He was President, head of state, party leader and commander-in-chief of the armed forces. If he, rather than the putschists, had established a state of emergency, the clock would have been well and truly turned back (just as it is being turned back by a Russian president in 2022). Of course, had Gorbachev conferred a veneer of legitimacy on a comprehensive crackdown in January or on that which actually occurred in August, he would not have lasted long. Those who took matters into their own hands in August would never forgive him for undermining their hitherto unaccountable power and for destroying the pillars of the system and the Union.

Conclusion

The peoples of the Baltic States deserve great credit for establishing the most democratic political systems of the fifteen successor states to the Soviet Union. The facilitating conditions for their independence were, however, the pluralisation of the Soviet political system which got seriously underway in 1987 and accelerated in each subsequent year. A new tolerance, freedom of speech and, increasingly, of publication played a huge part in enabling the peaceful pursuit of greater national autonomy and, ultimately of independent statehood. The latter aspiration was given a tremendous psychological boost by Gorbachev's calm acceptance in 1989 of the East European countries casting aside their Communist rulers and Soviet overlordship. Contested elections for a new Soviet legislature, which Gorbachev announced in mid-1988, would take place the following year—and the actual elections in 1989, 1990 and 1991 provided institutional pathways for the pressing of national goals. Even Gorbachev's zigzags and compromises may have been a necessary evil for the peoples of the Baltic States; without them, it is more likely than not that those who sought a return to highly authoritarian rule would have struck earlier and with a greater chance of success. Not least, Gorbachev's aversion to bloodshed was for Estonians, Latvians and Lithuanians an unmitigated good. The August 1991 putschists regarded as treachery Gorbachev's refusal to preserve the Union by force. It is a view shared by Vladimir Putin and his closest associates in the Kremlin of 2022. Who the top leader is matters in any country. In Russia it matters more than in most.

10

THE HOUSE DIVIDED

Professor Vladislav Zubok

The pro-independence movements of the Baltic republics rose in synchronisation with Mikhail Gorbachev's reforms. They took advantage of glasnost and perestroika to legitimise their national discourse eventually leading to a 'nationalisation' of their local communist parties. Today, some people look back on the late Gorbachev as some sort of sorcerer's apprentice, a hapless figure who did not know what he had started and could not put an end to it. Whatever the Balts think of him nowadays, I would like to offer a defence for Mikhail Sergeyevich. In my most recent book, I am rather critical of the Soviet General Secretary, and it is proper to balance this criticism out.[1] Without Gorbachev's reforms and his principled rejection of force, it would have been infinitely harder, if not impossible, for the Balts to mobilise themselves and receive so much support from other peoples in the Soviet Union for their cause. The Baltic people, whose foundational national narrative is a rebellion against a totalitarian communist regime and Moscow's 'empire', should remember to whom they owe a big debt for their relatively quick and bloodless access to independence.

The Baltic 'republics' also exploited the fact that the Soviet Union was originally a constitutional confederation. This confederation, as it was conceived by Lenin against the vehement objections of Josef Stalin, was, of course, only a confederation on paper. It was a brutal and ruthless unitary state held together by the Party dictatorship, the army, and the KGB. Yet Gorbachev, in a fit of socialist idealism, decided to change it. He was a legalist and a graduate from the faculty of law at Moscow State University. To him Soviet constitution and confederal structure of the Soviet state mattered. This stance also offered him a clear stance in opposition to the Stalinist methods of rule, as the Soviet leader attempted to go 'back to Lenin'—i.e., back to the ideals of the revolution that had proclaimed national liberation from imperial and colonial shackles all over the world. The Balts took full advantage of this amazingly idealistic attitude to demand economic and then political sovereignty for their three republics. The legal mechanisms were not guaranteed or specified in great detail, but the Soviet constitution did proclaim the right for any republic to exit from the Soviet Union. This was a legal implication from the Leninist, confederal interpretation which the pro-independence elites in the Baltics were keen to exploit.

Gorbachev and his allies in the Politburo declared that in a new political environment of perestroika regional autonomy must be respected. Suddenly the possibilities of vague constitutional structures, that existed mostly on paper, seemed more attainable. The 'cardboard' and subordinate republican institutions, including a government, a Supreme Soviet, a republican Party branch, an Academy, and other national cultural institutions, suddenly got a lease to become flesh-and-blood institutions.

Politically, Gorbachev encouraged mobilisation of intelligentsia and working people in support of perestroika: he needed a lever to overcome resistance to his initiatives from the ossified Party and state bureaucracies. This allowed the Baltic intelligentsia, with the support of Moscow, to launch the mass movements that quickly turned into a political opposition and became an umbrella for diverse forces that opposed the old regime and demanded radical change. Economic reform, Gorbachev's priority in 1987–8, played an additional and very important role in this transformation. The Soviet government began to dismantle the system of central Party controls over economic management in Moscow and elsewhere, introducing unprecedented decrees on state enterprises and cooperatives. These policy decisions set in motion a process of economic decentralisation, that the Soviet Union had not experienced since 1927. As this process was not accompanied by a creation of financial and trade markets, it had very destructive implications for the highly integrated Soviet economy. The Baltic elites, most of them still Party-controlled yet with distinct national aspirations, saw in those economic reforms their greatest chance for legal promotion of their autonomy, if not independence, from the Kremlin. They turned to the central leadership with an offer to showcase the economic reforms to other republics, whilst at the same time gaining greater independence for themselves.

The Balts also profited from a massive Gorbachev purge of the Brezhnev era cadres which had previously overseen governance in the three territories. The purge made space for such leaders as Algirdas Brazauskas in Lithuania and Anatolijs Gorbunovs in Latvia, as well as others such as Edgar Savisaar. These people were anti-Stalinists, who sympathised with national aspirations and knew that radical changes were necessary. In 1987–9 they were given the opportunity to become leaders of the local parties and the head of cultural-political movements.

It should be stressed that it was very early on that the Baltic pro-independence actors realised the most viable strategy for them to gain independence would be to promote independence of all titular nationalities of the Soviet Union. These nationalities included the Ukrainians, Belarusians and above all the Russians. From their point of view, there would be no liberation of the Baltic States without liberation of the Slavic core of 'the socialist empire.' The nationalist movements in the Baltic republics established Russian language media to promote Baltic democracy as an example for other republics. The first gatherings of 'popular fronts' from Belorussia, Georgia, Moscow and Leningrad, took place in Baltic venues, with the logistics for them being offered by Baltic activists. This was a very smart strategy that would ultimately yield results surpassing even the boldest imagination of the Baltic national movements when they formulated their initial plans back in 1987/88.

In retrospect, we can see that the Balts began to develop a highly effective strategy for deconstruction of the Soviet Union as a unitary state at a very early stage. On the contrary, Gorbachev and his entourage in Moscow lacked a strategy to deal with separatists. The term 'separatists' naturally reflects the viewpoint of the Soviet leadership, including Gorbachev, who wanted to reform the Soviet Union, not to see it imploding at republican seams. Gorbachev realised that the Balts cleverly checkmated him on the issue of a constitutional confederal statehood. Yet he continued to regard any exit from any part of the Soviet Union as an act of secession and considered it the beginning of a domino effect which would lead to economic troubles and huge political crisis.

At the end of 1988, there was an interesting attempt to confront the issue of Baltic autonomy, just as Gorbachev in his very narrow, indeed shockingly narrow circle, began to discuss constitutional and political reforms in the Soviet Union. One of

Gorbachev's lieutenants, Anatoly Lukyanov, who would later become known negatively for his role during the coup of 1991, proposed the creation of a legal firewall to prevent probable Baltic secession. This safety mechanism had one eye on all the other republics, should they be inspired to follow the Baltic example. Lukyanov was absolutely convinced that the exit of the Baltic republics from the USSR could trigger a constitutional crisis on a Union-wide scale. The way to proceed, Lukyanov argued, was to create the Congress of People's Deputies in Moscow as an all-Union body, a powerhouse that would be able to cancel laws from the republics when they clashed with the laws of the Union.

Lukyanov, like Gorbachev, was a lawyer. Alexander Yakovlev, Vadim Medvedev and many of Gorbachev's other aides, who did not have this legal background, all protested this design. Such a proposal, they argued, would lead back to a unitary Stalinist state that went against the principles of 'democratic socialism' and would be applauded by Russian chauvinists, fascists and Stalin's admirers. Gorbachev also ended up objecting to the project and so it was buried. Why did Gorbachev, along with others, resist Lukyanov's suggestion? One reason was that Lukyanov's project was conservative, and Gorbachev saw himself as a socialist in a Leninist style, who promoted, rather than thwarted, national aspirations. Another reason was that Gorbachev and other reformers at the time expected the greater danger to be the resistance of the conservative Party nomenklatura to economic and political reforms. On the contrary, he saw reformist Party cadres in the Baltic republics as his allies.

In February 1989, Georgy Shakhnazarov, one of Gorbachev's aides and highly sensitive to nationalism, wrote to the General Secretary to tell him that the only alternative to conflict in the Baltics was the incorporation of 'people's fronts' into the emerging political system. They would then serve as a check on the

Party conservatives. Shakhnazarov also urged for the implementation of a law that would only allow the exit of a republic from the USSR if a popular referendum mandated it. He argued that Lithuania's nationalists would not be able to pass the test. In fact, the Balts had already made very clear choices: they wanted out of the Soviet Union.

In my view, Gorbachev himself and the party reformers stubbornly steadied their course. Even in the early Fall of 1989, Gorbachev and other figures in the government, such as Alexander Yakovlev and Nikolai Ryzhkov, still hoped 'against hope' that Baltic nationalism would not go as far as secession. They continued to promote the Baltic republics as a testing ground for economic and political reforms, while branding nationalists as 'radicals' and the enemies of perestroika. Their worst fear was to provoke civil confrontation between different forces in the Baltics, primarily between the Balts and Russian-speakers. This would have mobilised Russian nationalism and possibly buried perestroika.

The history of revolutionary change consists of such delusions and fears: the inability of reformers and revolutionaries to understand the obvious, but their determination not to deviate from the designated course, etc. At this point, I cannot resist the temptation to tell you a personal story. In the summer of 1988, I travelled to Lithuania for a vacation. Before that, I had been very active in glasnost and created a discussion club in Moscow. In the spring of 1988, we in that club discussed the Molotov-Ribbentrop Pact. There could be, of course, KGB agents in the audience, but nobody muzzled or harassed us. This made us feel exhilarated about how progressive and liberal we were and how much we were contributing to glasnost. In the summer, I went on vacation to Lithuania and rented a place near a missile base from a Lithuanian captain who served in the Soviet army. We had a drink with him and after one bottle and a half of vodka, all of a sudden, this captain told me, 'I know you're Russian. I'm Lithuanian. Listen, if tomorrow they in Vilnius create any alternative political party to the Communist Party, be it Nazi, fascist, doesn't matter; I would join this party.' For me, being from the liberal intelligentsia in Moscow, it was a shocking realisation that things were not working out so straightforwardly in terms of aligning with the Balts and bringing them into the wonderful pro-reform camp against the conservatives. They perhaps had their own liberals and conservatives, but they definitely wanted out of the whole structure of the Soviet Union. Yet this realisation still sank in very slowly. I guess my instinct forbade me to think about this complexity. And my imperial mentality as a Muscovite was still very strong.

This perspective may well have been true for Gorbachev too. The first major reform to come to fruition was the Congress of People's Deputies, which opened in spring 1989. The Balts had almost 100 delegates, all freely elected on a platform of pro-independence. These representatives aligned with the Russians and with the Moscow intelligentsia to defend perestroika. However, it was part of their own game. They had not come to support Gorbachev or Moscow reformist intellectuals, but to agitate, doing everything they could to gain allies and undermine Soviet power structures. The Balts, and in particular the Lithuanians, used the new parliamentary debates and investigating commission to delegitimise the Soviet annexation of the Baltic States in 1940—linking this annexation to the 'secret protocols' of the Molotov-Ribbentrop Pact of 1939. During the Congress of the USSR in session, the Balts approached Jack F. Matlock, the US ambassador to Moscow, with the first Congress in session. They made specific requests for the United States to recognise their independence. Matlock was quite shocked by this appeal, but it was also a surprise to the Balts that the ambassador told them that the United States could not provide them with such recognition as long as they had no 'sovereign' control over their own territory.

When did Gorbachev's eyes finally open to the problem? Only in August 1989 after the Baltic Way stretched from Tallinn to Vilnius, across all three Baltic republics. We know that in late July, Gorbachev was preparing a new Union treaty which was very liberal and worked to make the Soviet confederation into a reality. After the Baltic Way he shelved this proposal and issued a very hard-line declaration from the Central Committee, which described the Baltic popular fronts as a conspiracy of 'anti-Soviet international elements' who whipped up 'nationalist hysteria.' This statement was so far out of sync with what he had said before when he ushered in the new political atmosphere in the country that the Balts suspected that this document had been concocted by the Party hardliners behind Gorbachev's back. In reality, the document did indeed belong to Gorbachev. For the first time the architect of perestroika felt he was squeezed between the Party conservatives and Russian nationalist forces in the Soviet power structures on the one hand, and the radicalised forces of secession with a minority of liberal intelligentsia on the other. In response to these pressures, he began to zigzag in an increasingly desperate effort to avoid polarisation and violence, which for him was synonymous with the end of his reforms.

The sudden fall of the Berlin Wall and communist regimes across Eastern Europe changed the whole situation. Indeed, it revolutionised it. In December 1989, at a summit in Malta, Gorbachev made a pledge to President George Bush to proceed with a light touch in regard to the Balts and, to the furthest extent possible, to refrain from employing violence. The Lithuanians, however, put this pledge into doubt. Encouraged by the parade of peaceful revolutions in Eastern Europe, they declared an open secession in March 1990, against Western advice. Lithuania's announcement placed Gorbachev in real trouble.

THE HOUSE DIVIDED

I should stress that the Baltic States were not central to Gorbachev's agenda, just like the Baltic States were not central to the agenda of the Western powers. They wanted to settle the German question to begin with and they wanted to get this Baltic problem out of their way at least for half a year or maybe a year. Hans-Dietrich Genscher, the German Foreign Minister in conversation with Bush, stated that the Baltic question exploded in Gorbachev's face six to twelve months too early. Both Gorbachev and the West were quite interested to slow history's pace.

Now Gorbachev essentially faced two alternatives. The first was to negotiate a hard-nosed divorce between the Union state and the Balts. The head of the State Planning Committee or Gosplan, Yuri Masliukov, proposed to offer Lithuania independence from the Union, but without the territories of Vilnius and Klaipeda, that had become attached to Lithuania after the German-Soviet Non-Aggression Pact of 1939. Prime Minister Nikolay Ryzhkov warned Gorbachev, however, that letting the Balts go through negotiation would encourage Russian and Ukrainian nationalists. He proposed the dilution of republican sovereignty. The extraordinary Congress of the Soviet Union in March 1990 voted to make Gorbachev the president of the USSR, but also declared Lithuanian independence 'illegal' and passed the law of exit that made constitutional secession for Vilnius almost impossible.

The second option was to respond to the Lithuanian challenge with force. There were plenty of hardliners among the military and members of the Congress, who demanded military action. Gorbachev sent General Valentin Varennikov to Lithuania to ensure vital assets of the economy and communication stayed under Moscow's control. Varennikov recommended that the parliament in Vilnius be seized by the military, but Gorbachev did not want to use violence, fearing a 'massacre in Lithuania.'

As we know, Gorbachev ultimately found a third option between stepping back and using force: he used a blockade. If we

145

praise John F Kennedy for using quarantine during the Cuban Missile Crisis, we should probably praise Gorbachev for using the blockade against Lithuania, however distasteful it was for Lithuanians at the time. Washington, it has to be said, had prepared for something worse. Under the circumstances, Gorbachev chose probably the most realistic way to deal with the situation, but the decision to impose a blockade heavily angered the Soviet Minister of Defence, Marshall Yazov, who claimed that the Baltic situation could be fixed in 'three to five days, maximum a week.' It could almost be a quote from Russia's Minister of Defence in 2022, Sergei Shoigu, telling Putin how long it would take to 'fix' Ukraine. Yazov's solution was opposed by Ryzhkov, who, with Gorbachev nodding in support, stressed that such an action could lead to 'a civil war.'

We know, instead, that the blockade of Lithuania lasted for four months, and it was a classic opportunity for Gorbachev to buy time but not to resolve the problem itself. The approach was supported in the West where the issue of Lithuania also interfered with attempts to deal with German reunification and its accession to NATO. There was also worry about undermining Gorbachev. President François Mitterrand intoned at his meeting with Bush: 'We should encourage the Lithuanians to be wise.' If other dominoes in the Soviet Empire began to fall, he continued, then 'Gorbachev is gone; a military dictatorship would result.' Instead, the Balts gained allies in Moscow. On 12 June 1990, the new Congress of People's Deputies of the Russian Federation voted for 'sovereignty' of the largest republic of the Soviet Union. The Russian legislature acted in revolutionary style, by claiming all economic and financial assets on its territory to be 'national' rather than belonging to the 'Union.' Although Lithuania had suspended it succession, lacking Western support, the pro-independence actors now felt that time was on their side. Lithuanian leaders, such as Vytautas Landsbergis, now understood that the Soviet Union could be undermined from within.

At the beginning of the last year of Soviet history—1991—the next crisis and the bloodshed which followed it came rather unexpectedly. In the growing political polarisation between pro-independence majority and the pro-centre minority in Lithuania, the leaders of the latter decided to invite the Soviet Army to introduce 'presidential rule' in Lithuania. The two camps were set for a confrontation. On 10 January, Marshal Yazov ordered General Varennikov to return to Vilnius. The head of the KGB, Vladimir Kryuchkov, instructed his colonel, Mikhail Golovatov, to fly to Vilnius with 'Alfa', a small well-trained group of KGB commandos. The next day, the Lithuanian communists pro-claimed 'the committee of national salvation.'

According to Condoleezza Rice, who was working in the White House at the time, had Gorbachev supported the use of force and sustained this support, the Soviet Union could have still been preserved. However, in Rice's view, it was probably the last moment in which such a resolute attempt could have succeeded. Instead, Gorbachev stepped back and ordered his ministers to cancel the 'special operation', removing support for the bloodshed. The Baltic affair left the military camp and the KGB let down and demoralised. It was debilitating for the conservative camp, but for the Baltic States, it gave rise to a new hope.

At least two pro-independence leaders from the Baltic, Arnold Rüütel and Lennart Meri, came to the White House to talk to Bush about a new strategy. The best way, they said, to help Gorbachev survive, would be to support Russian democracy and Boris Yeltsin. By this time, Yeltsin, the most popular leader of the Russian opposition to the Soviet state, had openly aligned himself and 'sovereign Russia' with the leader of the three Baltic States. Rüütel and Meri's proposition to Bush meant supporting, not only Baltic independence, but also Yeltsin in his course of seceding from the Soviet Union, initiated in summer 1990. Gorbachev, they claimed, was a prisoner of the seven thousand generals in the army and the KGB. If Gorbachev was to receive support from Yeltsin and from the Balts, he would overthrow all of these generals, rid himself of the KGB and everything would be wonderful. Bush was genuinely puzzled by this novel idea and did not know how to react. It did not seem realistic at all for him to believe what these Baltic leaders were telling him.

In March 1991, Gorbachev carried out a national referendum that granted him a qualified majority in favour of preserving the Soviet Union. Contrary to strong fears in the Baltics and among Russian democrats, Gorbachev interpreted the results of this referendum not as an invitation for dictatorial rule, but in favour of further devolution of political power to the separate republics. He also attempted to dilute the power of Russian separatism by appealing to non-Russian autonomies within the Russian Federation. His ultimate goal now was to transform the old Soviet Union into a new voluntary Union that would be a real, not fictional confederation. He hoped, however, to preserve his presidential power on top of this new set-up.

By the end of July 1991, the Baltic strategy of creating a coalition of Gorbachev, Yeltsin, and the West seemed to have succeeded. Gorbachev accepted all Yeltsin's demands of Russian sovereignty; he tacitly seemed to agree that the Balts would be treated separately from the future Union (although he continued to drag his feet on formal talks about letting the Balts go, despite repeated advice of his US partners).

On 18–19 August, Kryuchkov triggered the Emergency Rule and launched the coup in Russia, while making Gorbachev incommunicado at his villa in Crimea. This changed the game. From the documents describing events of the first day of the coup in the Baltic States, as well as Georgia and Ukraine, the picture is of absolute calm. Nobody protested and nobody went out into the streets. The coup seemed to be a complete success. The Baltic republics suddenly fell silent, as they were under total military control. It was only the surprising resistance of Yeltsin in Moscow, encapsulated by the scene of him on the tank shown on CNN, that broke the spell of fear. Maybe resistance would have happened later, but the fact remains that it was Yeltsin and his ragtag 'democratic' coalition in Russia who broke the hard-line momentum, followed by the central Soviet state structures.

For the Balts the unexpected melting away of the coup in Moscow was a moment of golden opportunity. The Western countries hesitated to extend recognition of their independence, as they were uncertain how Gorbachev and Yeltsin would pro-ceed. There was a widespread fear in the West about the future of Soviet nuclear weapons in both Russia and Ukraine. Conse-quently, the Balts again decided to take matters into their own hands. On 22 August 1991, Rüütel, who was a personal friend of Yeltsin, called him to congratulate him on his amazing demo-cratic victory. On the next day he flew to meet with Yeltsin, accompanied by legal experts; 23 August was the anniversary of the Molotov-Ribbentrop Pact, and Rüütel hoped that Yeltsin would sign a declaration recognising Estonian independence. The Latvian leader Anatolijs Gorbunovs flew to Moscow to join his Estonian counterpart. Yeltsin was busy with consolidating his power in Moscow, so it was not until 24 August that they met. Essentially Yeltsin took the draft, composed completely by Estonian legal advisors, from the Estonians and signed it off without even reading it. The act was an amazing grand gesture, not of divorce, but a type of birthday gift to celebrate indepen-dence, given by the Russia leader to the Balts. Just like Gorbachev, Yeltsin had a much broader game in mind in which he wanted to leapfrog over Gorbachev into Europe, NATO and European structures. What Gorbachev failed to achieve, the common European home, Yeltsin wanted to achieve. That may explain, at least in part, his act of generosity to the Estonians.

Yeltsin's signature on the independence documents did open a floodgate of Western recognition of the Baltic States. The next day, Norway and Finland, previously hesitant, recognised the state sovereignty of the Baltic republics. Germany and France followed. If the Russian democrat, the Russian leader elected by all Russian people, recognised the Baltic States then, of course, it would follow that everyone else should do the same and acknowledge the Baltic leaders. Yet one Estonian legal expert would admit that 'legally this recognition was nonsense. Russia was not sovereign, and its act of recognition had no legal force.' The USSR was still the only legitimate subject of international law. Figures such as Edgar Savisaar remained unsure. Savisaar attended the meeting of the makeshift state council, Gorbachev's new attempt at government, essentially out of fear that at some point the independence deal could still fall through.

The second sceptic was President George Bush. He and his close friend Brent Scowcroft talked about the possibility of future Russian nationalists or Russian fascists rising up to claim that Baltic independence had been imposed on the USSR 'under duress in a weakened condition.' As Scowcroft wrote very frankly in his memoirs, he and Bush 'were striving to make a permanent solution to the Baltic question.' This could only be done with Gorbachev as Bush did not know if Yeltsin's 'Russian revolution would last.' He wanted Gorbachev and the structures of the Soviet Union to recognise Baltic sovereignty before Washington did so itself.

These considerations put the story of heroic Baltic mobilisation in a proper historical perspective. The Baltic determination and will to regain independence played a big role in the drama of the Soviet demise. Nevertheless, it is vital to keep the context to these events in the Baltic republics in view. In Moscow, Gorbachev's reforms offered a green light to Baltic national mobilisation and separatism. From the fall of 1989 onwards, the end of the Cold War, Western cooperation with Gorbachev, and the situation of a 'house divided' in Moscow, created revolutionary opportunities that surpassed any Baltic dreams. Ultimately, aside from their own energy and determination, the cause of Baltic independence was resolved by the unique and surprising rise of the Russian democratic movement and Yeltsin's leadership. The latter paralysed the power of Russian right-wing nationalism and Yeltsin was the first to acknowledge the Baltic independence. The Western leaders and other Western actors played a peripheral role in the drama, acted with utmost prudence, and with the aim of ensuring the lasting solution of the Baltic Question. We must also not allow ourselves to indulge too much in a triumphalist discourse and telescope the Baltic experience of liberation, so that it seems like a simple and easy game. We should recognise that at every point there were pitfalls and dangers. The Soviet Union was not a paper tiger.

11

RUSSIA AND THE BALTIC

THE LONG VIEW

Sir Rodric Braithwaite

In May 1991, as the Soviet Union fell apart, Michael Alexander, the British ambassador to NATO, gave a lecture in Moscow to the Soviet general staff. It was very professional and he pulled no punches. He reminded his listeners that Soviet special forces had recently killed peaceful demonstrators in Vilnius, the capital of Lithuania, and Riga the capital of Latvia. Half a century earlier the Soviet Union had invaded and occupied all three Baltic States. Britain wanted to cooperate with the Soviet Union as it reformed itself. That would be hard if it did not modify its attitudes towards its neighbours.

The generals were incensed. The Baltic nations, they cried, had voluntarily asked to join the Soviet Union in 1940. The Russians had moved in to protect them, and to provide themselves with enough strategic space to stop the impending German onslaught. How could the British, the Soviets' wartime allies, now criticise them for taking such an essential measure? The ambassador forbore to point out that in 1940 the Soviet Union was allied to the Nazis, whom the British were fighting on their own.

* * *

Three decades later President Vladimir Putin told the audience at an exhibition on Peter the Great's empire that Peter had fought the Swedes for decades in order to recover territory that had been Russian from time immemorial. Russia today, he went on, faced a similar task of recovering what had been lost. People's blood ran cold. Was he saying that he would deal with Russia's Baltic neighbours after he had finished off Ukraine?

What Putin said was of course significant. But it was not new. He was simply reflecting a view of the past on which most Russians have been brought up for centuries. Like most national histories, the stories Russians tell themselves are a mixture of fact and myth. Whether they are 'true' in any rigorous sense is not the most important thing about them. They intimately inform the way Russians think about themselves and their country, about its relationships with the surrounding world, and about its future. They are the basis for Russian patriotism, for the willingness of so many ordinary Russians to suffer and die for their country even when the suffering is inflicted by their own rulers, as it so often has been.

These stories generate emotions which have affected Russian policymaking for centuries. They may seem alien to the outside observer. But if we do not understand what lies behind them, we will find it harder to devise adequate ways of dealing with Russian policy as it develops. What follows is therefore a brief outline of Russia's involvement with the Baltic region against the wider background of Russian history.

Some time towards the end of the first millennium, according to legend, a band of Viking raiders established a trading post at the head of the Baltic on land hitherto inhabited by Finns. They were called or called themselves Varangians, or 'Rus' after an old Norse word meaning 'the men who row'. Their legendary leader Ryurik allegedly went on to found the nearby city of Novgorod the Great, which later traded profitably with the members of the Hanseatic League all along the Baltic. The story is partly supported by the remains of a wooden trading post which can be securely dated by dendrochronology to 753. There is no adequate documentation.

The Varangians continued raiding down the great Russian rivers towards Byzantium and the other rich empires of the south. On their way they met another predatory people called Slavs, who had been a thorn in the flesh of Byzantium, and had begun to move up river to try their luck in the north. The Slavs increasingly adopted the ways of the Varangians and the Varangians adopted the language of the Slavs.

These diverse peoples created a sprawling empire from the Baltic to the Black Sea based on the city of Kiev (now Kyiv, the capital of Ukraine). For a while this 'Kievan Rus' was one of the largest, most sophisticated, most literate, and most ramshackle states in Europe, ruled by a dynasty descended from Ryurik which lasted for seven hundred years. Today's Russia, Ukraine and Belarus are situated on its territory. Each lays passionate claim to its inheritance. The whole story is hotly contested by historians, politicians and journalists on all sides. Outsiders get involved at their peril.

Near the end of the tenth century Grand Prince Vladimir of Kiev—Volodymyr is his Ukrainian name—adopted Christianity for himself and his people. He chose the Orthodox form of Christianity based in Byzantium. That made more geographical, commercial and military sense than an alliance with the more distant Catholics or Muslims. But the choice divided the Rus and their descendants from Catholic Europe and its increasingly sophisticated civilisation. It has indelibly marked Russia's relations with the rest of Europe ever since.

Kievan Rus was destroyed in the thirteenth century by the Mongols. It ceased to exist as a political organisation. Galicia to the south-west briefly survived under a Ryurik prince, until it was incorporated into Catholic Poland. The north-west part of Kievan Rus was absorbed into pagan Lithuania. An independent state based on Kiev did not re-emerge until 1918.

But in the north-east the principalities survived under princes from the Ryurik dynasty. They preserved some autonomy by collaborating with the Mongols more or less enthusiastically. Foreigners regard this 'Mongol Yoke' as an explanation of Russia's backwardness and the brutality of its politics. Russians regard it as an excuse for both those things, and also as grounds for believing that Russia is a separate 'Euro-Asian' civilisation poised between the two great continents. Both views are exaggerated.

As the Mongols slowly withdrew, riven by internal discord, a new power slowly emerged. It was called 'Muscovy' and was based in the city of Moscow. It was still ruled by a descendant of Ryurik. Its rulers set out systematically to impose their rule over the other surviving Russian principalities and to reassemble the fragments of Kievan Rus. At the beginning of the seventeenth century the Ryurik dynasty petered out after ruling for seven hundred years. Muscovy nearly collapsed under the pressures of internal intrigue, popular despair after a series of failed harvests, and invasion by foreign enemies, notably the Poles and the Lithuanians. But the Russian people rallied, and a new dynasty, the Romanovs, took over and expelled the foreigners. Under Peter the Great and his successors Muscovy was transformed into imperial Russia, a dominant force in European politics.

Much of what we know about the early history of the Baltic people is based on the observations of foreigners who invaded and ruled but rarely understood them. Along the coastline people mostly lived on farmsteads or in small villages. They were roughly organised into tribes but had no towns or larger political organisations. The languages they spoke evolved over the centuries into modern Latvian and Estonian.

Foreigners had been moving into the Baltic region for a couple of centuries, but from the twelfth century they began arriving in strength, mainly from Central Europe. Because the local people were pagans, many of the incomers were German missionaries, churchmen and crusading knights who had been given a free hand by the Pope to convert them by whatever means—however brutal. Bishop Albert from Bremen founded the city of Riga, the capital of today's Latvia, in 1201. He and his successors used it as their base to promote trade as well as Christianity.

The bishops soon found themselves in a protracted conflict with the crusaders who were nominally on their side. Bishop Albert founded the Livonian Brothers of the Sword in 1202 to promote Christianity by force. The Order soon suffered a devastating defeat at the hands of the ancestors of today's Lithuanians and Latvians. It was absorbed by the Teutonic Order but maintained a shadowy existence and continued to exercise control over the Baltic littoral.

The Teutonic Knights were founded in the Holy Land, but the (German) Holy Roman Emperor recruited them to subdue and convert the Prussians. They arrived in 1225 and all but exterminated the Prussians in an exceptionally bloody campaign. They then ruled Prussia as a sovereign state, from which they regularly campaigned against Poland, the Grand Duchy of Lithuania, and the Russian principalities. Their defeat in 1410 at the hands of the Poles and the Lithuanians at the Battle of Grunwald (Tannenberg) marked the beginning of a long decline. A later Grand Master of the Order, Gotthard Kettler, became a Lutheran Protestant and carved out the secular Duchy of Courland in 1561 out of what is now part of Latvia. It soon became a vassal state of Lithuania. Peter the Great's niece Anna married its duke in 1710 and gave it to her Baltic German adviser and (presumed) lover Ernst von Biron after she became empress in 1730. It disappeared along with the rest of Poland-Lithuania when the Commonwealth was partitioned for the third time.

As they moved Eastwards, the German and Polish invaders came up against the Russian principalities of Polotsk, Pskov and Novgorod. By then the Russians were already beginning to invade Estonian territories from the east, in an attempt to promote trade and Christianity. The Swedes and the Danes were also taking a rapacious hand. Both Germans and Swedes were briefly stopped in the mid thirteenth century by Alexander Nevsky, the hero of Sergei Eisenstein's great film, who remains an image of Russian heroism for Russian leaders and people alike.

The rulers of Muscovy remained determined to open—or reopen, as they saw it—the outlet to the Baltic. Fighting there was almost continuous over the next two centuries, and drew in Germans, Danes, Poles, Lithuanians and Swedes on one side or the other. None secured a permanent advantage. Ivan the Terrible launched the 'Livonian Wars' (1558–83) in yet another attempt to secure a Baltic foothold. He failed to achieve his aim, crippling his country.

The battle for the Baltic resumed under the Romanovs. It drew in Poles, Germans, Danes, Swedes and even the British. But Peter the Great's defeat of Sweden in the Great Northern War (1700–25) cemented Russia's dominance in the area and gave it the southern littoral. In 1809 it took over the northern littoral as well when it acquired Finland from Sweden, which had ruled it for over six centuries.

By then the southern Baltic coast was a patchwork of duchies and principalities, ruled mostly by Germans organised into four aristocratic corporations or Ritterschaften (knighthoods), which had emerged from the Teutonic Knights. Overall sovereignty was exercised by whichever great power happened to be dominant in the area at a particular time: Prussia, Sweden, Denmark, Poland, Lithuania. The land was owned by Germans and worked by local peasants or serfs. The towns were mainly inhabited by Germans, but the merchants and traders based there were also drawn from the indigenous peoples. The cultural split between the governing elites and the peasant population was all but complete. The German landowners imposed a harsh form of serfdom on their peasantry, although their Swedish and to a lesser extent their Russian overlords tried with limited success to regulate their behaviour.

Nevertheless, the German elite was the most convenient instrument of Russian rule in the Baltic lands. The Swedes had reduced their privileges. The Russians restored most of them. German remained the language of government and foreign trade. A few Russian administrators moved in to ensure that the Tsar's will ultimately prevailed: they naturally used their own language for the conduct of business.

The Baltic Germans feared that peasant literacy would encourage sedition. But enlightened churchmen—Catholic priests and Lutheran pastors—studied the languages of their peasant flock and printed the first catechisms in the local languages. The Swedes founded a university in Tartu in Estonia in 1632, but until well into the nineteenth century, locals who wanted to make a career could only do so in one of the elite languages.

The Germans were concerned equally by the spread of revolutionary ideas from France and by the reforming instinct of the more enlightened Russian tsars as they moved towards the abolition of serfdom. Their response was to make themselves as indispensable as they could both in the Baltic lands and in St Petersburg, where their administrative and political skills were appreciated by successive Russian governments.

The history of the Lithuanians was very different from that of the future Latvians and Estonians. They too began as a collection of disorganised tribal societies. But by the thirteenth century they had been organised by powerful leaders into a state which, as the Grand Duchy of Lithuania, included present-day Lithuania, Belarus, most of Ukraine and parts of Poland and Russia. In the sixteenth century the Grand Duchy combined with the Kingdom of Poland into a Commonwealth to form the largest state in Europe, powerful enough to invade Russia on several occasions, and to occupy Moscow at the beginning of the seventeenth century. In 1570 a university was founded in the Lithuanian capital, Vilnius, which itself had been founded early in the fourteenth century. Yet, after a last brief moment of glory when Jan Sobieski, the King of Poland, raised the Turkish siege of Vienna in 1683, the Commonwealth fell into an irreversible decline.

Russia, Austria and Prussia competed for the loot. In 1797 they shared out what remained, agreeing to 'abolish everything that could revive the memory of the existence of the Kingdom of Poland.' The country's name, they announced, would 'remain suppressed as from the present and forever.'

As a result of the carve-up, Prussia received most of western Poland, and East Prussia was no longer separated from the rest. The Austrians received Galicia, which they encouraged to shake off the influence of its previous Polish masters. The Russians took over Lithuania, acquiring the two capitals of the Commonwealth, Warsaw and Vilnius, and moved their border three hundred kilometres to the west.

Catherine the Great saw no reason to apologise. 'There is no need to present the reasons compelling us to unite to our state,' she wrote, 'and that, having become part of the Polish Republic, belonged in antiquity to Russia, where the cities were built by Russian princes and the population descends from the same tribe as the Russians and are also of our same [Orthodox] faith.' She struck a medal which read: 'I have recovered what was torn away.' The logic was the same as Putin's today.

For more than a century thereafter, until 1918, successive Russian governments hovered uneasily between a belief that the Poles, the Lithuanians, the Latvians and the Estonians would assimilate naturally into their empire, and a determination to accelerate the process by policies of harsh repression, including imprisonment, exile, and the banning of publications and education in local languages.

History was against them. Influenced partly by German Romanticism, partly by the French Revolutionary Wars, the idea that states should be organised on the basis of a common culture was gaining ground all over Europe. The Poles, with their long history as a state, twice rose in bloody but futile rebellion. The Lithuanians were sucked into the resulting repressions, which included a policy of Russification under which they had to use Russian rather than their national language for their everyday business.

Now, almost entirely separated from their ancient state tradition, the Lithuanians, together with the Latvians and Estonians, concentrated on developing their strong sense of cultural and linguistic unity as a basis for eventual political action. The Estonians and the Latvians used the national song festival as a device for expressing their national feelings in a manner to which the authorities could hardly object: they used it again to defy Moscow in the last years of the Soviet Union. They and the Lithuanians waited and planned for the opportunity that would eventually allow them to achieve independence.

The revolution of 1905 was a false start: in the Baltic territories the peasants rose against their German, Russian and Polish masters, but the risings were ruthlessly suppressed or petered out. The true opportunity arrived with the collapse of the

Russian empire in 1918. The Poles, who had acquired a good deal of military experience fighting on both sides of the war, immediately declared their independence, and set about recreating the old Commonwealth from the Baltic to the Black Sea. They seized the Galician town of Lviv and the Lithuanian capital of Vilnius, in both of which there were large Polish majorities, and briefly occupied Kiev until they were expelled by the Bolsheviks. Along the Baltic coast there was confused fighting among Poles, Germans, Russians and local freedom fighters aided by the British Navy. The Lithuanians, denied their ancient capital of Vilnius by the Poles, built their new state round their second city, Kaunas. The Estonians and Latvians rose against their German landowners and set up viable states with their capitals in Tallinn and Riga. The Finns successfully asserted their independence by force of arms. The Russians thus lost the hold on the Baltic they had so painfully acquired over the centuries.

The three new Baltic States had to cope with some very difficult problems: putting together independent and viable political and administrative structures, accommodating entrenched Russian, German and Polish minorities without compromising their new national status, restoring their economies after the destruction of the war. Not surprisingly, they were not entirely successful. Lithuania, followed by Estonia and Latvia, tried to cope by modifying their parliamentary constitutions to concentrate greater power in the hands of their presidents. They were following the example of the Poles, who in 1926 had adopted a form of veiled dictatorship under Józef Piłsudski, who had led them to independence and victory over the Russians.

The collapse of the European empires in 1918 resulted in the emergence of some fifteen new countries on the map of Europe. Lenin was willing to accept this outcome. He allowed the former non-Russian members of the empire to go their own way: a policy which Putin has now denounced. His successors were much less enthusiastic: in due course Stalin practically reversed his policy.

The international environment became increasingly hostile for small countries like the three Baltic States as Europe moved towards war. After their initial support for Baltic nations after 1918, the Western record was unimpressive. The French, the British and the Russians all behaved shamefully, appeasing Hitler at the expense of smaller countries in the hope of diverting his aggressive energies elsewhere. The Poles also attempted to accommodate themselves to Hitler and cooperated with him in dismantling Czechoslovakia in the spring of 1939. All still bitterly resent any suggestion that they gave Hitler the green light to go to war.

In 1939, Hitler and Stalin wiped Poland—'this bastard of the Treaty of Versailles,' according to Stain's foreign minister—off the map of Europe yet again. The following year Stalin bullied the three Baltic States first into submission and then into oblivion when they 'voluntarily' agreed to become constituent republics of the Soviet Union. His soldiers and secret policemen arrested, executed, and deported hundreds of thousands of people in a ruthless imposition of Soviet rule. The Latvians and Estonians, like the Ukrainians, had some hope the invading Germans might restore their sovereignty. Some went so far as to fight alongside them. But the Germans had never had any intention to free the Baltic nations or Ukraine: all were mere objects for German occupation and settlement. An underground struggle against the Russians nevertheless continued after the war, and those who fought on are still widely regarded as patriotic heroes.

Britain and France did at least declare war on Hitler, though they paid for their lack of serious commitment. He roundly defeated their armies in six weeks flat in May–June 1940. A year later the Russians were equally rapidly expelled from their new conquests when the Germans attacked in June 1941. The buffer zone so vociferously praised by the generals at the Soviet staff college fifty years later proved almost useless.

America, Britain and France refused to recognise the new 'Soviet Baltic Republics.' The Americans continued to deal with the three Baltic embassies in Washington; Britain allowed them to stay open in London but did not do business with them. Both were willing to work with the Soviet Baltic republics on economic and commercial matters: they called it 'de facto' recognition. During the war the British, in particular, inevitably placed more weight on their own strategic needs than on the interests of the Baltic States. After the war they maintained their ineffective moral support for the Baltic nations. As the Soviet Union lurched towards collapse under the impact of Gorbachev's reforms, their verbal support for the Baltic peoples increased and they protested vigorously at the Soviet use of force in Vilnius and Riga in 1991.

As Gorbachev's reforms unfolded there was nevertheless always an undercurrent of concern in London and even in Washington that they might be derailed by Baltic intransigence. That of course changed when it became clear that Gorbachev's project had failed. Once Yeltsin recognised the independence of the Baltic States in August 1991, the British and Americans quickly followed suit.

In subsequent years they gave considerable political and economic assistance and advice to all three Baltic States. A major issue was whether they should be admitted to NATO along with the former members of the Warsaw Pact, and if so, when. After some strenuous argument the political and moral arguments prevailed. NATO was expanded to include first the countries of Eastern Europe, and then the Baltic States. That was probably inevitable. It was bitterly resented by the Russians and has been used by Putin to justify his invasion of Ukraine. I expand in an Annex.

* * *

I used to tell Russian friends that in Western Europe we had finally learned after the Second World War that we were no longer allowed to invade Belgium every twenty-five years: they needed to reach a similar conclusion about the Baltic States. Few were ever convinced.

* * *

ANNEX: The Enlargement of NATO

The Russians maintain that, in the period immediately before and after the signature of the Treaty on the reunification of Germany in autumn 1990, Western leaders gave them oral assurances that they had no intention of enlarging NATO. They do not claim that anything was put in writing: indeed, they criticise Gorbachev for failing to pin down formally the promises that were made to him.

Western politicians and many academics argue that no assurances were given, and that a false narrative has been built up by Vladimir Putin into a major grievance and a justification for his aggressive moves towards Ukraine since 2004.

In fact, the record has always been reasonably clear. It is further bolstered as documents continue to emerge from the archives.

Things were said to the Russians during the negotiations for German reunification in 1990, especially by US Secretary of State, James Baker, and the German Foreign Minister, Dietrich Genscher, which could only be interpreted as assurances that NATO would not be enlarged beyond the boundaries of reunited Germany.

The story has been scrupulously told by Mary Sarotte in her recent book *Not One Inch: America, Russia, and the Making of the Post-Cold War Stalemate* (London 2022). She nevertheless comes to one wrong conclusion. The German negotiations nearly stalled at the very last minute when the British insisted on

165

including a phrase making it clear that German NATO forces could deploy freely right across united Germany, and that Allied NATO forces could deploy within Germany, east of the Elbe for limited periods at the invitation of the German government. The Russians threatened to walk out, but the phrase was eventually adopted. Sarotte argues that this means that the Russians accepted in principle that NATO could expand into what had previously been Warsaw Pact territory. I know of no evidence that those who participated in the talks drew that conclusion.

In March 1991, Prime Minister Major was asked by the Soviet Defence Minister to comment on a recent demand by President Havel of Czechoslovakia that the Visegrad countries (Czechoslovakia, Poland and Hungary) be brought into NATO. Major replied that he 'did not himself foresee circumstances now or in the future where East European countries would become members of NATO.' Foreign Secretary Hurd gave the same reply to the Soviet foreign minister in April. They made these statements in my presence. They accurately reflected official thinking: on 7 March 1991 senior officials from Britain, France, Germany, and America, meeting in secret in the so-called QUAD, approved a British paper which said 'We could not offer East Europeans membership or associate membership of NATO. Nor could we offer explicit or implicit security guarantees.'

The intentions had already begun to change by October 1993, when American officials indicated to their QUAD partners that they were no longer prepared to rule out enlargement. NATO governments were already under strong pressure to offer membership to Eastern European countries that had been bullied for centuries by the Russians. The East Europeans did not believe the Russians would long remain flat on their backs: for them it was painfully obvious that only NATO membership could guarantee their future. Many in the West, fuelled by guilt for previous betrayals—Munich, Yalta, Hungary,

Prague—supported their aspirations. So did the descendants of Poles, Balts and others who lived in places crucial to the outcome of American elections.

In the years that followed, the British government and others claimed that whatever was said while the Soviet Union was still in existence became irrelevant when it was replaced by Russia in January 1992. Apart from implying that Western politicians did indeed say ambiguous things in 1990–91, this curious argument seems to say that though we were willing to protect the Eastern Europeans against an emerging 'democratic' Russia, we were not prepared to protect them against the Soviet Union which preceded it.

George Kennan and others thought that enlargement was a gross strategic error, which would scupper Russian attempts at democratic reform. Defence establishments in London and Washington feared that enlargement would place obligations on NATO that it would be unable to meet. Some argued that it might be feasible to bring in the former East European members of the Warsaw Pact, but that extending membership to countries that had been part of the Soviet Union would provoke the Russians beyond measure. If Ukraine were to be brought in, it would have to be together with Russia itself. But all attempts to associate Russia formally with NATO failed: the Americans were unwilling to accept the Russians as equals, and the Russians rejected any lesser status as humiliating.

Some claim that the Russians were initially willing to accept enlargement and that neither Gorbachev nor his immediate successors ever expressed their opposition. That is incorrect. The view of Yeltsin and other Russians that enlargement would have a bad effect on Russia's relationship with the West is well documented. But the Russians' negotiating position was hopelessly weak, and they were in no state to resist.

I myself believe enlargement was all but inevitable. No American president would have found it easy, or even possible, to resist the domestic and international pressures to push ahead. Most American officials believed that America could and should exploit its apparently unchallengeable primacy in Europe to pursue American interests as they perceived them. Many Europeans, especially in Eastern Europe, believed that they would need American protection against Russia for the foreseeable future. Even if enlargement hadn't gone ahead there could be no guarantee that the Russians would change the tradition of centuries and at last adopt a settled and viable system of democracy and a cooperative attitude towards its neighbours.

But against this background the belief of so many Russians that they were double-crossed is understandable: it didn't have to be manufactured by Putin. We would be seething if the situation were reversed.

12

TOO 'GREAT' TO THRIVE?

Sturla Sigurjónsson

Iceland and the Soviet Union established diplomatic relations in 1943, which were maintained following the creation of the Russian Federation in 1991. Through the decades, Icelandic relations on different levels with the Soviets and Russians have been pragmatic and people-to-people contacts have traditionally been mostly friendly. However, there have always been substantive differences between Iceland and Russia, which pertain to how the Russian government views its status and role in the world and which affects the way it interacts with other countries, not least smaller states.

Fundamental Principles

The main principles of Icelandic foreign policy were set in the years following the establishment of an independent republic in

1944 and still apply. They include the importance of international law, including the sovereign equality of states, self-determination of nations and respect for universal human rights, as well as the need for security and solidarity amongst democracies and constructive regional cooperation. This was manifested by Iceland joining the UN in 1946 and becoming a founding member of NATO in 1949 and the Nordic Council in 1952, as well as through active participation in various other international and regional fora.

Hence the Icelandic support for the Baltic States in 1991, Georgia in 2008 and Ukraine from 2014 onwards. This support was rendered despite the risk of endangering a long-standing bilateral relationship with first the Soviet Union and later Russia. The principles at stake were considered to be so fundamental that they outweighed shorter-term political and commercial interests. Throughout the Cold War, the Soviet Union was one of Iceland's single largest trading partners but the value and volume was drastically reduced in the early 1990s. Similarly, having joined in targeted Western sanctions against Russia following the annexation of Crimea in 2014, Russian counter-sanctions had a substantial negative effect on Iceland's primary exports to Russia, i.e. seafood. Subsequently, trade in other sectors increased, mainly maritime and fisheries technology, and cooperation on Arctic affairs continued, including within the Arctic Council. However, the horrendous Russian invasion of Ukraine in February 2022 reversed what little progress had been made and Iceland joined its allies and partners in applying further sanctions on Russia. This includes discontinuing meetings with Russian representatives in the Arctic Council. As a result, Iceland is in good company amongst countries currently defined as 'unfriendly' by the Russian government.

TOO 'GREAT' TO THRIVE?

Confronting an Existential Threat

So, why has a small state in the middle of the North Atlantic taken such a firm stance on distant events? Icelanders feel no hostility towards the Russian people but Iceland holds dear values and interests which the Russian government is currently violating in Ukraine. The values relate to the sanctity of human life, respect for universal human rights, adherence to the letter and spirit of international law, the peaceful resolution of disputes, national self-determination and democratic governance. The interests are broad and long-term in safeguarding the security and freedom of Iceland as a sovereign, albeit small, state by supporting a rules-based international order, where voluntarily agreed treaties equally commit all states regardless of geographic, demographic or economic size or military capability. If Russia's unprovoked and illegal invasion of a large country like Ukraine were to be successful, it would not only cause further prolonged instability and conflict in the whole of Europe but also undermine the principle of sovereign equality, which is a prerequisite for the existence of small states. Russian authorities have offered contradictory justification for the invasion but essentially the rationale appears to be national chauvinist if not imperialist, including the negation of Ukrainian national identity. This in and of itself constitutes a threat to all European countries, including Iceland, and may explain why a large number of states have joined NATO since the end of the Cold War and still more aspire to membership, including Finland and Sweden.

Great Power Obsession Inhibited Cooperation

Historical and cultural attitudes affect government policies and, therefore, matter in international relations. The 'great power' obsession of many former and current Russian leaders and the

171

long destructive trail of their conquests affects how most other European countries, particularly neighbouring countries, view Russia and interact with its government. Despite this, Western democracies have during past decades demonstrated countless times that they wanted to build and maintain peaceful and constructive relations with the Soviet Union and then Russia, without departing from basic principles. Lately, there has been a narrative in some Western circles on how the West 'lost' Russia through a lack of understanding and consideration. For many reasons, this is a false narrative and two examples relating to Iceland show how Russia's sometimes myopic attitudes could spoil opportunities for closer cooperation.

The NATO and Russia Founding Act was signed in 1997 and the Permanent Joint Council (PJC) was established as a forum for consultations and coordination. It was chaired by a troika of NATO's Secretary General, one of the NATO member states on a rotation basis and a representative of Russia. When it fell to Iceland to represent the NATO member states on the PJC troika in 1998, I attended a meeting as Iceland's Deputy Permanent Representative in the Secretary General's private office and it was quite apparent that the Russian Ambassador was not satisfied with an arrangement based on equivalence with a small state. This was subsequently confirmed in what seemed to be Russian-inspired media reports. Russia wanted a privileged status in the PJC. Russian representatives did not seem to understand or accept that the reason for the Alliance's success was the fact that in the North-Atlantic Council and subordinate bodies all member states had a voice and role and all decisions were taken by consensus. At this time, Russian representatives all but acknowledged that in the absence of a right to veto NATO decisions, their government's goal was to disrupt any NATO activities it found inimical to its interests. They carried this negative stance into the NATO-Russia Council when it replaced the PJC in

2002. The narrative about NATO failing to engage with Russia is simply wrong. Russia wanted security only on Russian terms.

Lost Opportunity

A second example relates to the closure of the United States military base in Iceland in 2006. This was a unilateral decision made in Washington DC and it was clear that the government of Iceland felt it was imprudent. But the reasoning was that the bilateral Defence Agreement between the United States and Iceland would still be in place, that Russia was a partner and there was no imminent threat, and that valuable resources were required elsewhere. Therefore, it came as an unpleasant surprise that immediately following the departure of US forces, Russia resumed unannounced flights of strategic bombers close to Iceland. They had hardly been seen since the end of the Cold War. The government of Iceland did not know what to make of these patrols, including the close circumnavigation of the country, in an area where there was no longer any NATO military presence to speak of. Furthermore, being responsible for significant civilian air traffic control over the North Atlantic, Iceland was concerned about the sudden appearance of Russian military aircraft flying with their transponders turned off. This was one of the reasons why Iceland decided to continue the operation of the integrated Iceland Air Defence System previously run by the United States and requested intermittent NATO air policing.

The Russian patrols continued and diplomatic expressions of concern were made by Iceland to Russia, without any effect. Consequently, at the NATO-Russia Council summit in Bucharest in 2008, the Prime Minister of Iceland raised the issue briefly in the presence of the President of Russia. I was present as the Prime Minister's foreign policy advisor. Shortly thereafter, the Russian ambassador in Reykjavik requested a meeting with me and expressed dissatisfaction over what he said was an unwarranted intervention by the Prime Minister, as the patrols were directed against the United States and not Iceland. In response, it was pointed out that there were no United States forces based in Iceland and as a sovereign state Iceland was responsible for its national security, as well as the security of civil aviation in the region. This made no impression on the ambassador, who in so many words reiterated that the patrols were none of Iceland's business. This interaction gave the impression that Russia viewed Iceland's concerns over its own security as trifling. Moreover, one can conclude that the reason for the Russian irritation was that Iceland's complaints were in contradiction to the myth of Russia's military encirclement by NATO. So, with regard to the narrative that the West 'lost' Russia through a lack of understanding and consideration, this example again shows who was pushing whom away. Russia immediately reacted to the departure of United States forces from Iceland by flexing its military muscles in the North Atlantic, instead of using the opportunity to maintain mutually a low level of tension.

The two above-mentioned examples did not affect the bilateral relationship between Iceland and Russia but reflected a mindset which seems to be prevalent in Russian government circles and has already led to aggression against Georgia and Ukraine. This explains why other countries, which are Russia's neighbours and share history with Russia, are particularly concerned and seek safeguards. They have reacted by applying for membership of NATO and the European Union.

Sanctions as an Expression of Public Repugnance

Iceland is the only member state of NATO without national armed forces. Therefore, the country is uniquely dependent on the collective defence commitments which underpin the Alliance.

Solidarity and a willingness to make sacrifices for the common good is what makes NATO work. Unlike a commercial insurance scheme, it is a political relationship based on mutual trust, provided with the resources for deterrence and collective defence. It is viable and effective so long as every member state contributes politically, militarily and financially in accordance with real ability. Unlike the former Warsaw Pact, there has never been any coercion against individual member states of NATO. Iceland's contribution is political and financial, through the deployment of civilian experts to headquarters and operations. Iceland is also a host nation to Allies and partners.

Iceland joined other countries in applying sanctions on Russia in reaction to the aggression against Ukraine. Economic sanctions are not within NATO's remit, so such decisions made by Allies and partners are national or in coordination with relevant fora like the European Union. Sanctions are controversial because they can be a blunt and expensive tool. But, for obvious reasons, they are by far a preferable alternative to armed conflict. In the face of an unprovoked and illegal invasion of a sovereign European state, threatening security and stability in the whole region and beyond, it was out of the question to remain passive. Ideally, sanctions make an economic impact and inhibit the aggressor but, regardless of practical implications, they are an expression of a public repugnance and refusal to have normal relations with the country in question as long as the aggression continues.

Can We Ever Have Normal Relations?

History shows that it can be easier to begin a conflict than to bring it to a conclusion, but wars do end. It has become clear that Russia has failed to defeat Ukraine through conventional means and that a negotiated peace will eventually be concluded. However, it must not be a ceasefire and has to meet the legitimate expectations of Ukrainians for a guaranteed settlement maintaining the sovereignty, independence and restoration of the territorial integrity of Ukraine, including Crimea, and an accountability mechanism for Russia's actions. Of course, it will be Ukraine's prerogative to set out terms that it deems to be acceptable. This would strengthen security and stability for all in the region and in due course pave the way for 'new' normal relations between Western democracies and Russia. In terms of European and global security, the effects of the war in Ukraine will be profound and long-lasting. Much will depend upon Russia's willingness to re-engage in a responsible way. Iceland, for one, is a European and Arctic state and hopes for cordial and constructive future relations with a democratic, stable and peaceful Russia.

PART V

THE BRITISH ANGLE

13

MOSCOW AND THE BALTICS

A WESTERN CORRESPONDENT'S VIEW

Bridget Kendall

In late 1989 and early 1990 the world watched in amazement as Moscow's hold over the Warsaw Pact countries of Central and Eastern Europe disintegrated. Meanwhile I was busy observing events from my vantage point in Moscow, where I was based as BBC Moscow correspondent. There too, intense political dramas were being played out, but I also needed to understand what was happening away from the Soviet capital. So I accompanied the Soviet leader, Mikhail Gorbachev, on major trips—including to East Berlin in October 1989 for the celebrations to mark the fortieth anniversary of the East German State—and I travelled extensively around other parts of the Soviet Union, including regular trips to the Baltic States. The snapshots and vignettes from some of my experiences from that time are perhaps illustrative of the flavour of that extraordinary era.

UNDERSTANDING THE BALTIC STATES

When I first arrived in Moscow as BBC correspondent in July 1989, I quickly made arrangements to pay early visits to all three of the Baltic republics, returning several times over the course of that summer. Events there were moving fast and I wanted to see at first hand what was happening. From my first visit I was struck by how swiftly all three places seemed to be shifting into a parallel universe. By the summer of 1989 they were already on a totally different track from Moscow, working to a different reform timetable and beginning to use different terms of reference from the rest of the Soviet Union.

I recall one visit to Tallinn in Estonia in August 1989 when I came across a group of activists sitting at a desk, their heads down as they intently conferred over a list of voters they were compiling for upcoming elections. I was somewhat mystified by this. Elections had been held across the Soviet Union earlier in the spring, but I was unaware of any elections of significance due to take place in Estonia. I raised my puzzlement with the Tallinn activists. They quickly put me right. 'Oh no, no', they asserted, 'these voter lists are not for Soviet elections; they will be Estonian elections. They are nothing at all to do with the Soviet Union.' They explained that their plan involved electing a Congress of Estonian nationals, to represent those who had been citizens or were direct descendants of citizens who had lived in Estonia prior to Soviet occupation in 1940. Anyone who had moved to Estonia more recently from the Soviet Union would be excluded. It was the first sign of Estonia taking steps to regain statehood and it was in startling contrast to Moscow, where tentative plans for increasing the powers of self-government in Soviet republics had so far been limited only to ideas of cultural autonomy, not economic independence and certainly not political secession. It was my first lesson that if you were going to deal with the Baltic States, you had to deal with them on their terms. They inhabited a very different space from the rest of the Soviet Union.

This Baltic mindset was also visible at the two inaugural sessions of the all-important USSR Congress of People's Deputies, held in Moscow in May and December of 1989. This was a bold new initiative, created by Mikhail Gorbachev, to establish a semi-democratic alternative to the Communist Party's Central Committee in order to try to speed up a programme of major political reform.

The delegates thronged to Moscow for the long sessions of intense debate in the colossal Palace of Congresses in the Kremlin, coming from all over the Soviet Union. Local political elites from each region and republic joined leading academic and cultural figures (including former dissidents such as the physicist and human rights campaigner Andrei Sakharov), as well as government ministers and all the country's most senior communist officials. Most regional delegates came from the top ranks of their local communist parties, 'apparatchiks' who could be relied upon to take their lead from the Kremlin. But it soon became clear that when it came to the Baltic delegations, their loyalties lay more with Lithuania, Latvia and Estonia than Moscow, and they were impatient to push the agenda into politically sensitive areas, especially those which affected the Baltics. So, they wanted to raise the so-called Molotov-Ribbentrop non-aggression Pact between Stalin and Hitler in 1939, whose secret protocol assigned the Baltic States to a Soviet sphere of influence; they wanted to talk about the subsequent repressions of the late Stalin era which had affected Baltic citizens; and they wanted debate about the provision in the Soviet Constitution which theoretically gave each republic the right freely to secede from the Soviet Union.

In a methodical, determined way, the Baltic delegates helped radicalise the agenda of the Congress. And because the extraordinary sessions were for the first time ever being conducted live on Soviet television, they were also instrumental in radicalising popular opinion. Up until now Soviet citizens had been used to all political discourse being tightly controlled by the Communist Party. Now, astonishingly, everyone was privy to live debate about some of the most sensitive issues which went to the heart of how the country was governed, being broadcast throughout the Soviet Union. I remember finding myself in small towns where the old ladies charged with handing out hotel keys would be clustered around television sets on each corridor, watching in fascination as those in power were taken to task and criticised. The fact that proceedings were being held in public had a powerful impact on everyone. It indicated that challenging political leaders and pushing the limits of what could be discussed was now sanctioned from the very top. It was a green light which signalled that people could now confidently discuss their views everywhere without fear of reprimand. The Baltic delegations did a very important job in pushing that dialogue, opening up new areas for debate that had not been allowed before.

Throughout this volume we have been discussing how the Baltic republics and their campaigns for the restoration of statehood were in the vanguard, but also how others were not that far behind. Archie Brown very deliberately mentions Western Ukraine, where the People's Movement of Ukraine, or Rukh, was founded as a civil-political movement in 1989. Western Ukraine was another area that had been part of the planned carve-up by Hitler and Stalin in the Molotov-Ribbentrop Pact, and it was incorporated into the Soviet Union after the war. As a result, the Soviet authorities were always nervous of the possibility of resentment or even rebellion against Soviet rule and kept a firm political grip, especially in western parts of Ukraine.

In 1987, a couple of years into Gorbachev's perestroika reforms, I found that, even in the Ukrainian capital, locals were wary of making contact with a foreign journalist for fear of KGB reprisals. It seemed a very repressive place. Even local dissidents whom I had managed to get in touch with were terrified in case the authorities found out. They urged me to cover my tracks and take a circuitous route from and back to my hotel to ensure I was not followed, and they would not be traced and arrested for meeting a foreigner. It was striking how frightened they were of the Ukrainian secret police at a time when criticism of the Kremlin was commonplace in Moscow, and ordinary Russians had become far more relaxed about contact with foreigners. The Russian dissident Andrei Sakharov had been released from internal exile, censorship was being lifted and it felt as though the place was waking up from a long-enforced slumber. But Ukraine was still being kept in the dark ages.

However, in Ukraine too, events eventually moved swiftly. In September 1989 a rare weekend protest meeting was organised outside the West Ukrainian city of Lvov (as Lviv was then known). From Moscow I received reports of how Ukrainian riot police had broken up the crowd by unleashing dogs on them. Many people were arrested and some savagely bitten. Nonetheless Ukrainian activists scheduled another protest for the following weekend, so my BBC editors asked me to travel there to report on it first-hand.

I was expecting an event where the police would once again attack the crowd. This time, however, the authorities took a different tack. There was almost no police presence and therefore no police dogs either. Instead, the massive gathering was allowed to assemble peacefully and deliver speeches without any intervention. It turned into an impromptu, jubilant expression of nationalist fervour. I remember an incredibly moving scene of a man who agreed to be interviewed by me and then in the middle of the interview suddenly dropped to his knees in front of the crowd who were listening in to testify the fact that he felt he had for years been a passive collaborator with the Soviet regime, and now wanted to beg for his fellow Ukrainians' forgiveness. All that time since the Second World War he had been quiet, he said, but now he wanted to repent and speak up for a free Ukraine.

The Ukrainian situation felt like an overnight flip. Shortly after that memorable weekend rally, the First Party Secretary of the Ukrainian Communist Party—the boss in Ukraine—a hardliner called Vladimir Shcherbitsky (or Volodymyr Shcherbytsky in Ukrainian) was removed by the Kremlin and replaced by a more moderate figure, Vladimir Ivashko. Rukh's numbers swelled seemingly instantaneously. Almost within the space of a day, it felt as though the lid had been lifted on Ukraine.

The focus of this volume sets itself firmly on the Baltics, but we must not forget that other places such as Ukraine and also Georgia, which had suffered a brutal crackdown at a protest in April 1989, likewise took advantage of the increasingly lenient attitude in Moscow, transforming whispers of nationalist sympathy into a full-scale national awakening. These movements also occurred in Armenia, Azerbaijan, Belarus and even Kazakhstan, and eventually emerged inside Russia itself under the leadership of Boris Yeltsin, all following a path first laid down by Estonia, Latvia and Lithuania.

Nonetheless, the Baltic States considered themselves a special case. They insisted that their story was not part of the same history as the rest of the USSR, since the Baltic States had been forcibly and illegally occupied by the Soviet Union as a result of the Second World War. Therefore, they could not be counted among the Soviet republics and could not be seen as the instigators of the waves of protest which subsequently encompassed the entirety of the USSR and led to its downfall.

Yet I believe that for other areas of the USSR, the Baltic republics were indeed an important model, a prototype for how any constituent part could extract itself from Moscow's grip. The Baltic push for language laws to be changed, for the Kremlin's legal right to restrict regional autonomy to be challenged, and the right for individual states to rule on their own sovereignty, all laid the groundwork for other republics.

Tensions between Moscow and the Baltics intensified from late 1989 onwards, after Mikhail Gorbachev allowed Eastern Europe to go its own way but argued heatedly that independence for the Baltic States was a red line that should not be crossed. He feared that if they were to break away, others would follow. It also seems that he genuinely could not conceive why the Baltic republics should consider themselves better off without the Soviet Union, given the economic advantages, as he saw it, of remaining part of the Union and benefitting from the access it offered to cheap energy. Indeed, Gorbachev imposed an energy blockade on the Baltic republics precisely to drive home this point, not realising that instead of increasing dependence on Moscow, such punitive action would instead strengthen Baltic resolve to break away.

Gorbachev also repeatedly voiced his concerns that any move by the Baltics to try to leave the Union might, if replicated elsewhere, lead to violent upheavals. Time and again he would warn that if the Soviet Union were to split up, there could be *grazhdanskaya rozn*, or civil strife (for some reason he steered clear of presaging *grazhdanskaya voyna*, or civil war).

I remember that at the time, I and other foreign correspondents saw this plea as rather self-serving; the complaint of a leader whose power was waning and who was worried that he would be forced to step down if the Union dissolved. In fact, there were already indications that territorial disputes were on the rise. Conflict had already erupted between Azerbaijan and Armenia in 1988 over the disputed enclave of Nagorno-Karabakh region. Tensions were already emerging over the breakaway states of Transnistria in Moldova and Abkhazia on Georgia's Black Sea coast. In Central Asia, access to resources and border tensions were beginning to lead to outbreaks of violence in the Fergana valley which connects Kyrgyzstan, Uzbekistan and Tajikistan. And after the Soviet collapse, it did not take long for the autonomous Russian republic of Chechnya in the North Caucasus to challenge Moscow. The hot-headed new Chechen President, Dzhokhar Dudayev, recently retired from his position as a Soviet air force general based in Estonia and fired up by what he had experienced there, declared that Chechnya should follow the Baltic lead. His call for Chechnya to secede from Russia would trigger two wars and an uneasy peace over the next three decades.

But all that only became clearer with hindsight. Until the attempted Soviet coup by hardliners in August 1991, I do not think that most foreign correspondents based in Moscow thought that the breakup of the Soviet Union was imminent, or that wide-scale bloodshed was a likely outcome. Indeed, the transformation which Gorbachev's perestroika reforms unleashed was hailed as 'a revolution without shots'. Even when Soviet republics decided to dissolve the Soviet Union at the end of 1991, with the exception of Chechnya and a string of 'frozen conflicts', it did not seem as though any serious civil war or civil strife, or any great scale of bloodshed, was on the cards.

Unfortunately, history has proved us wrong: the decision by Russia's President Vladimir Putin to launch an unprovoked invasion of Ukraine in February 2022 tragically turned the fear of a full-scale war between the two former leading republics of the Soviet Union into a reality. We now know from an interview given to the Reuters news agency by his former interpreter, Pavel Palazchenko, just after the Soviet leader died in August 2022, that at the end of his life Mikhail Gorbachev had been left shocked and bewildered by the Ukraine conflict and psychologically crushed in recent years by Moscow's worsening ties with Kyiv.

Returning to the events of 1991, I was not there to witness at first hand the attacks on the Baltic States in January of that year, most prominently in Lithuania. They came after the resignation of Eduard Shevardnadze as the Soviet Foreign Minister in December 1990, who publicly warned of a 'creeping dictatorship.' We soon understood what he meant. Under pressure, Gorbachev reshuffled his cabinet to include more hardliners from the KGB, Defence and Interior Ministries, the same men who would try to stage a coup against him in August 1991.

Once this new cabinet was installed, the next move in January 1991 was to take steps to rein in the Baltics. Soldiers from the local Soviet garrison in Vilnius led an attack to attempt to capture the television station and the parliament. They were unsuccessful, in part because of popular resistance, but it also seems because those in Moscow lost their nerve or changed their mind. The Kremlin, still under the leadership of Gorbachev, called off the military assault and the troops were ordered back to barracks.

A week or so after the failed suppression of the Baltics, I went to Lithuania to observe the consequences of this dramatic episode. The whole place was under curfew and governance was in confusion. A system of parallel institutions was being established, one Soviet and one Lithuanian. So, on one street there was a Lithuanian Interior Ministry, guarded by armed Lithuanian Interior police troops, while on another street the Soviet Interior Ministry had its own Soviet guards. Such competitions for power were being enacted all over Vilnius.

One incident particularly sticks in my mind. One evening just as the overnight curfew was starting, I approached a Soviet checkpoint on the edge of the city and asked for an interview. I was taken to the commanding officer who turned out not only to be a major in the Soviet army, in charge of one of the local garrisons, but also one of the officers who had led the assault on the Lithuanian parliament. A loyal Soviet patriot and military man, he was unashamedly proud of the fact.

As we talked, it emerged that his wife was an English speaker and he agreed to invite me to their home to meet her and their small son. She was initially terrified at coming face to face with a foreigner, but soon relaxed and the meeting was friendly. It was interesting to talk to someone whose immersion in Soviet propaganda meant she was fearful of any contact with a Westerner, but even more intriguing to gain an insight into her husband's thinking and try to understand why this Soviet officer was so sure the military operation to subdue Lithuania had been the right thing to do.

A year later, after the Soviet Union had collapsed, he and his wife dropped in on me in Moscow. He revealed that, although a Russian speaker who had spent his entire career in the Soviet army, he was in fact Ukrainian, born in Kiev. Now the USSR had gone he said his plan was to join the Ukrainian army, although with a wink he pulled out his Communist Party card and said he would be locking it safely away, just in case the old Soviet regime came back and he could use it again.

In the weeks following the Russian invasion of Ukraine in February 2022, I often wondered whether he found himself among the Ukrainian troops defending their country from the Russian army, or whether he was one of those who switched their allegiance to fight on the Russian side. Whatever his fate, his example is a perhaps useful illustration of how some people, seemingly loyal to one set of the authorities, may, as circumstances change, adopt quite different and fluid positions.

The importance of the international media coverage during the attempted Soviet crackdown on Lithuania in January 1991 is also worth noting. Most members of the foreign press corps in Moscow kept closely in touch with contacts in all three Baltic States, and so in early 1991, we all received warnings that a Soviet military attack might be imminent. Because of these prior tip-offs, many foreign journalists—including colleagues from the BBC—were on site to witness the violent attack in Vilnius and those attempted in Tallinn and Riga.

This international media coverage was significant. One crucial logistical aid for foreign reporters in the Baltic States in those years was a rare direct line available for making telephone calls abroad from the national parliaments. In most other parts of the Soviet Union outside Moscow, it was always a challenge to find a way to tell the world what was happening. Booking international phone calls from provincial hotels could take hours and sometimes days. But in Vilnius, Riga and Tallinn, you could dial on the parliamentary phone line via Warsaw direct into your news desk in Washington, London or Paris. It meant any attempt to impose a media blackout by Moscow on what was happening in the Baltics was never successful, and the world was kept well informed about every important Baltic development.

I remember one occasion in Riga on the afternoon in May 1990 when the Latvian parliament voted for the restoration of independence. Foreign correspondents queued up to use the phone line. I called in the result of the vote direct to the BBC newsroom, in time for the World News bulletin at the top of the hour. Afterwards, I went out onto the banks of the nearby River Daugava where there was a massive demonstration. Many people were singing Latvian songs, waiting to hear the vote outcome. I walked around the perimeter of the gathering attempting to count it, which is what we used to do as journalists in those days to try to gauge how big the crowd was. At a certain point, an MP came out from the parliament building and announced something in Latvian which I could not understand. Everyone cheered loudly and began a chant: 'BBC! BBC!' I asked my Latvian translator what had made the people so enthusiastic about the BBC. It turned out that the MP had not only formally declared that the parliament had voted to restore independence, but also that he had been listening to his shortwave radio and the news had featured as a headline on the BBC News. 'So now we know it is true,' my translator remarked.

That anecdote illustrates one powerful aspect of the role that international news reporting played in directing the focus of the outside world to what was happening in the former Soviet space. The Baltics were assured of instant coverage in Western media outlets, and crackdowns like those attempted in January 1991 evoked an immediate response from Western capitals.

But I have often thought how different their experience of January 1991 was from what happened in Baku in Azerbaijan in January 1990, a year earlier. In this era before the use of the internet or even mobile phones, if foreign observers could not be present to offer eye witness accounts and could not find a way to file their reports quickly, there was always a risk that the Soviet authorities would be able to get away with repressions in outlying areas, confident that the outside world would fail to pay attention. In this instance, violence sparked between Armenians and Azerbaijanis led to a brutal security crackdown in Baku which killed hundreds and put many more in police custody. It became known as the January Massacre. Yet there was nothing like the international outcry there would be a year later after the 1991 January events in Vilnius.

Activists from Azerbaijan's Popular Front had warned Western correspondents in Moscow that something was brewing. But the Soviet authorities successfully blocked us from travelling there. I well remember the frustration over the 'Catch-22' which was all too common for foreigners in that era. At the Aeroflot ticket office, you would be told that you first had to obtain Foreign Ministry permission to travel to Baku before buying a plane ticket; but on applying to the Foreign Ministry for the right documents to travel, you would be told to get a plane ticket first. So, there were no independent western eyewitnesses when the Baku crackdown happened, only indirect reports from local stringers and very few pictures. Soviet Azerbaijan was, it seemed, too far away and events too murky and ill-understood for the Western world to pay much attention.

It is a lesson, I believe, which holds true even for today. Even in this social media age, those parts of Russia or of former Soviet republics which are further away from Europe and its capitals, feel far more vulnerable and likely to be ignored by the outside world if rights are infringed or events turn violent.

In conclusion, I would argue that as far as the ultimate Soviet collapse at the end of 1991 was concerned, the influence of the Baltic States was more significant at the start of the process of disintegration, in 1989 and in early 1990, than in its final denouement. By 1991, the Baltic peoples and their parliaments had passed votes to restore independence. Psychologically and politically, they were already inhabiting a new post-Soviet era, no longer much interested in the turbulence which continued to rock Soviet domestic politics. By the summer and autumn of 1991, the blocks of seats set aside for Baltic delegations at the sessions of the Soviet parliament in Moscow were always empty. Their delegates simply ceased to bother to turn up.

Arguably the old guard of hardliners who held power in Moscow in 1991 were no longer much focused on the Baltic States either. When the attempted coup took place on 19 August 1991, early that same morning I rang my Baltic stringers to see if the local Soviet garrisons had once again tried to storm the parliament or take over the TV tower, as they had in January 1991. My Baltic contacts sleepily answered that all was quiet. We soon found out that the main drama of those remarkable three August days would unfold in the Soviet capital. The coup's leaders were more concerned with trying to arrest Boris Yeltsin, the President of Russia, and it was when he managed to slip through their fingers and appeal to the people and armed forces of Russia to defy the coup that the stage was set for an inevitable show down.

The Yeltsin factor surfaced in Soviet politics from the mid-1990 onwards. I will never forget in the spring of 1990 when the Russian Supreme Soviet—once a rubber stamp parliament but now beginning to find real political purpose—held a meeting to elect its new Chairman of the Praesidium. It was pretty clear that the victor was going to be Boris Yeltsin and the position would serve as a launching pad for his comeback as a new type of Russian leader. Having been removed from the Communist Party's Central Committee in 1987, he had reinvented himself, allied himself to Russian activists pushing for democratic reform, and returned to the political scene through popular Russian elections. His resounding landslide victory instantly made him a political threat to Gorbachev, who had always avoided testing his popularity in nationwide direct elections.

At that symbolic meeting of the Russian parliament to endorse Yeltsin as its leader, Mikhail Gorbachev sat alone on a balcony high above the Kremlin hall looking down on proceedings and intently following them. He sat there alone for hours and hours, an astonishing thing for a Soviet President to do, given everything else to which he might have needed to attend within his day. It was a very visual indication that he understood that a new threat to his power was in the process of being established—that of the leader of the Russian Federation.

When I interviewed Gorbachev in later years, he would often say that the collapse of the Soviet Union came about in large part because of Boris Yeltsin and his ambition to take over as Kremlin leader. But in an interview with me in 2011, for the first time he added the thought that not only Yeltsin's role was critical; the collapse of the Soviet Union had also been heavily influenced by Ukraine's vote for sovereignty.

I think that this was right. By the second half of 1991, the new reality of the Soviet Union was that the Baltic republics had gone, and what really mattered now were the actions of Boris Yeltsin and other republican leaders. The most important issue for the survival of the Soviet Union was what the three big Slavic nations, Russia, Ukraine and Belarus, intended to do. Thus, the key moment was the signing of the Belovezh Accords in December 1991 whereby the leaders of these three republics took the critical step of deciding to end the existence of the Soviet Union and replace it with the so-called CIS, the Commonwealth of Independent States.

So while by 1991 the Soviet Union could have survived without the Baltics, it could not survive without Ukraine or Russia. Yet the ambition of the Baltic States to strive for independence had earlier played an important role in this political drama. The Balts forced open a door so they could leave, and they left it open behind them for Ukraine and Russia to follow in their footsteps.

14

BRITISH POLICY TOWARDS THE
BALTIC STATES IN 1991

Patrick Salmon

Like other Western countries, the United Kingdom confronted a series of dilemmas as the Baltic crisis deepened at the beginning of 1991. On the one hand the British government wished to maintain Gorbachev's position in power as he faced increasing challenges both from hard-liners within the Soviet Union and from nationalists in the Baltic republics and elsewhere, and as Gorbachev himself reacted to those challenges in unpredictable, sometimes violent ways. On the other hand, fulfilling Britain's historic commitment to Baltic independence threatened to undermine Gorbachev and ultimately implied dismemberment of the Soviet Union. All this, of course, was taking place as the Gulf crisis reached its crescendo and it seemed imperative to keep Gorbachev on side. But there was also a specifically British dimension in that the last months of 1990 and the first months of 1991 were a time of transition—in foreign policy as in other spheres—from the eleven-year premiership of Margaret Thatcher (brought to a brutal end by her cabinet colleagues in November 1990) to that of her relatively inexperienced former chancellor of the exchequer, John Major. The government remained Conservative, but the mood music was often very different. Writing about these events in a 1993 postscript to a book first published in 1991 (and completed in November 1990), the late John Hiden and I thought that the departure of Thatcher had had 'a liberating effect on Britain's policy towards the Baltic problem.' It was, we went on to claim (contentiously),

> almost as if Major were feeling his way back to the curiously dogged concern which the British showed for the welfare of the Baltic states up to 1940. The tradition of appeasing the Soviet Union, maintained by British leaders from Anthony Eden to Margaret Thatcher, seems at last to have been broken.[1]

It is now possible to test this judgement, based only on sources publicly available at the time, against the evidence of Foreign and Commonwealth Office (FCO) documents released to the National Archives (TNA) in 2021. Not surprisingly, the tale the documents tell is more nuanced and more contradictory than the one we thought we had identified. The documents confirm the main outlines of the story we told, but sometimes modify it in unexpected ways. This chapter draws on only a small selection of files: the FCO 28 Soviet Department series covering 'Internal Situation in the Baltic States'.[2] The files dealing with the three republics individually—Estonia, Latvia and Lithuania—have not been consulted at all; nor have those dealing with important bilateral issues such as the question of Baltic Gold. These will have to await further, more detailed, research which will no doubt modify or contradict the conclusions I have reached.

Policy towards the Soviet Union developed in dialogue between London and the British embassy in Moscow, which had been headed since 1988 by Sir Rodric Braithwaite. A remarkable scholar of Russian history and culture in his own right, as his many subsequent publications testify, Braithwaite led an exceptionally able team. It included David Logan, the deputy head of mission responsible for the Baltic republics; David Manning, head of the political section; Tim Barrow as second secretary; and, in her first overseas posting, third secretary Sian MacLeod.[3] All of these diplomats acquired first-hand knowledge of conditions in the Baltic republics through numerous visits in the course of 1991 (always travelling in pairs or with a partner). Only Braithwaite himself was unable to take the trip, since an ambassadorial visit would have implied British recognition of Soviet sovereignty over the three republics and abandonment of the principle the United Kingdom had maintained since 1940. In London, contacts with Moscow were mediated in the first instance by the Soviet Department, which had been headed since the previous autumn by Roderic Lyne, formerly deputy head of mission in Moscow. Depending on their seriousness, issues were then escalated up the FCO hierarchy, sometimes involving other Foreign Office departments, sometimes junior ministers—in the first instance the minister for Europe, Douglas Hogg—and ultimately the foreign secretary himself. Hogg had held his post only since November 1990, but Douglas Hurd had considerable international experience, having served as a diplomat and junior Foreign Office minister before becoming foreign secretary in October 1989. Finally, of course, the new prime minister, John Major, was rapidly finding his feet and developing his own views on relations with the Soviet Union.

Naturally tensions and disagreements arose between the Moscow embassy and London—often, but not always, when the people on the ground wanted to move faster than those at home.

But there was broad consensus on the main priorities. Some related to global politics: it was imperative to avoid reversion to East-West confrontation and to keep Gorbachev on side until the Gulf War came to its unexpectedly rapid conclusion on 28 February. Others were specific to the situation on the ground. Somehow a balance had to be struck between encouraging Baltic aspirations and preserving what was left of the reformist movement in the Soviet Union as a whole, including keeping Gorbachev in power. At the same time Britain must keep in step with its allies: meaning, in the first instance, the United States and the European Community. Above all, the job of British diplomats was to pursue Britain's national interest. This meant doing their best to ensure that the UK got ahead of the game: without jeopardising Gorbachev's survival or Western solidarity, Britain should gain as much credit as possible by responding to Baltic appeals a little more quickly, and providing the Baltic republics with practical support a little more visibly, than its Western partners.

There were two major flashpoints: first, the military crackdown in the Baltic republics in January 1991; secondly, the failed coup against Gorbachev and the Estonian and Latvian declarations of independence in late August. Between the two came a lull of several months in which British diplomats set about learning more about Baltic conditions and aspirations. Then, in the autumn of 1991, the period after diplomatic recognition saw the establishment of embassies in the three Baltic capitals while, in London, ministers and officials debated the nature of Britain's future relationship with the Baltic States, often in surprisingly conservative terms.

The January Crisis

As the year 1990 ended, the stalemate between Moscow and the Baltic republics continued. Lithuania had declared its independence in March 1990; the pro-independence governments elected by popular majorities in Estonia and Latvia were preparing to follow suit; all three republics were laying the economic groundwork for a viable existence outside the Soviet Union. At the beginning of January 1991 came the first sign that the central authorities—or elements within them, or local activists—might be trying to break the deadlock. Moving paratroopers into Latvia and Lithuania to round up young men seeking to avoid conscription seemed a minor issue, but might be a sign that the army was putting pressure on Gorbachev to take a tougher line. More ominous was a statement by Gorbachev on 10 January that used language which seem to imply, without stating outright, a threat to impose presidential rule on Lithuania and effectively demanding that it give up its claim to independence.[4]

Following a meeting with Douglas Hogg, Roderic Lyne asked: 'How should we react?' The answer, agreed with Rodric Braithwaite in Moscow, was 'a response which is strong, but which does not throw the whole book at the Russians after the first act of repression': in other words, a calibrated set of responses depending on the severity of Soviet actions.[5] On 11 January the FCO's political director, John Weston, delivered a démarche to the Soviet chargé d'affaires. The message was later reinforced by Douglas Hurd and repeated in Moscow on the personal instructions of the secretary of state.[6] Assessing Gorbachev's statement, Braithwaite judged that Soviet actions were haphazard rather than carefully planned.[7] However, they revealed the growing influence of the military, and Gorbachev's language recalled that used before the Warsaw Pact invasion of Czechoslovakia in 1968. It looked as though local hardliners had been pressing Moscow for a crackdown and using provocations to make that happen. Gorbachev knew how much damage such action would do to relations with the United States, but the trend was likely to be towards greater conflict and increasing use of force by Moscow. The hardliners were on the offensive; the liberals were in retreat. Embassy officials, Braithwaite noted, were due to visit the Baltic republics over the next week.

David Manning was in Tallinn by 12 January. He reported that Soviet paratroopers were expected in the city the following day and that a large demonstration by ethnic Russians was planned for 15 January. It was not yet clear whether this was a deliberate provocation.[8] Elsewhere, violence had intensified with the storming of the Press House in Vilnius on 11 January; it culminated on the night of 12–13 January in an attack on crowds surrounding the TV tower and the parliament building, in which thirteen people were killed and several hundred injured. Similar events, it was reported, might be planned for Estonia and Latvia.[9] The violence was strongly condemned by both the prime minister and the foreign secretary, the latter warning that the Soviet Union must not think it could get away with repression while the world's attention was focused on the crisis in Kuwait.[10] David Logan visited Riga and Vilnius with his wife on 14–16 January.[11] 'The problem,' he recalled, 'was that here was the Prime Minister of Latvia, as far as he was aware under attack by the Soviet forces, saying to the Brits, "What are you going to do to help us?" To which there wasn't a great deal you could say as reassurance. You did your best.'[12] By 17 January, however, Braithwaite was able to report that the immediate crisis had passed.[13] Influenced by international opinion, the Soviet authorities seemed to have had second thoughts about an immediate crackdown.[14] Yet, on the eve of Operation Desert Storm, it remained imperative to keep international attention focused on the Gulf. The UK's mission to the UN in New York (UKMIS) was advised: 'We would not wish to see Lithuania raised in the Security Council, above all at a time when Soviet cooperation over the Gulf is of vital importance.' The UK's commitment to the Baltic States remained strictly limited. While Britain did not recognise the legality of the Soviet takeover,

UKMIS was advised, 'This does not imply recognition of any continued existence after 1940.'[15]

In this context, Britain's policy objectives remained the familiar ones: to sustain Soviet cooperation internationally and in the Gulf: to deter the Soviet government, by carrot and stick, from extending internal repression; and to keep open channels to reformers and republican leaders.[16] In pursuit of these last two objectives, on 23 January, Braithwaite was instructed to call on the new Soviet foreign minister, Alexander Bessmertnykh, to express concern about events in Baltic States and hope that cooperation could continue, while on the same day the Latvian foreign minister, Jānis Jurkāns, and prime minister, Ivars Godmanis, called on Major at 10 Downing Street. Braithwaite had been frustrated when his American, French and German colleagues delivered démarches to the Soviet government on 22 January while he had to wait until the following day before being instructed to do so. He finally called on Bessmertnykh on 25 January, finding him worried that Baltic situation might jeopardise relations with the West, but failing fully to appreciate the force of Baltic nationalism, or the impact the crisis was having on the West.

In his first extended reflections on the Baltic crisis Braithwaite acknowledged that Baltic leaders had not handled their case well but were inexperienced. Gorbachev, for his part, was not necessarily the prisoner of the reactionaries. The Baltic crisis might spin out of control, but genuine negotiations might follow, and the West could encourage both parties to move in that direction.[17] Four days later Braithwaite was able to report a temporary pause, although tension remained high.[18] The Balts had made it too easy for hardliners to mount provocations against them: they had not been wise in their tactics. The Russians could suppress them by force if necessary, even if they thereby lost much of what they had gained since 1985. But Britain's policy, Braithwaite concluded, had been 'just right': we had condemned the use of violence in the Baltic republics but were supporting Gorbachev as long as his reforms continued. Major's first visit as prime minister to Moscow, scheduled for early March, would offer the best opportunity to reinforce these points. On 1 February Braithwaite urged that the prime minister should send a personal message to Gorbachev soon even though they had not yet met: Britain was suffering by comparison with other Western countries by its lack of a direct personal line to the man at the top. Gorbachev's adviser Anatoly Chernyaev, he reported, had spoken wistfully of Mrs Thatcher.[19] A week later, Braithwaite reported the return of Manning and Barrow from their latest visit to the Baltic States.[20] They had found deep gratitude for Britain's firm stance and a willingness to get negotiations going, but doubt whether Gorbachev was prepared to negotiate seriously. The hardliners were regrouping and there were fears of a new crackdown.

Major visited Moscow on 5 March, immediately after referendums in Estonia and Latvia had shown clear majorities in favour of independence. Before meeting Gorbachev, Major met Baltic representatives; to Gorbachev himself he explained

> the dismay that I felt and that the West generally had felt about the events in January of this year and I expressed also our hope that the way forward would be through negotiations. Mr Gorbachev contested some of the statements and decisions and comments that had been made in the West and emphasised the difficulties that he faced. He also emphasised in our discussion that he believed in a constitutional process to solve the problem of the Baltics. He emphasised also that if the Baltics followed that process then independence was a possible outcome.[21]

His discussions over the Baltic States had been 'intense', Major admitted, but not 'ill-humoured': 'there were some frank and free exchanges; it was a candid but good-natured discussion.' Major had, therefore, shifted the balance in favour of support for the Baltic States without jeopardising Britain's relations with Gorbachev. British diplomats could not have asked for more.

Interlude

Once the immediate crisis had passed, thoughts in both London and Moscow turned to the wider implications of recognising Baltic independence. The FCO's Historical Branch provided information on the history of the independent Baltic States between the wars and noted the publication, for the first time, of the Soviet text of the Nazi-Soviet Pact of 23 August 1939.[22] From Moscow, Sian MacLeod sent what would become the first in a series of fortnightly summaries of recent events in the Baltic States. 'More, please!', replied Susan Miller of the Soviet Department.[23] The permanent under-secretary, Sir Patrick Wright, asked the policy planning staff to look at the way the FCO handled 'representatives of various national movements and national territorial entities which are not states', including Baltic representatives.[24] On 12 April, Lyne wrote to Braithwaite to test his reactions to 'three small steps' which might gradually ratchet up our relationship with the Baltic republics: first, a series of one-off payments to help them set up information offices in London; second, a 'private' ambassadorial visit to a Baltic republic; third, further visits by British officials to the Baltic republics. Braithwaite favoured only the last of these.[25] If he went to the Baltic as ambassador, it would send a confusing signal both to the Balts and to the Soviet authorities. Funding information offices would contradict Hurd's repeated statements that Britain was not trying to promote the break-up of the Soviet Union. Nevertheless, in early July it was agreed to grant sums of £3,000 (not £5,000 as originally proposed) to each of the three information offices, to the great satisfaction of Baltic representatives.[26]

In a background brief of 9 August, the Soviet Department summarised British policy towards the Baltic States.[27] The UK had never recognised their seizure by Stalin in 1940, but they did not meet its criteria for recognition as independent countries as they did not properly control their own affairs. But once independence had been agreed between republican and central Soviet authorities, the UK would deal with them as with any independent state. Meanwhile, the UK continued to develop contacts with the elected authorities of the Baltic republics. Baltic leaders had visited London, and the prime minister had met Baltic representatives in Moscow during his visit in March. British diplomats had visited the republics; British ministers had met the Latvian and Estonian foreign ministers; a significant part of the Know How Fund had been directed towards Baltic projects; educational and cultural links were expanding through the British Council; Baltic information offices had been established in London. Nothing, however, had happened to break the deadlock.

Recognition

Ten days later the impasse was broken dramatically by the coup against Gorbachev and its failure. Immediately afterwards, on 22 August, Estonia and Latvia followed Lithuania in declaring their independence; all three republics called for Western recognition and the restoration of full diplomatic relations. Major was quick to respond. On 23 August, one day before he was to leave for the Baltic republics, Manning was instructed to 'tell Baltic leaders that the prime minister has asked him to go to see the situation and report back'. Major himself hoped to visit Moscow soon and would welcome the opportunity to meet Baltic leaders there. The foreign secretary was also quick off the mark. Rather than favouring the obvious next step, a visit by the ambassador, he thought 'something more high profile might be desirable' and that Hogg should visit the Baltics in the week following the prime minister's visit to Moscow.[28] Sir Arthur Watts, the FCO's legal adviser, confirmed that ministerial visits 'would not necessarily imply *de jure* recognition of the incorporation of the Baltic Republics into the Soviet Union, any more than that would necessarily imply recognition of their independence. The political signal, of course, will be strong, but that is another matter (and is what is intended anyway).'[29]

The situation was complicated. The Russian government had recognised Baltic sovereignty but not independence. Negotiating independence was a matter for the Soviet government but, as Braithwaite noted, 'these days Gorbachev follows where Yeltsin leads.'[30] Having received no instructions, Braithwaite now pushed urgently for British recognition. On 25 August he noted that 'a race amongst Western European countries to get in first is already beginning' and warned that the UK risked falling behind: 'Iceland and Denmark have already recognised them and ... Canada is moving the same way.'[31] He recommended an early statement to 'reinforce our position in the Baltics (though it will not go as far as they would like) without undermining it here [i.e. in Moscow]': it should welcome the Russian recognition of Estonian and Latvian independence; look forward to negotiations between the Soviet Union and Baltic governments; and promise to open diplomatic relations with the Baltic States as soon as they reached agreement with Moscow.

Manning phoned from Riga early in the morning of 25 August, shortly after Braithwaite's telegram had been sent. Both the Estonians and Latvians had 'expressed very great gratitude for the support that Britain has been giving them'; they were also grateful for Manning's visit, the first of its kind so far. They remained very nervous, fearing 'a resurgence of Russian imperialism', and therefore 'expressed great hope that we can recognise their independence very soon'. 'At present they regard us as ahead of the wave': they believed that with Yeltsin having recognised them and Gorbachev weakened, 'there is a window of opportunity during which our recognition would strengthen their position without damaging ours.' Braithwaite urged that the recommendations in his previous telegram should be regarded as a minimum.[32] Following his return to Moscow, Manning reported on his final visit, to Lithuania, where he had met Landsbergis.[33] The latter repeated the arguments of his Estonian and Latvian counterparts, 'in typical Landsbergis needling style', claiming that Britain was falling behind other countries: a suggestion that Manning 'contested forcefully … reminding Landsbergis of our long and strong advocacy of the Baltic cause.' Manning's overall conclusion from his visit was that the Balts were grateful for British support but wanted 'immediate recognition, not least because they believe that where we lead others will follow.' They explicitly recalled the historical reasons why Britain should be in the vanguard, citing the events of 1918–19 and 1940. They also wanted practical support in the form of advice, especially on setting up foreign ministries and diplomatic services.[34]

Hurd held an office meeting on the Baltic States and the Soviet Union on 27 August. There was no discussion of when to recognise Baltic independence: it was simply assumed that recognition would happen soon, presumably in coordination with other EC members—there was no suggestion that Britain might go it alone. On the basis of that assumption, the meeting decided that Hogg should visit the Baltic States on 3 September, the day after the prime minister's visit to Moscow. Hurd favoured establishing diplomatic relations as soon as possible after Hogg's visit, 'notwithstanding the difficulty of withdrawing representation once it had been sent.' He also wanted Britain and France to help the Baltic States in their applications for UN membership. Baltic Gold was identified as a problem still to be tackled. Early in the evening of 27 August, Manning telephoned the Baltic capitals to 'let them know informally that British recognition was imminent, almost certainly in concert with that of our EC partners ... He said that you [Hurd] favoured immediate recognition by the 12 and would be speaking strongly in this sense in Brussels. You were likely to carry your colleagues... All three Baltic interlocutors were delighted and grateful ... Judging from the surprise and excitement, we were first to pass the news to the Baltic capitals.'[35]

Official visits quickly followed. Major met the three Baltic prime ministers in Moscow on 1 September, a meeting rounded off with a champagne toast. He was assured that although challenges would lie ahead, they could be resolved. The Baltic States 'had enjoyed close relations with Britain before the war and looked forward to developing these once again'.[36] Hogg visited the three Baltic States between 3 and 6 September. He reported that they were 'following [a] business-like and cautious approach'.[37] On diplomatic relations, Hogg's preliminary view was that 'we should have an Ambassador in Riga ... served by small subordinate posts in the other two capitals'—in other words, a throwback to the arrangement between the wars. 'On the awkward question of the Baltic gold ... We really must resolve this fairly.'

Baltic independence

By late September a paper seeking to define the main lines of British policy towards the newly independent Baltic States was in draft: the final version was registered on 7 October.[38] Its most striking assumption, while paying due homage to their long struggle for independence, was how *unimportant* they were likely to be to British policy in the future. Other more important republics, above all Russia and Ukraine, would now become the main focus of British interest: by comparison, 'the Baltic states will be of small future bilateral importance to the UK':

A large part of our future relations, especially in the trade and economic fields, will be conducted through the EC. Likewise with fewer than eight million inhabitants between them and a total area less than half that of Finland, they will not play a significant role in Europe. They will aspire to EC membership, but will take many years to attain this. Their economies are backward and must be restructured completely. They have few natural resources. However their geographical position and knowledge of the Soviet market in due course should allow them to resume their former role as a natural entrepôt for trade between Western Europe and the Russian hinterland.

This last assumption is particularly revealing, because it is a throwback not to the interwar period—when the Baltic States were largely cut off from the Soviet Union and successfully reoriented almost their entire production and foreign trade towards Western European markets—but much further back to the period before 1914, the last time when cities such as Riga did act as an entrepôt between Russia and the West.

These priorities were reinforced by a paper on policy towards the Soviet Union produced by an interdepartmental Political Steering Group chaired by Weston.[39] Envisaging the future Soviet Union as, at best, a loose association of essentially independent republics, it foresaw them gravitating in different directions: 'the Ukraine, for example, will look Westwards and the Central Asian Republics to the South'. The future trajectory of the Baltic States was depicted in remarkably pessimistic terms. Their independence would be constrained for many years by the presence of Soviet armed forces and Russian minorities, as well as by economic interdependence with the Soviet Union: 'As time passes, the Baltic States will attract less attention and less Western sympathy—especially if the illiberal treatment of minorities by Landsbergis's Lithuania government becomes endemic. Collectively they muster only 8 million people and few economic resources.' The UK should pay its part in helping to bring the Baltic States into European and international orbits, but they would be 'of small importance to the UK by comparison, say, with the Ukraine, and we should deploy our resources accordingly. They will look primarily to the Scandinavian countries for help and partnership, and are natural candidates for a Nordic sub-grouping.'

These discouraging assessments were belied by the facts on the ground. By October British ambassadors had arrived in all three Baltic capitals—Richard Samuel to Riga, Michael Peart to Vilnius and Brian Low to Tallinn—and were building embassies from scratch in conditions that were challenging, to say the least. From Tallinn, Low wrote:

> Sony short-wave working well. BBC clearly audible. Cellnet phone lit up and making the right noises, but unable to raise either Duty Officer Stockholm or Embassy Helsinki. Could be my power but propose taking it to Helsinki for Embassy to check.
>
> ... The Department will be relieved (as am I) to learn that the US10,000 issued to me in Stockholm is now safely in the US Embassy strongbox pending deposit in a bank.
>
> ... The Estonians will happily show us round property for both office and residential use. Both are pretty awful.[40]

By the autumn practical assistance was in full swing. The Know How Fund had been extended to the Baltic States and very deliberately demarcated from the Fund's activities in the Soviet Union.[41] It organised training for the police, helped to reorganise ministries of foreign affairs and provided advice on parliamentary practice and legal training. Technical assistance was offered to banks and businesses. The British Council was active with fellowship and scholarship programmes. Links were established with the Centre for Baltic Studies at Bradford University, the University of Leeds and the School of Slavonic and East European Studies in London. Even the problem of Baltic Gold was being discussed in a friendly and positive spirit.

What the Baltic States were doing, of course, was to recon-
struct their economies and orientate them towards the West
precisely as they had done during the interwar period. It seems
that in their preoccupation with grand strategy some people in
London had forgotten this particular lesson from history. By
offering practical support and building on the contacts forged
during the tense months preceding the recovery of Baltic independence, British diplomats were helping to establish UK-Baltic
relations on a firm foundation of friendship and cooperation, just
as the Royal Navy's intervention in Estonia and Latvia had done
in 1918–19. Nevertheless, Britain had not encouraged Baltic
aspirations quite as decisively as John Hiden and I had thought
in 1993. Until the failed coup, moves in that direction had been
checked by the perceived need to sustain Gorbachev in power and
to prevent in some degree the disintegration of the Soviet Union.
By the end of 1991 at the latest, there was no further need for
such restraint.

15

THE CONTEMPORARY POLITICAL DIMENSION

Rt Hon Sir David Lidington

In 1987 I was appointed as a special adviser to Douglas Hurd, who was then Home Secretary. I moved with him to the Foreign Office when he was appointed Foreign Secretary, beginning on his very first day in office, 26 October 1989. A special adviser is a political appointee hired to support ministers. They give party political advice and support that would be inappropriate for the civil service to provide but also have the freedom to comment on civil service policy advice to Ministers.

I held this post only up until the early weeks of 1991 since the rules obliged me to resign from my advisory role when I was selected as a candidate for the parliamentary constituency of Aylesbury at the very end of 1990. As a consequence, I did not witness first-hand the developments throughout 1991 which have been described elsewhere in this book.

I can nevertheless speak to the atmosphere in the Foreign Office in the months leading up to the collapse of the Soviet Union as Europe experienced seismic change. It was clear to see that the astonishing events that led to the drawing back of the Iron Curtain, had taken even the most skilled in the department completely by surprise. The accounts of both Patrick Salmon and Bridget Kendall tally well with my own memories of the time. My short piece therefore serves as a political reflection of the time, which may be able to put a gloss on the first-rate analysis provided earlier in this volume. The presentations at the Centre for Geopolitics symposium in March 2022, 'The Baltic contribution to the dissolution of the Soviet Union in 1991' have reminded me of a number of interesting and enlightening experiences from my time in the Foreign Office.

My initial recollection of the Foreign Office as an institution was that I believe it very often framed its thinking in terms of a Russian sphere of interest. Despite the fact that the United Kingdom had never recognised Stalin's seizure of the three Baltic republics and Estonian, Latvian and Lithuanian embassies remained in London throughout the period of Soviet occupation, the understanding of the Baltics in the department was generally linked to Russia in some way, rather than viewing them in isolation.

Something that rings true in my memory, as the Baltic States began to break away, is the British belief in the idea that the Baltics, which officials hoped would enjoy greater freedom and autonomy in a Soviet Union reformed by glasnost and perestroika, might return to their traditional role as an entrepôt between the West and Russia. This frame of reference probably went right back to the eighteenth century in terms of institutional memory and practice within the Foreign Office. It was at that time, of course, that the Baltics were first incorporated into the Russian Empire.

But my memory is that in 1990 and even in January 1991, senior levels of the department were totally taken aback by the rapid emergence of nationalism in the region. To them the sense of an assertive desire for independence was just as much of a surprise when it first emerged in all the Central European countries of the Warsaw Pact as it was subsequently in the USSR itself and in Yugoslavia after that. A complete cession from the Russian zone of influence was simply not seen as a possibility or in the character of the Baltic region. This was perhaps surprising given the history of the independence of the Baltic countries between the great wars.

I can remember the winter of 1989/90, when so many dramatic developments unfurled in front of us. I was fresh in the Foreign Office having just come in with Douglas Hurd, as I mentioned above, on 26 October 1989. Little over two weeks later, on 12 November, the Berlin Wall came down. At that time, I talked with a very senior, very distinguished diplomat who was then in overall charge of the two Germanies. I asked him about what had happened in Berlin and whether it was at all conceivable that we could be talking about a type of German unity coming onto the agenda at some point in the near future. As I spoke, I felt that I must be sounding terribly naive! But my job as a special adviser was to ask questions. The response of the diplomat is still very vivid in my mind. Considering my question, he leant back in his seat and told me, 'Well David, perhaps in 25 years we might talk about a confederation between the two German states.' As we all know, the situation moved rather quicker than that!

In the weeks that followed I read the daily telegrams from British Ambassadors in Prague, Warsaw, Budapest and so on. They wrote in a tone of genuine wonder and amazement at the events that they were seeing unfold. Hard-bitten, experienced, worldly-wise ambassadors openly admitted that they did not know what was going to come tomorrow. Much of their news seemed barely believable, for instance the transmission from the ambassador in Prague who reported that Alexander Dubček, the figurehead of the 1968 Prague Spring who had been in exile from the Communist Party ever since, was now on his way to the capital. In all corners of the British diplomatic service and the corridors of the Foreign Office there was this sense of utter astonishment.

That sense of shock became even more intense when the Soviet Union itself started to crack apart. I can remember a meeting in 1990 which centred around Russia and the Soviet Union, in which I raised the subject of Boris Yeltsin, who was then the Chairman of the Supreme Soviet of the Russian SFSR. I had observed that Yeltsin was being talked up in the British press as some sort of conceivable alternative to the Communist Party leadership. I put it to the attendees of this meeting that he clearly had something in mind. Could he possibly be manoeuvring into a position of power? Might he challenge the authority of Gorbachev? The general response was fairly dismissive of this notion. 'He's clearly ambitious', remarked one senior official, 'but he does not have control of any of the levers: he does not have the partners in the party, he does not have the military contacts, nor the security and intelligence network needed for such a coup.' There was simply no way, according to this official, in which he could ever take power; it was simply not going to happen.

From the very start, British diplomats did not fully recognise the upsurge and desire for change in Eastern and Central Europe. These were good diplomats, but they were hindered by the restrictive conditions which came with working in authoritarian countries. The Kremlin did not allow Western diplomats to travel freely within the Soviet Union. Most of the people whom British officials met were either part of or allied to the regime. They were unable to gauge accurately the depth and scale of public discontent.

To both officials and senior political leaders, the historic role that Russia had played in European politics and diplomacy since at least the eighteenth century, shaped a world-view which saw Russia (and the Soviet Union in Russia's shoes) as an inevitable and permanent part of the European balance of power.

Margaret Thatcher, Prime Minister until 28 November 1990, had also invested heavily in Mikhail Gorbachev, to whom she felt a strong personal commitment. From their very first meeting at her official country residence, Chequers, in 1984, when he attended at her invitation as a very new Politburo member, she famously remarked, 'I like Mr Gorbachev, I could do business with him.' Mrs Thatcher regarded sustaining his authority as critically important to the interests of the United Kingdom.

Thatcher had been born in 1925. Her teenage memories were of German militarism and aggression and of Britain's battle for survival. For her, the prospect of German unification and the resurgence of German power which she believed would follow, threatened to upset the balance of power in Europe and also destabilise a reformist Soviet leader whom she wanted to see continue in power.

Her commitment to Gorbachev also made her extremely reluctant to give any sort of support to the push for Baltic independence.

I remember one Foreign Office discussion in which we were preparing for a potential Lithuanian delegation to the UK, who wanted to set up a ministerial meeting. The matter had been referred up to Number Ten and Charles Powell, who was the Foreign Affairs Private Secretary to the Prime Minister. The message from him basically said 'no Balts.' Number Ten's view, in Margaret Thatcher's time, was that such overtures to prominent figures from the Baltics posed much too big a risk to the relationship with Mikhail Gorbachev and to his authority.

There were, of course, some good reasons for this approach. We may look back in hindsight and say that this policy was mistaken, but Gorbachev was seen, first of all, as vital to achieving success from the Four plus Two talks on the future of Germany. In 1990 we were contending with an accelerated push for German unification, but with Soviet and other Warsaw Pact troops stationed in East Germany. How would we manage that? How would we manage it without talking to Gorbachev, indeed without his support? Throughout 1990 the German question was central to the priorities of the Foreign Secretary and the Prime Minister in the United Kingdom and so it took precedence over any push to destabilise the Soviet Union.

Second, the USSR still had a massive nuclear arsenal. If it started to look as if the Soviet regime was at risk of tipping over, what might follow Gorbachev? It was not guaranteed to be somebody who was more liberal or more friendly towards the West, as indeed the botched coup in 1991 showed. If there were a chaotic succession contest then the treaties that existed on arms control and the Soviet nuclear stockpile in particular, would all be at risk.

Then, of course, on 2 August 1990 Saddam Hussein invaded and annexed Kuwait. Throughout the latter months of 1990 and into the launch of Operation Desert Storm in January 1991, United States, United Kingdom and other Western diplomacy was dominated by the effort to assemble the widest possible international coalition of support for military action to restore Kuwait's independence. Gorbachev's Soviet Union was willing to line up, at least as a non-participating supporter of the coalition that President Bush and others had assembled. Preparation for what we now call the Gulf War was the overriding priority, again pushing issues in the Baltic down the list.

During 1990, Gorbachev's role in Germany and the Middle East was too valuable to undermine.

The change of Prime Minister in late 1990 made it easier for the United Kingdom to shift towards more overt support for

Baltic independence. John Major, born in 1943, had lived all his life knowing Germany as a reliable, democratic partner that had demonstrably rejected the horror of Nazism and built a thriving capitalist economy and liberal society. He did not fear a united, democratic Germany.

There was also an important change in circumstances by the time, in the middle of 1991, that the Baltic States' drive to recover their independence gathered pace.

The German question had been settled with the whole of Germany inside both NATO and the European Union. Soviet troops had left German territory peacefully.

The Gulf War had been won. Victory was seen as representing a triumph for international coalitions and the democratic world. A small sovereign country had been rescued from a much more powerful neighbour. The principle of national self-determination had been upheld. If Kuwait, then why not the Baltic States?

The political background of mid-1991, in contrast to the situation of early 1990, made it much easier for the British government to view Baltic independence with a favourable eye.

PART VI

THE CONTEMPORARY USE OF HISTORY

16

HISTORICAL PROPAGANDA IN PRO-KREMLIN MEDIA

THE CASE OF THE COLLAPSE OF THE SOVIET UNION

Dr Inga Zakšauskienė*

Introduction, Sources, Techniques

Russian state propaganda and disinformation campaigns against Ukraine exploit different parts of history, from the Rurik dynasty and the foundation of Kievan Rus to the collapse of the USSR. Pro-Kremlin state media employs methods of history manipulation to create a convenient narrative for propagated discourse, such as manipulation or selective presentation of histori-

---

* I am grateful to Agnė Eidimtaitė and Magdalena Wilczyńska from DebunkEU.org, who undertook the empirical analysis of pro-Kremlin discourse for this chapter.

cal facts, falsification of historical facts, or the denial of war crimes. For example, Russian state propaganda omits the mass repressions of the Soviet era such as the crimes committed by Stalin's regime, including the Holodomor famine in Ukraine and the Great Terror. This practice aims to convince Russian and international audiences of the legality of the Molotov-Ribbentrop Pact and the subsequent occupation of the Baltic States. The pro-Kremlin adjusted narratives target different audiences: vesti.ru and ria.ru target Russia, while Sputnik news agency, baltnews.ru and ukraina.ru attempt to influence countries in the former communist bloc.

The media sources mentioned above are controlled by the Russian government, therefore they uphold the state propaganda narratives. History can be conveniently exploited in propaganda and misleading information campaigns in two opposing ways: to build up a picture of alleged enemy countries and, on the contrary, to find memory allies by promoting Russia's view of historical events.[1] Russian influence is bolstered not only by media campaigns and pop culture, but also by symbols and memories that are exported to other countries, mostly targeting Russian minorities abroad.[2] One of the most successful informational campaigns is the promotion of the St. George Ribbon as a visual symbol worn on 9 May, the day of victory in the Great Patriotic War. Nostalgia for Soviet times is exported to post-Soviet, communist bloc countries, whilst narratives supporting an image of the Soviet Union's great power seek to reach further than just those countries in Russia's zone of influence, the so-called 'near abroad' (Russian: *blizhneye zarubezh'ye*).[3] Yet, according to the NATO Strategic Communications Centre of Excellence, Russian speaking minorities outside the Russian border are one of the main target audiences, and are the most vulnerable, as they have a less critical approach to their information sources.[4] These groups potentially might accept the Russian state propaganda discourse and react to the various Russia-initiated information campaigns, leading to polarization, destabilization, internal unrest, and the creation of further social and political threats.

Since state organized information campaigns usually tend to exploit prominent state anniversaries to consolidate propagated narratives, Kremlin-related and pro-Kremlin media presumably would have reacted to the 30th anniversary of the dissolution of the USSR as an opportunity to create new narratives and messages. The media analysis presented here is written in collaboration with the Lithuanian independent technology think tank and non-governmental organization, DebunkEU.org. They have created an open-source monitoring tool which researches disinformation, in order to detect the Russian state media information campaign exploiting the dissolution of the Soviet Union, by inspecting the media environment and the reaction to the mentioned historical events. The report presents analysis of textual, audio and video content from the digital environment which includes detection of historical topics, crucial events, repetitive messages and disinformation techniques exploited by the Pro-Kremlin media reacting to the anniversary of dissolution of the USSR.[5]

The analysis of the historical discourse around the collapse of the USSR leads back to the famous phrase uttered by Vladimir Putin during his annual address to the Federal Assembly of the Russian Federation in 2005, frequently repeated by the Russian media; 'the collapse of the Soviet Union was the greatest geopolitical disaster of the century.'[6] Analysis has demonstrated several instances in which Russian state propaganda applied the USSR history narrative, showing: 1) that the collapse of USSR was a great tragedy to the Russian people at home and abroad; 2) that the collapse had a negative effect on global stability; 3) that Russia actively held onto the idea that it was the legal successor of the Soviet Union and the history of the USSR was perceived as a part of Russia's history. These attitudes indicated that pro-

Kremlin and Kremlin-related media promoted historical narratives concerning the Soviet era that would comply with official Russian propaganda.

The goals of the media analysis were three-fold: 1) to research how certain events and the collapse of the USSR as a whole have been presented in pro-Kremlin media, what the main messages were, and how they could have been exploited to support the Russian state's perspective of history and its bid to find memory allies or discredit particular political actors; 2) to discover whether and what kind of techniques were used in pro-Kremlin media to manipulate historical facts, rewrite history or present the collapse of the USSR in a misleading way; 3) to find the main targets blamed for the dissolution of the USSR, what reasons were given to explain the collapse, and what political figures, countries or organizations were presented as responsible for the collapse of the USSR.

To reach the set goals, DebunkEU.org analysts researched all articles related to the dissolution of the USSR from the period 1 August 2021 to 16 January 2022 that were published in pro-Kremlin and Kremlin-related media sources. The research categorized the articles it analysed according to narratives and sub-narratives, in order to identify the main messages and distinguish the techniques used in potentially harmful content. The full analysis of the view of the Soviet Union's collapse, and events related to it, was based on 655 content pieces identified in the information environment of the pro-Kremlin media.

DebunkEU.org methodology evaluated published content pieces and their disinformation in terms of writers' intentions to exploit events or situations to attract readers' attention to an issue, promote preferable messages, and mould opinions on the event or a certain target. In the case of historical topics, anniversaries of historical events caused an increase in the dissemination of content pieces; however, this reaction was an ordinary trait in the media landscape around the globe. The study shows that pro-Kremlin media tended to spread repetitive messages in order to form an opinion and sentiment toward the dissolution of the USSR around particular dates. Pro-Kremlin media reacted significantly to two crucial historical events of the ending Soviet era: the August coup (19–22 August 1991) and the signing of the Belovezha Accords (8 December 1991). These events were conceived as crucial points in the process of dissolution of the USSR, and propaganda articles presented the events as tragic with the participating political leaders presented as traitors and enemies of the motherland.

The leading media distributor of articles that manipulatively presented historical facts on the collapse of the Soviet Union was cont.ws, a Russian internet blog that publishes opinions in favour of Kremlin narratives. It quoted various Russian experts on war, history and politics. Articles were often presented as analytical, containing historical facts or shared memories about the allegedly true sequence of events. The media sources which were studied reached a wider Russian audience, however, they also gained a decent audience in the post-Soviet countries or among Russian speaking readers in Western Europe. For instance, around 11% of cont.ws readers are from Ukraine,[7] while tehnowar.ru also reaches audiences in Kazakhstan, Ukraine, and the Netherlands.[8]

It is worth noting that, although most of the Russian articles were published in pro-Kremlin media, most news sources cannot be associated with the Russian government. While cont.ws, tehnowar.ru, and top-war.ru support state propaganda narratives, when it comes to their sources, direct subordination to the government cannot be traced. However, the above-mentioned media sources are not just used to share original content pieces, but also to disseminate articles or opinion pieces from other media organizations, including some funded by the Russian state.

On the contrary, such sources as ukraina.ru, news-front.info, sputniknews.ru and ria.ru are owned by the Russian state, and cases of misleading information detected in these sources demonstrated direct Kremlin intentions to manipulate internal and external audiences. Ukraina.ru specifically concentrated on the situation in Ukraine, trying to present 'different points of view'. The analysis revealed that both pro-Kremlin (proxy sites) and Kremlin-owned (state-funded) media sources shared similar narratives concerning the collapse of the USSR, frequently blaming former high-level Soviet officers and Western or post-Soviet countries for the event, as well as supporting Russia's state propaganda. Moreover, identical articles were disseminated in several sources creating a wider reach in audiences. According to DebunkReach®, content pieces that manipulatively presented historical facts about the Soviet Union and its collapse had potentially reached approximately 236 million contacts all around the world.[9]

False, misinformative or propagandistic content in pro-Kremlin media applied rhetorical techniques to increase the credibility of the propagated message. When undermining historical facts, as in the case of the collapse of the Soviet Union, particular techniques were used more often than others. Hyperbolization stood out as a dominant rhetoric technique in the cases of historical manipulation (37.2%). In these cases, the media provided exaggerated information or provided two opposing sides, deliberately exacerbated on the basis of assumptions which were only partly true, featuring one side having a very negative/positive connotation and trying to discredit an opposing view. This technique was used most frequently to spread pro-Kremlin propaganda. Regarding the history of the collapse of the USSR, hyperbolization was used to exaggerate the alleged Western influence and interference in the process and magnify the 'tragic consequences' that were caused.

Information selection techniques were detected as the second most dominant feature in pro-Kremlin media, a trait identified in almost a quarter of all problematic articles. Selection techniques were applied that presented information out of context, intentionally omitting important aspects of the situation, background to the events etc. This method was also often adopted in the articles undermining the independence referendums held in the Baltic States, alleging that the polls were illegal under the Soviet law. These articles purposefully omitted information regarding the existence of national constitutions and the rulings of national supreme courts that confirmed the legal status of the Baltic States. Therefore, selective presentation of arguments in a historical debate (in this case the legitimacy of the referendum), although resolved under national legislation and case law, was presented misleadingly to confuse the reader. The goal of authors spreading imprecise information was to undermine the sovereignty and independence of the post-Soviet states, backing up the major narrative of collapse of the USSR.

The technique of association, which entails the inclusion of quotes, confirmations, endorsements by well-known figures in Russian politics, appeared in about one fifth of the pro-Kremlin media publications under analysis. Adoption of association techniques requires the cooperation of journalists and other partners, such as witnesses, public figures, or former politicians. In many articles, former Soviet officials were interviewed in order to authenticate the message. In some publications, witnesses of the events also shared their memories about the Soviet times or dissolution. Self-reflective interviews and personally-focused documents (memoirs, autobiographies, etc.) in this type of publication were assessed without precaution, ignoring the fact that retrospective views of the past are more open to being moulded to fit a preferred discourse. Witnesses in the published interviews intentionally presented themselves in a positive light and their stories were not double-checked.

UNDERSTANDING THE BALTIC STATES

Dominant Narratives and Sub-Narratives

The categorization of narratives provides a deeper understanding of the main messages presented by pro-Kremlin media. The predominant narrative in the media: 'the Soviet elite led the USSR to collapse' shows that the content pieces focused on portraying Soviet officials negatively and presented their actions as crucial points in the process of the USSR's collapse. Sharp increases of the above-mentioned narrative were noticed around the anniversaries of the August coup and the Belovezha Accords; almost one-third of detected messages highlighted the topics of internal political affairs in the last year of the USSR's existence.

Data analysis demonstrated that pro-Kremlin media not only chose a certain target for its information campaign (the Soviet elite) but indicated how the collapse was portrayed. The second dominant narrative: 'the collapse of the USSR led to great tragedy' pointed to pro-Kremlin media efforts to apply the official state propaganda and efforts to amplify negative emotions toward the dissolution. Surprisingly, media focused on negative aspects of the dissolution in considerably higher scope than on the promotion of positive feelings toward the Soviet past. In both cases, the narratives disseminated in the Russian state media tried to tempt an emotional response from the audience.

The media analysis revealed the efforts of pro-Kremlin media to accuse the Soviet officials of the collapse of the USSR. The analysis of sub-narratives revealed Mikhail Gorbachev as the most discredited person in the country and his political decisions were presented in a negative light, referring to his political activities as illegal or malicious. While the analysis sought to research pro-Kremlin media coverage around the events related to collapse of the USSR in 1991, the stories exhibited traits similar to conspiracies, which exploited political figures and events in the late Soviet era to support their claims that the process of the collapse of the USSR was organized and implemented years before 1991. Therefore, former heads of the USSR Yuri Andropov and Leonid Brezhnev, as well as the Soviet ambassador to Canada (1973–83) and later head of the propaganda department, Alexander Yakovlev, were mentioned commonly. In the framework of the narrative: 'the collapse of the USSR led to great tragedy', media messages focused on negative circumstances following the dissolution of the USSR, which, it was claimed, had a great impact not only the life of citizens in the former USSR but also global stability.

Political Figures and Countries—Traitors and Enemies
in Pro-Kremlin Media

The pro-Kremlin and Kremlin-related media put the blame for the collapse of the USSR on certain political personalities or accused Western countries of external interference. Around one third of all misleading articles that were detected, disseminated the narrative: 'the Soviet elite led the USSR to collapse', while the dominant sub-narrative called the dissolution of the USSR, Gorbachev's personal crime. Media analysis indicated several versions adopted to showcase the role of the president of the USSR in executing the destruction of the country. Some of them aimed to display Gorbachev as incompetent, a weak leader, who had not taken necessary measures to stop the tragic processes evolving in the country. Other more repetitive stories in media messages attempted to display Gorbachev's policies, primarily perestroika, as conscious actions aiming to destroy the whole communist system. References to the first president of the Russian Federation, Boris Yeltsin, and the first president of Ukraine, Leonid Kravchuk, in pro-Kremlin media have increased rapidly since December 2021 along with stories about the Belovezha Accords. Boris Yeltsin, an opposition leader during the last year of the

USSR, was accused more rarely in comparison to Gorbachev. Attempts to discredit him appeared most prominently around the anniversary of the Belovezha Accords, which in the studied media articles were considered as illegal.

Although the majority of articles in pro-Kremlin media concentrated on the events that happened in the last year of the USSR, they also targeted personalities in the political elite, responsible for the collapse of the USSR even before the start of perestroika. Yuri Andropov, the head of the KGB and the short-reigned (1982–4) leader of the USSR, was shown as the real architect of the destructive politics of perestroika, who paved the way for Gorbachev to gain power and start a disruptive process within the Soviet Union. Yuri Andropov often appeared in conspiracy-like stories which tried to prove the fact that destruction of the USSR started right after the death of Leonid Brezhnev and was organized by close proponents of Yuri Andropov and Western agents. Andropov, during his short period of rule, did start some reforms to curb corruption, yet historians perceive him as a 'fundamental communist'. It is worth mentioning that the relation between Andropov's policies and the implemented liberal reforms were not investigated in the analyzed media messages.

As the collapse of the USSR historically could be considered as a recent past, the analysis searched for the use of memoirs or interviews from former officers in the USSR. The study showed that these dominated in pro-Kremlin media. Witnesses shared their memories about the last events in the Soviet Union and frequently searched for targets in the Soviet political elite to accuse them of malicious and deliberate political decisions, leading to the dissolution of the country. Proving the accuracy of the details presented by witnesses was ignored by pro-Kremlin media; memories were actively used as a tactic to support state propaganda.

HISTORICAL PRO-KREMLIN MEDIA

Interference From the Outside

Dominant narratives in the Russian disinformation media focused heavily on interference from outside powers, who supposedly carried out systematic and subversive activities against the Soviet Union. The narrative: 'Soviet authorities started the destruction process years before the USSR collapsed' joins together with: 'the collapse of the USSR was the work of outsiders.' It is claimed in these media narratives that Western agents took continuous action, working hand in hand with the Soviet elite, to destroy the country from the inside.

The narrative: 'the collapse of the USSR was the work of outsiders' was detected in 163 of the 552 cases studied. The US was mentioned in every tenth article related to the topic of the Soviet Union's dissolution, portrayed as being directly involved in activities against the Soviet Union. However, it is worth noting that not all articles presented the US as the major reason for the USSR's collapse. Of those that did, several different stories were disseminated by pro-Kremlin media regarding how the assumed US involvement in the dissolution took place. These included: alleged information warfare against the USSR; involvement of CIA agents in elite Soviet circles with specific plans for the US to destroy the Soviet Union from the inside; and equipping soft power agents for starting a revolution. The United States were presented mostly as the main foreign power that had influence on the events of the Soviet Union's dissolution. This US involvement was proclaimed as a hidden, even secret mission conducted by the special services. Media messages claimed that the operation was complex and planned vividly. The narratives accused the United States of deep infiltration into the Soviet regime and society.

One of the dominant tactics of pro-Kremlin media was to point to the depravity of interference by the US and its allies (NATO,

UNDERSTANDING THE BALTIC STATES

EU, and other Western European countries) in the events of the post-Soviet countries.[10] The message that 'popular movements were US-sponsored "Colour Revolutions"'[11] targets Western countries, claiming they illegitimately instigated uprisings or plotted so-called 'colour revolutions' in Georgia, Kazakhstan, Belarus and Ukraine. By employing such disinformation campaigns containing unproven and often hyperbolized messages, Russia seeks to maintain its influence in the post-Soviet region.

Post-Soviet Countries as a Sphere of Influence in Pro-Kremlin Media

In the context of the dissolution of the USSR, almost all post-Soviet states were presented as traitors to the idea of the Union in pro-Kremlin media. Some countries gathered more focus than others; Ukraine was one of the most vivid examples. One third of articles of potentially harmful content within the period of analysis, were related to Ukraine in some way. Ukraine's domestic and foreign policy problems were presented as a result of its decision to secede from the Soviet Union. Thus, the most distinctive narrative disseminated in relation to Ukraine was that Ukraine contributed to the tragic destruction of Soviet civilization. Ukraine was mentioned 54 times in the media messages containing the narrative, 'the Soviet elite led the USSR to collapse.' Even Ukrainian politicians were presented as traitors, having independently (or in cooperation with Russian politicians) planned and organized the collapse of the USSR.

The data has revealed that pro-Kremlin media actively incorporated discourses about freedom fighters in republics who resisted Soviet occupation during the post-WWII period, in order to portray any nationalistic sentiments as aggressive or threatening to Russia, Russian minorities, and the accused countries themselves. To strengthen the negative image of freedom fighter groups (for example Bandera's followers in Ukraine[12] and the 'Forest Brothers'[13] in the Baltic countries), pro-Kremlin media portrayed national movements as fascist. Putin had actively revived the heroic story line of the victory of the USSR against Nazi Germany, while this discourse was exploited the portrayal of modern Russia as a fighter against rising fascism in post-Soviet and Western countries.[14] Russian media has continually tried to compromise civic movements by labelling them fascist: it can be traced back to the Orange Revolution in Ukraine in 2004[15] or the Maidan Revolution in 2014, as in both examples civic movements and their leaders were labelled fascists, Nazis,[16] or Bandera followers.[17] The 'Forest Brothers', a historical topic of huge importance in the Baltic countries, has also been a target for disinformation for years.[18] Nationalistic movements and their leaders in the Soviet republics were labelled as the followers of Bandera's men and 'Forest Brothers';[19] anti-Soviet, nearly 'criminal'[20] groups which destroyed the Soviet civilization and fraternal unity. Malign rhetoric was commonly used in the articles disseminating these messages.[21] Pro-Kremlin media content concerning the Baltic States has generally aimed to subvert the statehood and sovereignty of these countries. One especially vivid disinformation message claimed that the statehood of Latvia, Estonia, and Lithuania was questionable or unjustified since, according to the author, the restoration of independence of the Baltic States in 1991 was illegal.[22]

The fact that pro-Kremlin media has intensively covered the political and economic events in the post-Soviet countries, and especially their ties with Western organizations and democratic movements, indicates that Russia still considers the former Soviet space as its sphere of influence. While radical suggestions of restoring the Soviet Union were not detected in the analysed cases, several vivid examples expressed Russia's willingness to preserve its geopolitical domination in the post-Soviet countries.

Conclusions

The monitoring of pro-Kremlin and Kremlin-related media outlets around the major anniversary events of the USSR's dissolution (1 August 2021–16 January 2022) by DebunkEU.org, detected 552 content pieces containing manipulation of historical facts in pro-Kremlin media.

The leading distributor of manipulated content (23.9% of all detected cases) was cont.ws, a Russian internet blog that tended to publish opinions favouring the Kremlin's historical narratives and quoted various Russian experts. Articles were often presented as analytical, containing historical facts or shared memories of the alleged sequence of events. Hyperbolization, selection, and association were employed as the predominant rhetoric techniques in misleading articles.

Analysis on how pro-Kremlin and Kremlin-related media portrayed the process of the collapse of the USSR through the major events of 1991 (the referendum on the future of the Soviet Union, the August Coup, and the signing of Belovezha Accords) demonstrated repeated narratives exploited by the Russian state media. Pro-Kremlin and Kremlin-related media denied or at least attempted to omit the socio-economic and political issues that greatly influenced the process of fragmentation.

Pro-Kremlin media actively searched for enemies and traitors inside and outside the country. Such accusations targeted three main groups of actors: the Soviet elite, Western countries, and former Soviet republics (Ukraine and the Baltic States).

Mikhail Gorbachev appeared as the most discredited former Soviet officer in the cases analysed. As the most prominently denounced political leader, he was accused of causing the destruction of the Soviet Union. Boris Yeltsin, Leonid Kravchuk and Stanislav Shushkevich were also labelled as traitors due to their participation in the signing the Belovezha Accords.

HISTORICAL PRO-KREMLIN MEDIA

The US was presented as an active initiator and executor of the USSR dissolution process. The United States was mentioned in the narrative promulgating that 'the collapse of the USSR was outsiders' work.' At the same time the content drew parallels with information warfare instigated against the USSR, claiming involvement of the CIA agents within the Soviet elite and identifying specific American plans to destroy the Soviet Union from the inside. The final stage of this conspiracy was the preparation of soft power agents to start a revolution.

Post-Soviet countries, first and foremost Ukraine and the Baltic States, were targeted and presented as traitors to the USSR. Nationalistic movements and their leaders in the Soviet republics, through reference to them as the followers of Bandera's men and 'Forest Brothers', were presented as anti-Soviet, nearly 'criminal' groups, which destroyed Soviet civilization and fraternal unity. Moreover, several vivid examples expressed a Russian goal to preserve its geopolitical domination in the post-Soviet countries.

235

17

THE UKRAINIAN DIMENSION

Professor Andrew Wilson

It is often argued that the Baltic States played the same role in the dissolution of the USSR as Poland did in the Romanov Empire.[1] First imperial Russia and then the Soviet Union erred by over-expanding. As Rousseau advised the Poles in his *Considerations on the Government of Poland and on its Proposed Reformation* (1772): 'You may not prevent [your neighbours] from swallowing you up; see to it at least that they will not be able to digest you.'[2] The Baltic States in the Gorbachev era played the same role as Poland between 1772 and 1917: they were not only indigestible; they radicalised other nationalities, creating stronger separatist movements than would otherwise have been the case.[3] So did the other territories that the USSR annexed along with the Baltic States after the Molotov-Ribbentrop Pact in 1939 and 1940. West Belarus was relatively quiet; but Moldova and Western Ukraine, especially eastern Galicia, the stronghold of Ukrainian nationalism by the middle of the twentieth century, helped increase the multiplier effect.[4] In the Gorbachev era, both Ukraine and Belarus were tightly controlled politically until at least the end of 1989. But the then Baltic republics provided an inspiration and a template for increasingly radical opposition.

Ukraine was never as radically rejectionist as the Citizens' Congress movements in Estonia, which opposed all forms of collaboration with Soviet occupation, although a small equivalent movement in Ukraine made some impact in 1990–1. Ukraine adopted a different strategy of building up sovereign institutions within the USSR; even paying some lip-service to the 1990 Law on Secession from the USSR when it declared independence in August 1991. Ukraine was therefore independent but structurally post-Soviet after 1991.

But if modern Ukraine was founded in 1991, it has been refounded three times. First the Orange Revolution in 2004 and then the Revolution of Dignity in 2013–14 were conceived as catch-up revolutions; reconnecting Ukraine with the energy and radical reformism of 1989 in central Europe and 1989–91 in the Baltic States. The Revolution of Dignity was much more explicitly anti-colonial. And thirdly, war-torn Ukraine in 2022 is even more committed to building back better and 'winning the peace.' Covert Russian invasion in 2014 and then full-scale war in 2022 have strengthened the psychology of catch-up; and the idea that Ukraine can become what Putin dubs the 'anti-Russia' in a positive sense—opposing authoritarian and imperial Russia. By 2014, and even more so after 2022, Ukraine was increasingly framing itself in Baltic terms: as unequivocally European, as an Antemurale of European civilisation against Russia; and as part of a common geopolitical Intermarium stretching from the Baltic to the Black Sea.

Baltic Tutelage

Political liberalisation came late to Ukraine in the Gorbachev era. Despite the Chernobyl disaster in 1986, and in part because of the unrest that it threatened, it suited Gorbachev to leave the conservative stalwart of the Brezhnev era Volodymyr Shcherbytsky in charge until as late as September 1989. Small informal groups appeared in 1987–9 (*neformaly*—non-Communist parties were still banned); but were often based in, or ran their print operations from, the Baltic republics. In neighbouring Belarus, under similar conditions, the first congress of the Belarusian People's Front had to be held in Vilnius in June 1989. A Co-ordinating Committee of Patriotic Movements of Peoples of the USSR could also only meet in Riga and Vilnius.

It was only as Shcherbytsky's grip began to loosen in late 1989 that opposition groups began to coalesce in Ukraine. Although Article 5 of the Soviet constitution defining the Communist Party's 'leading role' (monopoly of power) was not formally abolished until March 1990. It was widely assumed that Shcherbytsky's removal for ill-health was a cover story; but he was dead by February 1990, either from pneumonia or suicide.

Popular Fronts

Hence the idea of setting up a Popular Front 'in support of perestroika'—half in and half out of the Party. An idea that also came from the Baltic Republics. Lithuania came first, with Sąjūdis holding its founding conference in October 1988, after events in the summer; with the Latvian Popular Front convening a few days before and the Estonian in November 1988. Ukrainian activists first tried to set up their own Popular Front in the summer of 1988; but the authorities were still prepared to make mass arrests and break up meetings. Again, it was only when

Shcherbytsky was on the way out that a Ukrainian Popular Front was set up in September 1989. Its name was Rukh, the same as Sąjūdis, meaning simply 'movement'. The Communist Party attempted to control Rukh 'from above', as an alternative to a more radical grassroots movement.[5] A fifth of the delegates at the founding congress were Communist Party members, more than three times the figure for the general population.[6] There were also agents of influence inside Rukh. This was also true of the Baltic republics' Popular Fronts; but the number in Ukraine was high. Though there is a debate as to whether that meant a more moderate position.[7] Rukh's first congress and programme were close to reform Communist positions. Rukh only switched to backing independence at its second congress in October 1990.

Human Chains

On 23 August 1989 Baltic activists commemorated the fiftieth anniversary of the 1939 Molotov-Ribbentrop Pact with the 'Baltic Way', a human chain of two million people stretching from Tallinn to Riga to Vilnius. This time the copying process was quicker. Rukh organised a similar human chain from L'viv to Kyiv in January 1990. Approximately 750,000 were involved.[8] This was a much smaller percentage of the Ukrainian population—less than 2% compared to over a quarter for the Baltic Way. Nevertheless, this helped mobilise support for Rukh in advance of the March 1990 republican elections. Standing as the 'Democratic Bloc' because opposition parties had only just been legalised, Rukh could only win about a quarter of the 450 seats. The Communist Party originally had 331, but defections soon reduced it to the 'Group of 239'—still a majority in the Ukrainian parliament. Rukh was never able to win decisive majority support like the Baltic Popular Fronts in elections and referenda in 1990–1.

THE UKRAINIAN DIMENSION

National Communists

Rukh was therefore forced to work more with reform Communists, although they were fewer in number than in the Baltic republics. The Communist Party of Lithuania declared itself independent from the Communist Party of the Soviet Union (CPSU) in December 1989 and refounded itself as the Democratic Labour Party. The Estonian and Latvian Communist Parties both split into independent and pro-Moscow parties in 1990. In Ukraine the party apparat remained largely loyal to Moscow; and backed the coup in August 1991. It was only in parliament that there was a growing split between 'national Communists' and 'imperial Communists' in 1990–1. This meant a growing de facto alliance between Rukh/the Democratic Bloc and the national communists as an alternative majority to the Group of 239. Popular mobilisation like the January 1990 human chain helped pressure the Communists in this direction.

Though if popular mobilisation was key in the drive to independence for the Baltic Republics, and in Georgia, Armenia and Moldova; while elite politics was key in Central Asia; Ukraine was somewhere in the middle. Elite politics and popular mobilisation coexisted and influenced each other. Large parts of public opinion were more conservative than Rukh in 1989–90; though public opinion could also be radicalised by elite example. In March 1991, 71.5% of voting Ukrainians backed Gorbachev in his referendum on 'the preservation of the Union of Soviet Socialist Republics as a renewed federation of equal sovereign republics'. But there were two other questions in Ukraine; 80.2% backed the question added by the national Communist camp: that 'Ukraine should be part of a Union of Soviet Sovereign States on the basis of the Declaration of State Sovereignty of Ukraine'. In only three oblasts of west Ukraine, 88% backed full independence. Rukh voters backed both the second and the third question, and a 'no' to Gorbachev.

Elite politics changed drastically with the August 1991 coup and its failure. The imperial Communists were forced to join the national Communists in allying with Rukh to back independence. A decisive parliamentary majority of 346 to 1 backed a formal Declaration of Independence on 24 August. The imperial Communists now backed independence because of an informal understanding with Rukh that they would keep their jobs if they did so. But parliament also decided that its decision would be subject to ratification by popular referendum on 1 December. Unfortunately, there were no reliable opinion polls to test how public opinion may have changed between March and August 1991. But by 1 December 1991, 90.3% of voters (later adjusted to 92.3%) backed full independence. It is often said that opinion could not have changed so quickly in eight months. But the political possibility set had changed radically. And all elites now backed independence, if only to save themselves.

1919 not 1940

As in the Baltic republics, the January 1990 Ukrainian human chain was also about history politics; but a different history. The Baltic Way in 1989 was designed to show the illegitimacy of Soviet occupation in 1940; and to remind the West that the USA and others had never formally recognised the loss of Estonian, Latvian and Lithuanian independence fifty years earlier (the Welles Declaration). In January 1990 Ukrainians were marking the Day of Unity, an unofficial diaspora holiday. After the 1917 Revolution, Ukrainians in Kyiv had established a Ukrainian People's Republic, which declared independence on 22 January 1918. Ukrainians living in the Habsburg Empire had to wait for a second imperial collapse, before declaring their own West Ukrainian People's Republic in November 1918. The two Ukrainian Republics then signed a nominal act of union on

22 January 1919. The government of the Ukrainian People's Republic was then forced into exile after belated Soviet victory in Ukraine (at the third attempt) in 1921. It was this 1919 Unity Day tradition that Ukrainians were reviving, not 1940.

Exile Governments and Citizens' Congress

The Baltic 'republics' saw themselves as the Baltic States. Estonia had a full government-in-exile. Latvia had a diplomatic service-in-exile. Lithuania had a diplomatic service-in-exile that became a government-in-exile. The principle of legal continuity was the basis of the reiteration of independence in 1990–1. Independence was not won or even declared; it was still a legal fact and so was reiterated.

In the Baltic 'republics', Soviet rule was therefore characterised as Soviet occupation, based on the 1932 Stimson Doctrine. In Estonia, the authority of the Estonian SSR was rejected, and elections to the Estonian Supreme Soviet in 1990 boycotted. Estonian Citizens' Committees were established instead, to register citizens of the 1940 state and their descendants, who then elected a rival Congress of Estonia in February 1990. After contesting power, the two rival parliaments formed a Constituent Assembly in equal numbers in September 1991 to draw up a new constitution.

In Ukraine, there was a similar strategy; but it was more marginal. The Interparty Assembly was an alliance of small parties to the right of Rukh set up in June–July 1990, backed by the émigré Organisation of Ukrainian Nationalists (OUN). In Ukraine there were too few survivors of 1919, compared to 1940. The much more radically anti-Communist Interparty Assembly's key idea was a signature campaign to revive the 1918 Ukrainian People's Republic as a rival to the Ukrainian Supreme Soviet, once more than half of current Ukrainian voters had signed. (Ironically the OUN and UNR had often been rivals in exile.)

The Interparty Assembly claimed 2.8 million signatures; but independent sources only verified 729,000 out of a then population of 52 million. More than half of these were from L'viv oblast alone in west Ukraine.[9] The total was only 1.4% of the population, compared to 93% of 'eligible citizens' in Estonia who had backed the Congress of Estonia.[10]

In the Baltic States and in Ukraine the exile governments symbolically handed over authority to homeland governments in 1991–2. In the Ukrainian case, this was in August 1992, on the first anniversary of the Declaration of Independence. In contrast, the exiled Belarusian People's Republic never had enough confidence in the former Communist rulers of post-1991 Belarus to make the same move. The Rada of the Belarusian Democratic Republic (BNR) is now the world's longest serving government-in-exile. In 2018 during the era of 'soft Belarusianisation' that lasted from 2014 to 2020, when Belarusian President Lukashenka wanted to broaden his power base to prevent Russia pressurising Belarus in the same way as it had undermined Ukraine, there were some experiments with some official positive commemorations.[11] But such rapprochement was killed by the brutal crackdown after the 2020 elections.

In Ukraine there was one interesting coda to the story of government-in-exile. Despite independence in 1991, the Soviet Ukrainian parliament (Rada or Council) elected in 1990 served until 1994 and was called the 'twelfth' Supreme Council since 1919—thereby accepting some continuity with Soviet rule. It was only in 2000 that the numbering was changed by law, so that the then fourteenth Rada reset the clock, to call itself the third Rada. That is, the first Rada was now deemed to have been in 1990–4.

Memory politics

A more radical change in Ukraine's history politics came after the Orange Revolution in 2004 and Revolution of Dignity in

2013–14. The Baltic States backed up their radical political opposition to Soviet occupation with radical decommunisation policies in historiography and culture in the 1990s. All three Baltic States have showpiece museums. Lithuania has the Museum of Occupations and Freedom Fights in Vilnius set up in 1992. Riga has the Museum of the Occupation of Latvia from 1993; Tallinn the Vabamu Museum of Occupations and Freedom from 2003. Lithuania banned the use of Soviet symbols in 2008; Latvia did so for public events in 2013. An Estonian ban only got as far as a parliamentary first reading in 2007.

The Lithuanian Center for the Research of Genocide and Resistance was set up in 1993. Estonia has the Estonian International Commission for Investigation of Crimes Against Humanity, established in 1998. The Estonian Institute of Historical Memory was set up in 2008. Though the Baltic States do not have all-encompassing decommunisation laws or memory laws. In this case, they have followed the Ukrainian example. Estonia began removing remaining Soviet monuments in 2022.

Ukraine established an Institute of National Memory (INM) in 2006. It passed radical decommunisation laws in 2015. In 2017 the INM was charged with drawing up a massive four-year rolling centenary programme to celebrate the achievements of the UNR in 2017 to 2021. If the Baltic States stressed their legal continuity with their inter-war selves, Ukraine now looked to the UNR, and took a much more positive, even celebratory attitude to 1917 than Putin's Russia. The idea of 'two revolutions' was endorsed, with a distinct and specifically Ukrainian Revolution separate to and different from Russia's. The slogan of 'Our Revolution'[12] stressed that the Ukrainian revolution was more about national issues than social or class concerns. Another slogan linked '100 Years of Struggle' for independence and against Russia from 1917 to 2017. Another was that 'today's Ukraine is the successor of the state-building traditions of the

Ukrainian revolution 1917–1921'.[13] Unlike the Bolsheviks' class-based and Soviet-model revolutionary rule, the UNR was a typical European democracy with a separation of powers between branches of state.

Diaspora Politics

The Baltic Republics had a small but politically powerful diaspora in the West, empowered by the Welles Declaration. The Ukrainian diaspora in North America was bigger: approximately a million in the USA, and a million and a quarter in Canada. But initially it lacked the clout of Washington's official policy of not recognising the 1940 annexations. The Baltic diaspora played a key role in pressuring the Bush administration to treat Estonia, Latvia and Lithuania as a special case, different to other Soviet Republics. As Serhii Plokhy put it, 'the administration made a clear distinction between its policy toward the Baltic republics and that toward the rest of the Soviet Union. What was good for the Baltics was considered bad for Ukraine'.[14] This meant swift recognition of the Baltic States' independence in September 1991; but still a relatively cautious line toward Ukraine. President Bush visited Kyiv on 1 August 1991; but made the notorious 'Chicken Kiev' speech, which warned against a 'suicidal nationalism based on ethnic hatred'.[15] It was only in the autumn of 1991 that policy began to change. Gorbachev had been pushed aside by Yeltsin. Opinion polls indicated that the vote for Ukrainian independence on 1 December was a fait accompli. The Ukrainian diaspora made at least some difference, as the million-odd Ukrainian Americans were concentrated in key swing states in the eastern USA like Pennsylvania and Ohio, and George Bush wanted their votes in the close-fought 1992 election that he would ultimately lose to Bill Clinton. On 27 November at a meeting with diaspora leaders, the US decision to recognise Ukrainian independence was leaked.[16]

Parade of sovereignties

The alliance between Rukh and the national communists came later than and adopted different tactics to the Baltic republics in 1989–91. The aim in Ukraine was not to boycott Soviet institutions, but to create parallel state structures within the USSR. This was the logic of the 'parade of sovereignties', beginning with the Ukrainian Declaration of State Sovereignty passed on 16 July 1990. This time Ukraine was copying from the Russian Declaration of State Sovereignty passed a month earlier on 12 June; not from Baltic rejectionism. Though the follow-up Law on the Economic Independence of Ukraine passed on 3 August 1990 was based in part on the earlier example of the Baltic republics' 'Republican self-accounting'.

A parliamentary committee on rewriting the constitution was set up in Ukraine as early as October 1990. Largely unnoticed by the outside world, Ukraine was taking radical steps to build 'sovereignty' or 'statehood'—the terms often overlapped—within the USSR; before the failed coup in August 1991; and during Gorbachev's attempts to rewrite a new Union Treaty. A March 1991 Law on Banks and Banking led to an embryonic National Bank of Ukraine. A Law on the Presidency of July 1991 created a Ukrainian President—making at least three in the USSR including Gorbachev and Boris Yeltsin as President of Russia since June 1991. Significantly, the key role of the Ukrainian presidency was then envisaged to be 'to protect the sovereignty of the Ukrainian SSR' against central institutions in Moscow. In July, before the failed coup in August, the first presidential election in Ukraine was scheduled for 1 December 1991. The coup was designed to forestall the new Union Treaty, which because it would not include six Republics—the Baltic three, Georgia, Armenia and Moldova—was too radical for communist conservatives. But significantly Ukraine was also not due to sign; but to consider its position after the summer holidays in September 1991.

Secession

Nevertheless, the Ukrainian declaration of independence in August 1991 and its subsequent ratification by referendum in December 1991 followed some of the provisions of the USSR Law on Secession passed in April 1990—if not all. The Baltic republics ignored the law, which made the right to secession long included in the Soviet constitution newly difficult. Secession required first either a Republican Supreme Soviet to call a popular referendum or a petition signed by one tenth of voters, with, second, a vote to be held 'no sooner than six and no later than nine months after the adoption of the decision to raise the question of the republic's secession from the USSR'. Third, such a vote would need a majority of two-thirds of voters. Fourth, there would then be approval by the national USSR Congress of People's Deputies, with the power to impose a transitional period 'not exceeding five years.' The Ukrainian case followed points one and three, but not two and four.

Alternative Possibilities

Ukraine did not only copy from the Baltic republics. There were other trends and possibilities that could have taken Ukraine in a less radical direction. Both were centred on the eastern city of Kharkiv, an alternative centre of gravity to Kyiv, as when it had been the first capital of Soviet Ukraine from 1919 to 1934.

The first alternative was a different Communist Party; not one split between national and imperial communists, but with a centrist sovereign agenda. In 1990 at least such a party could still plausibly have commanded a majority. Volodymyr Ivashko from

Kharkiv, who headed the Communist Party of Ukraine (CPU) from September 1989 to July 1990, was a more typical Russian-speaking Ukrainian than his successor Leonid Kravchuk, from Volyn in west Ukraine. Ivashko had strong links with Moscow networks. Unfortunately, that led him to leave for Moscow with indecent haste after the 28th Party Congress to become Gorbachev's number two in the CPSU. The CPU then lost much of its ability to portray itself as the defender of Ukrainian sovereignty. Its decline was compounded by the splitting of Ivashko's jobs. Kravchuk became chair of parliament; the more pro-Moscow Stanislav Hurenko headed an increasingly isolated party apparat.

A second alternative was the Democratic Platform within the CPSU, which in Ukraine bridged Ukrainian and Russian-speaking intelligentsia; again, with key representation from Kharkiv, not just Kyiv and west Ukraine—which was more the profile of Rukh. Ukrainian members of the Democratic Platform worked together with Democratic Russia and some Baltic radicals in the all-Soviet Inter-Regional Group; but ironically that was more difficult after the Platform left the CPSU after the party's 28th Congress in July 1990. The Ukrainian members, however, set up the Party of Democratic Revival of Ukraine (PDRU) in December 1990. The slightly cumbersome title was literal. Democratic revival had to come first in Ukraine, before national revival. The PDRU had 28 MPs in 1990; but few real allies. Nearly all of the other new parties were on the right, apart from the Greens. One PDRU leader, Vladimir Griniov, ran for president in 1991, coming fourth with 4.2%. He presciently warned against Rukh's Grand Bargain with the national communists—that the old elite would keep their jobs if they backed independence. Griniov argued that decommunisation had to come first.

Prelude to 2022?

The biggest difference between 1989–91 and later events in Ukraine in 2004, 2014 and 2022 was Russia's role. Conservative Communists in Moscow in 1989–91 also learnt from the Baltic republics. They helped set up the Intermovement to oppose the nascent Baltic Popular Fronts in July 1988, supported by a tour of hard-line Politburo members to the region in November 1988. The Ukrainian equivalent Intermovement, based in the Donbas, was set up in November 1990.[17] Though it made less of an impact than in the Baltic republics, because radicals were not in power in Kyiv. Trade unions, some increasingly independent, concentrated on their own issues. Even to Russian-speaking workers in the Donbas, the demand for economic 'sovereignty' from Moscow made sense. Nevertheless, some Ukrainophobic remnants survived to play a role in 2014.

More broadly, however, many of the same issues driving Russia's war against Ukraine in 2022 were already a problem in 1991. Many Russians reacted to the declaration of Ukrainian independence in August 1991 by threatening a revision of borders in the same places as in 2014 and 2022—Crimea and the Donbas. The most serious row erupted just after Ukraine's Declaration of Independence on 24 August 1991; when Yeltsin's Press Secretary, Pavel Voshchanov, asserted on 26 August that Russia and Ukraine had only recognised each other's borders because they were both part of the USSR. A delegation descended on Kyiv on 28–9 August. Ukraine promised not to create an army during 'transition'. Kravchuk promised to attend ongoing talks on the future of the Union at Novo-Ogaryovo.[18] But Ukraine got the better of this exchange, as no concrete moves on borders was made. The Russians also backed off because they faced bigger public demonstrations than seen in Ukraine during the coup.

But as the border issue was not directly addressed, it kept recurring through the autumn, amidst uncertainty and scheming on both sides in the run-up to the Ukrainian referendum on 1 December. In Ukraine, the last-minute coalition supporting independence in autumn 1991 had to be held together with multiple messaging and ambiguity. The case for independence was often instrumental, not existential as in the Baltic republics. Rukh's cultural, existential nationalism was part of the mix; but Kravchuk also stressed the practical economic benefits of independence, promising to maintain Soviet prices and subsidies; and there was studied ambiguity as to what 'sovereignty' and 'independence' might mean. This helped reassure Russia. Nevertheless, in October Gorbachev was presented with a covert plan drawn up by his aide Georgiy Shakhnazarov,[19] which proposed the same type of political technology subversion that Russia used to undermine Ukraine in 2014: running anti-independence agit-prop and working with separatist local leaders like Mykola Bahrov in Crimea and Soviet Ukrainian cultural figures like Borys Oliinyk in Kyiv. Though the main difference between 1991 and 2014 was that Gorbachev 'had no resources to implement even half of Shakhnazarov's proposals.'[20] Another key difference was that elite deal-making was possible in 1991 in a way that it wasn't in 2014 or 2022; both between Russia and Ukraine and within Ukraine. Kravchuk toured the Ukrainian regions—Crimea, the Donbas, Transcarpathia—to buy off local elites with promises of their continued local control. Yeltsin prevaricated whether to back more nationalist actors like his Vice President Rutskoy and the mayors of Leningrad and Moscow, Anatoliy Sobchak and Gavril Popov. Even while Yeltsin wanted to take-over power in Moscow, Democratic Russia's basic impulse was centripetal. It wanted to control natural resources and divest Russia of the responsibilities of empire, especially the subsidisation of poorer republics, especially Central Asia. Triangular relations with the Baltic republics also helped Yeltsin's camp conceptualise a path for all the republics to at least nominal independence. There were also then elements within Democratic Russia, such as Yuriy Afanasiev and Elena Bonner, who declared 'We welcome the fall of empire.'[21] Above all, Russia was about to launch its post-Soviet economic transformation project. As Vladislav Zubok puts it, 'the smartest of Russian liberals realised then that the dispute with Ukraine could bury the prospect of Russian democracy [and a market economy] under a deluge of nationalist resentment'.[22]

James Sherr has argued that Russia accepted Ukrainian independence; but has always opposed Ukrainian *samostoiatel'nost'*— Ukraine successfully standing on its own two feet.[23] To Zubok, Russian elites assumed in 1991 'that Russia had sufficient political and economic means, above all cheap gas and oil, to influence Kyiv's policies and choices, so didn't have to worry about its political independence.'[24] There was also the fact that Ukrainian independence came so suddenly. But Ukraine-Russian relations have not always been bad.[25] There were crises over Crimean separatism in 1992 and 1994, and over strike waves in the Donbas in 1993. However, there was then a relative golden age of relations after the signing of an Inter-State Treaty in 1997, with both sides recognising each other's independence and territorial integrity, and an Agreement on the Black Sea Fleet the same year.[26] Though it could be argued that this was also because more friendly relations allowed for closer relations. Ukrainian foreign policy was still officially 'multi-vector', before successive reiterations of Ukraine's European course, most importantly the changing of the constitution in 2019 to assert 'the European identity of the Ukrainian people and the irreversibility of the European and Euro-Atlantic course of Ukraine'. In the late 1990s Leonid Kuchma was still a relatively pro-Russian president of Ukraine, and Boris Yeltsin had still to be succeeded by Vladimir Putin.

Ukraine Plays Catch-Up

Ukraine was influenced by, but did not blindly copy, the Baltic republics in 1989–91. But the influence of their quicker path to Europe, to EU and NATO membership in 2004, was also strongly felt in due course. Ukraine became independent in 1991; but there was no transformative revolution. Ukraine did not make the same clean break as the Baltic States. It was therefore markedly post-Soviet. Modern Ukraine still has the semi-reformed economic and political system built by the central figure in post-independence politics, Leonid Kuchma, in office from 1994 to 2005. Kuchma ruled via patronal and informal politics; and created a Ukrainian oligarchy by privatising industry into his allies' hands. Semi-reform stabilised by the 2000s.

Hence why Ukraine had two would-be catch-up revolutions, the Orange Revolution in 2004 and the Revolution of Dignity in 2014. The Orange Revolution was framed as Ukraine's belated 1989. In retrospect, it was too late for Ukraine to gate-crash the admission of the Baltic and Central European States to the EU in 2004; but the coincidence of the events in the same year was symbolic at the time. The Orange Revolution was a relative failure because it placed too much faith in individual leaders and failed to follow the Baltic States' structurally trans-formative approach. The future Kyiv Mayor Leonid Chernovetskiy told economic adviser, Anders Åslund, 'Don't you understand? They are all victors. Why should they listen to anybody?' How right he was.[27]

The sense that Ukraine had missed the (first) boat on EU expansion fuelled the desire to try harder after the Revolution of Dignity. In 2014–16 there was a more concentrated effort to copy the Baltic States' big-bang approach to reform.[28] By then, there was also the experience of Georgia's 'late reform' efforts to deal explicitly with the post-Soviet condition of semi-reform.

Foreigners with direct experience of post-Soviet success were imported into government. Aivaras Abromavicius from Lithuania was Minister of Economy and Trade. Former Georgian Health Minister Aleksandre Kvitashvili now did the job in Ukraine. Vitaly Kasko and Davit Sakvarelidze were deputy chief prosecutors. Most famously, former Georgian President Mikheil Saakashvili tried to jump-start reforms on Odessa, on the other side of the Black Sea. However, nearly all the foreigners resigned when reform efforts began to slow in 2016. But the idea remains. Under President Zelensky, there has been more emphasis on e-government. Jaanika Merilo from Estonia was advisor to the Deputy Prime Minister and Minister of Digital Transformation of Ukraine.

The war of 2022 was also potentially radically transformative. There was a new consensus that Ukraine was fighting on behalf of, and to secure its place in, Europe; and to build a better post-war society. Commentators talked of 'war as a chance for restart'.[29] At the time of writing, military and economic outcomes were far from clear; but the transformation in social mood was clearly long-term.[30]

The Intermarium

A final catch-up phenomenon is the idea of Europe itself. Even more so than the Baltic States, Ukraine defines itself against Russia. Ukraine has to disentangle itself from a complex East Slavic past; but it is impractical and polarising to use ethnicity or language as defining markers. Ukraine therefore officially prefers civic rather than ethnic identity politics. All Russians and other minorities are citizens. Ukraine has a strong civil society; but one that is not well-integrated with the informal state. Even post-Soviet leaders like Leonid Kuchma without anything resembling an ideology therefore use the fall-back idea that the differentiating factor between Ukraine and Russia is a more 'European' political culture.[31]

Second, Ukraine increasingly embraces geopolitical imaginaries that can help it resist Russia's alternative project of 'Eurasia'. As well as a general European course, Ukraine has increasingly conceptualised its geopolitical position as part of the Baltic-Black Sea Intermarium. There are many versions of this idea.[32] Poland has the Three Seas Initiative, 'connecting twelve countries and three seas' (ABC, which in Polish is the Adriatic, Baltic and Black Seas), but mainly as a lobby within the EU to counterbalance Germany. The Bucharest 9, founded in 2015, groups the nine easternmost NATO members. Ukraine sees the Intermarium as more like the historical Polish-Lithuanian Commonwealth, the common interests of Ukraine, Poland, Lithuania and Belarus against Russia. Historically, this defensive role was best performed when Ukraine was allied with Poland and/or the Crimean Tatars and Ottoman Turks. Improving relations with Turkey is key to preventing Russian domination of the Black Sea. Polish security assistance and open door for Ukrainian refugees has rebooted relations since the nadir of the early Law and Justice (PiS) years after 2015, beset by constant history disputes. Ukraine even hopes that, through its leading role in resisting Russia, the agency of its armed forces in particular, it 'will become the new Central European tiger... a leader in the large region between the Baltic and Black Seas.'[33]

Conclusions

The example of the Baltic Republics helped set Ukraine on a path to independence in 1989–91. But Ukraine did not fully adopt the Baltic model at the time. Manoeuvring within the old Communist elite, both within Ukraine and between Ukraine and Russia, was a much more important factor in Ukraine. Ukraine's polity, economy and society therefore remained post-Soviet. Both the Orange Revolution in 2004 and the Revolution of Dignity in 2014 were attempts to catch up with the Baltic States' perceived success. But time makes a difference. Late reform has proved difficult in Ukraine. And in 2004, 2014 and 2022 Russia has chosen to be hostile to a more European Ukraine.

PART VII

FUTURE NEW CHALLENGES

18

THE BALTIC GEOPOLITICS CHALLENGES
FOR TODAY

Professor Brendan Simms and James Rogers

Thirty years ago, just after the Cold War, it seemed not only as if history had 'ended'—as Francis Fukuyama memorably suggested—but that geopolitics had also come to an end. Nowhere was this more true than in the Baltic Sea region, for hundreds of years the object of furious strategic contestation and latterly of east-west rivalry, struggles in which Britain had often played an important part. Even British strategists agreed: Robert Cooper, then advisor to Prime Minister Tony Blair, foresaw the emergence of a 'postmodern zone' in Europe, including the Baltic, where peace was more pronounced than anywhere else.[1] In his view, the collapse of the Soviet Union and globalisation would offer the possibility that 'modern' geopolitics would be overcome. Three decades on, in 2022, history turned full circle. With

Vladimir Putin's invasion of Ukraine that year, and the resulting increased tension between Russia and the west in the Baltic, it has become clear that 'modern' geopolitics was back (and that the United Kingdom was in the thick of it).

* * *

Historically, the Baltic Sea region has held considerable geostrategic significance. The exit point to the North Sea for most of Europe's great powers, including Germany and Russia, the Danish 'Sound' was the choke point through which most commercial traffic had to pass, particularly after the establishment of St Petersburg in 1703. This led Europe's great powers to compete for influence there, creating a potential threat to the security of the British Isles. For this reason, perhaps the most consistently important actor was the United Kingdom, which monitored and repeatedly intervened in the region. This was to: safeguard the supply of raw materials, including timber for the Royal Navy; pre-empt the emergence of naval rivals; safeguard the balance of power; and in the twentieth century, to protect the new-found independence of the Baltic States, as well as to contain Germany and the Soviet Union. During the Cold War, Britain was effectively the lead nation for the NATO collective defence effort in the western Baltic and Norway.

The collapse of communism, which as this volume shows was in no small part due to events in the Baltic in 1989–91, brought with it a geopolitical revolution. Soviet control over Eastern Europe ended and the USSR itself disintegrated. The result was a new map of the region as Estonia, Latvia and Lithuania became independent once again. If the eastern Baltic had largely been a Soviet lake, Russia was now reduced to two toeholds: St Petersburg and the enclave of Kaliningrad, the former Königsberg. Germany, which had greatly increased in size through unification in 1990, and now had a much longer

Baltic coastline, looked set to become a more powerful actor in the region.

In the early 1990s, the Baltic Sea region—like the rest of Europe—was characterised by a new geo-ideological configuration. There were, for now, no more fundamental clashes of belief like those which had dominated most of the twentieth century. Western democracy and the capitalist system had prevailed. Nor were there any obvious great power rivalries. Russia was no longer a threat, and many expected it to 'join' the west in quick order. The revival of German hegemonic ambitions—much discussed in 1989–90—did not materialise, at least in a geopolitical sense. There was a widespread belief, not least in London, that the Baltic had been 'solved' and did not warrant further attention. There were no immediate plans to expand either NATO or the EU eastwards (with the exception of the incorporation of the eastern part of Germany).

A steady Russian retreat from the region, comparable to that which took place after the First World War, continued over the decade. In September 1993, the last Russian troops left Poland and Lithuania. They departed Germany in June 1994 and Estonia and Latvia (with the exception of some specialists) two months later. Despite periodic attempts to reassert its old grandeur, Russia remained mired in economic restructuring and internal conflicts such as Chechnya. The falling price of oil and industrial unrest laid her economy low—in 1998 Russian economic output was comparable to that of London.[2] Some analysts, such as Dmitry Trenin, saw the new dispensation as an opportunity to put relations between east and west in the region on an entirely new footing.[3]

Below the surface, though, the Baltic was roiled by the usual problems of the post-Soviet space. Territorial disputes and minority issues, while never as virulent as in the former Yugoslavia or other parts of the former Soviet Union (such as

UNDERSTANDING THE BALTIC STATES

Transnistria) re-emerged. Poland and Lithuania tussled over the Polish minority. In Estonia and Latvia, the Russian minority provoked disputes about language, citizenship and the memory of the Second World War. All this was complicated by economic crisis and backlash against the new nationalist governments, sometimes leading to the re-election of former Soviet function-aries. As if this was not bad enough, organised crime was rife during this period and its tentacles spread into central and western Europe as well.

In fact, the promise of the fall of communism soon gave way to profound instability across large parts of the continent. Tension flared between Hungary and Romania over Transylvania. The 'velvet divorce' between Czechs and Slovaks, though peaceful, further fuelled the general sense of fragmentation. Above all, war and genocide in the former Yugoslavia threatened to suck in outside powers and to undermine the security order. This was perceived by Baltic Sea region actors, especially Poland, as a direct threat to their safety.

Against this background, the Clinton administration decided to accelerate Euro-Atlantic integration in order to contain ethnic tensions and pre-empt the revival of old territorial disputes. The US National Security advisor Tony Lake advocated a 'double enlargement' of both NATO and the European Union (EU). Britain was initially somewhat ambivalent about these plans. On the one hand London welcomed the 'widening' of the EU, partly to stabilise the new Europe economically and partly to slow the feared 'deepening' which would aggravate Eurosceptics at home. On the other hand, there was also concern that expanding NATO would antagonise Russia, and eastern Europe, especially the Baltic States; indeed, eastern Europe was seen as primarily a security consumer, not a provider.

Besides, Britain's strategic focus was elsewhere. The 1990 'Options for Change' and 1994 'Front Line First' defence reviews brought big cuts to the Cold War armed forces. The British Army of the Rhine was drastically reduced. The main deployments during the 1990s were to the Gulf and the Western Balkans. After 2001, the 'Global War on Terror', with its longest deployments to Afghanistan and Iraq, became an all-consuming preoccupation. Little thought was given to the Baltic Sea region, which was generally regarded as stable.

Meanwhile, NATO and EU enlargement went ahead with profound consequences for the Baltic. Finland and Sweden joined the EU in 1995. In 1999, Poland was admitted to NATO; that same year, the Baltic States were given a 'Membership Action Plan'. Three years after that they were invited to join the alliance at the Prague Summit, and in 2004 they finally became members. The southern and eastern Baltic now enjoyed the prized 'Article Five' collective security guarantee. That same year Poland and the three Baltic States were admitted to the EU. The Baltic Sea Region was now—with the exception of St Petersburg and Kaliningrad—a European lake.

After the Conservative election defeat in 1997, the new Labour government of Tony Blair became an advocate of European integration. In his November 2001 speech, the Prime Minister stressed that he not only saw Britain as part of 'Europe', but also as its potential leader, albeit on the basis of a confederation of nation states rather than a multi-national 'superstate' union. Britain was a strong supporter of enlargement. Euroscepticism was relegated to William Hague's weak and peripheral Conservative Party.

It was relatively little remarked upon at the time, but the West's honeymoon with Russia was ending. There had been tension over Bosnia and direct confrontation was narrowly averted over Kosovo in 1999.[4] After brief hopes of a rapprochement over the War on Terror, the invasion of Iraq brought matters to a new low. Russia acquiesced to the enlargement of NATO into the former Warsaw Pact and even into the three Baltic States only with great reluctance. It barked, but it did not bite. It was clear, though, that a line against further NATO enlargement was being drawn after 2004. At that point, EU enlargement seemed much less problematic from Moscow's point of view.[5]

* * *

By the end of the first decade of the twenty-first century, most of democratic Europe had been embraced by the enlargement of the EU and NATO. There were now plans to extend this mutually reinforcing stabilising system into Georgia and Ukraine (in the case of NATO) and into Ukraine (in the case of the EU). These had enthusiastic support from Washington and London, but there were reservations in Berlin and Paris, at least as far as NATO was concerned. For now, though, the two Western ordering systems in the Baltic Sea Region—EU and NATO—were largely aligned.

Nonetheless, strong destabilising forces were already observable. Enlargement led to a larger-than-anticipated surge in migration from Poland and the Baltic States into western Europe. It became problematic in Britain which failed to apply the available 'emergency brake', on the assumption that most would go to Germany. This changed the way 'Europe' was perceived in the UK and led to a revival of British Euro-scepticism. It was reflected in the rise of UKIP and the emergence of a new slate of Euro-sceptic Conservative MPs at the 2010 General Election.

On the other side of Europe, the Russian challenge was becoming clearer. The Putin regime and its propagandists made more and more strident (though misleading) claims that promises not to expand NATO eastwards had been broken.[6] There was now a much more active Russian effort to keep Ukraine in Russia's orbit, even though Putin's attempts to prevent a reformer from taking power in Kyiv in 2005 failed. In February 2007, these tensions surfaced in a blistering attack on the Euro-Atlantic democracies by Putin at the legendary Munich Security Conference.[7]

Deeds soon followed words. Between April and May 2007, there was a well-publicised series of cyber-attacks on Estonia, which were almost certainly launched from Russia. A year later, Russia fomented a crisis in Georgia by handing out Russian passports to Georgian citizens of Russian ethnicity in South Ossetia and Abkhazia. The Georgian government fell into the trap and initiated a military response. The Kremlin seized on this opportunity, launching an invasion of the country which got perilously close to Tbilisi, before recognising the independence of North Ossetia and Abkhazia.

Initially, the European response to Russian aggression was tepid. The EU set up a Nordic battlegroup which went operational in 2008. It was a small force and included the Republic of Ireland (not a NATO member) but not Denmark (because it was not part of Common Security and Defence Policy (CSDP)). The emblem of the battlegroup was a visibly-endowed lion rampant, but because this was criticised as overly 'macho', it was later changed to an emasculated lion. The incident seemed to epitomise the EU's image of itself as a 'post-modern' actor at the very moment when a 'modern' predator was once again on the loose in the neighbourhood.

NATO was little better. Its 2010 *Strategic Concept* still saw Russia as a 'partner', even if the language was somewhat guarded.[8] There was hardly any sense that serious deterrence would be required to keep Putin in check. Most European states were not only unwilling but unable to do this, having run down their military capacities after the end of the Cold War. The biggest offender here was Germany whose proportion of defence expenditure to GDP slipped well below the levels agreed, albeit informally, at the Riga Summit in 2006, but she was by no means alone.[9]

Britain, too, was slow to appreciate the extent to which Russia had gone rogue. Its main focus was still firmly on other areas of the world. The British did little in response to the murder of the Russian dissident Alexander Litvinenko by Russian intelligence operatives in November 2006 and they took active measures in the 2010 Strategic Defence and Security Review (SDSR) to cut back the conventional firepower of the British Armed Force.[10] Instead, the 2010 SDSR was primarily focused 'complex emergencies', in the form of intervention and counter-terrorism. Little consideration was given to geopolitical peer competition. It was decided to draw down UK forces in Germany entirely by 2020.[11] In 2016, the British Kiel Yacht Club closed along with the Sailing Training Centre, Kiel. They took their captured yachts ('prizes of war') with them.

Slowly, though, Britain at least was beginning to think more systematically about the Baltic region. In 2011, Prime Minister David Cameron founded the 'Nordic-Baltic Summit' which held its first meeting in London. It was later renamed the Northern Future Forum. Cameron's interest was not so much strategic, rather focusing on finding common ground on technology and de-carbonisation, but Moscow was still wary of the initiative as an antechamber to NATO membership for Finland and Sweden. That same year, Defence Secretary Liam Fox set up the Northern Group consisting of the Nordic and Baltic states, Germany, the Netherlands and the UK. It reflected his belief that Britain was not thinking enough about geopolitics in general and the Baltic Sea region in particular.

It was at this time that Russian activity in the area was stepping up. The first line of Nord Stream I went operational in 2011. This had two important consequences. First, it bypassed Poland and Ukraine and enabled Moscow to decouple the supply of energy from the deteriorating relationship with both countries. Secondly, it deepened Germany's dependence on Russian gas at a time when she was exiting other forms of energy, such as nuclear and coal. There were some who warned about the geopolitical consequences this created for Germany and its implications for the containment of Russia, but they were ignored.

Then, in 2014, the Russian threat could no longer be ignored. Putin invaded Ukraine and annexed Crimea, which was part of Ukraine, and then instigated a separatist revolt in the eastern part of the country. The consequences were immediately felt in the Baltic Sea region, especially Finland, Sweden, Poland and the three Baltic States, the countries most exposed to a Russian surprise attack. They were menaced by large Russian land forces, by missiles in Kaliningrad, and by growing 'anti-access' and 'area-denial' capabilities which made the Baltic area unsafe for western aircraft and warships.

The western reaction to the first Russian attack on Ukraine was substantial (though it appears insufficient in retrospect). At the annual NATO summit—convened in Wales—during autumn 2014, the allies agreed to take stiffer measures in response: first, they agreed to boost defence spending close to 2% of GDP by 2024; secondly, they agreed to establish a Very High Readiness Joint Task Force to deter Russian aggression. Under much pressure from the Baltic countries, two years later, in 2016, during the Warsaw Summit, NATO agreed to establish an 'Enhanced Forward Presence' in the region. This would involve the forward deployment of small pockets of conventional forces from 'framework nations' to establish 'tripwires' to deter Russia by denying it speedy access to Baltic nations' territory.[12]

Britain's role in all this was considerable. Already riled by deteriorating relations with Russia—the Kremlin denounced the country as a 'small island no-one pays attention to' in 2013[13]—the UK agreed not only to act as the framework nation for Estonia, but also to post troops to Poland. It was the only ally to deploy forces to more than one country and offered more troops than any other NATO ally, including the US. On the sidelines of the NATO Summit in Wales in 2014, Sir Michael Fallon, the

British Defence Secretary, also announced the formation of a 'Joint Expeditionary Force' (JEF) which would include Denmark, Estonia, Latvia, Lithuania, the Netherlands, Norway, and the UK. Providing military 'bite' to the Cameron government's broader 'Northern' initiatives, the JEF became fully operational in June 2018 and later grew to include, alongside the original members, Finland, Sweden and Iceland.

The Russian challenge was aggravated by the increasing geo-economic importance of the Baltic. It was now Germany's principal source of gas and critical to her industry and domestic heating. This dependency only increased when Angela Merkel, Germany's Chancellor, decided to push ahead with a second pipeline, Nord Stream II, between Russia and Germany in 2018. The volume of seaborne trade in the Baltic also more than doubled between 1995 and 2014.[14] The Northern Sea Route from the Far East to Europe looked increasingly viable; with the future widening and deepening of the White Sea Canal, the Baltic Sea's economic and political significance would be further compounded.[15]

Already, two geopolitical perspectives were starting to materialise in response to Russian aggression: on the one hand were the 'Atlanticists' led by the UK and Poland; on the other were the 'continentals' in the form of Germany and France. The former looked to boost NATO and keep North America and Europe united and implement stiffer deterrence measures to constrain Russian action. The latter sought to placate, if not appease, Russia, by encouraging dialogue and building up the EU as a geopolitical actor, albeit one deeply connected to Russian energy. The Baltic region was trapped: it depended on British and American security guarantees, but it was becoming more and more economically entwined with the EU, especially after the Baltic States adopted the Euro (between 2011 and 2015).

* * *

The region, and the western alliance in general, was then subjected to two further shocks. In June 2016, the people of the UK voted by a small margin to leave the EU. From now on the two 'ordering systems' in Europe—NATO and the EU—were no longer so seamlessly aligned.[16] London, Brussels and the individual member states were unclear about what this meant. What was indisputable was that French and German defence aspirations for the EU had received a serious blow insofar as British military capabilities would no longer be available to the bloc.[17] There was a distinct fear—hardly recognised either by Brussels or analysts—that EU reprisals against Britain (which would involve Finland, Sweden, Poland and the three Baltic States) would be hard to reconcile with the fact that Britain was of all European states the one most committed to their defence. A 2016 report by Estonia's International Centre for Defence and Security found that Baltic officials 'did not wish to see the UK treated too harshly in the Brexit negotiations'; indeed, they even 'hoped that arrangements could be found that would allow it [the UK] to participate as fully as possible in the CSDP after its departure.'[18]

Moreover, Britain spent the next three years absorbed by the Brexit process and its potential threat to the Integrity of the UK. The withdrawal negotiations spanned 2017–19 and were punctuated by furious rows over the Northern ireland 'backstop', Scottish National Party (SNP) demands for a second referendum on independence from the UK, and even SNP foreign policy ambitions. The Scottish administration set out its stall to the Nordic and Baltic region in its *Nordic-Baltic Policy Statement* of September 2017.[19]

The shock of Brexit was followed shortly after by that of the victory of Donald Trump. Before and during the US Presidential Election campaign of 2016 he had repeatedly questioned the value of America's foreign alliances, in particular NATO. His victory caused consternation in Europe, and Trump's initial remarks as president seemed to put NATO's 'Article Five' commitment in doubt. The anxiety began to ease as it became clear that his rhetoric was partly designed to force Europeans to pay more for their own defence—a longstanding US concern—and the Trump administration's defence leadership (headed by robust figures like Jim Mattis and H. R. McMaster) actually increased the US presence in Eastern Europe. Still, so long as the erratic Trump was at the helm, there was a question-mark over Washington's commitment.

Due to growing British concerns over Russia's intentions, particularly after Russian agents attempted to poison Sergei Skripal in Salisbury in March 2018, the UK stepped up its Baltic focus. It decided to abandon its 2010 decision to completely withdraw from Germany, instead retaining a presence to be able to support NATO allies further east.[20] Then, in 2019, the UK flaunted the maritime strength of the JEF with the first Baltic Protector exercise, which featured naval manoeuvres, beach landings and other complex operations. As the Minister for the Armed Forces, Mark Lancaster, remarked: 'From Denmark to Lithuania, from Sweden to Estonia, Baltic Protector will leave potential adversaries in no doubt of our collective resolve and ability to defend ourselves.'[21] The fact that all this was taking place a hundred years after the Royal Navy had played a vital role in securing the independence of Estonia and Latvia was much remarked upon.[22]

Indeed, London's role was widely recognised and prized in the Baltic region. For example, in a report for the Atlantic Council the Swedish defence expert Anna Wieslander wrote that the UK is 'a security and defence actor of major importance and prominence' and that 'countries in the North are dependent on UK presence and protection in their neighbourhood'.[23] She justified this assessment with reference to Britain's permanent seat on the United Nations Security Council, nuclear capability, and her naval and military 'lift' capability (by some margin the largest in

Europe). During autumn 2021 this was confirmed: when Belarus, with the Kremlin's backing, attempted to destabilise Poland by importing foreign migrants and pushing them to cross the Belarus-Polish border, Warsaw turned to London for assistance. In response the UK firstly sent a reconnaissance unit to help in November, followed by 140 military engineers in December.[24] During the same season, Boris Johnson, the then Prime Minister, and Liz Truss, the then British Foreign Secretary, began to openly condemn the Nord Stream II gas pipeline in an attempt to compel Germany not to open it.[25]

* * *

Geopolitics in the Baltic was already undergoing 'de-postmodernisation'. Russia's renewed assault on Ukraine in February 2022 would ensure that it became thoroughly 'modern' again. With Russian troops now operating out of Belarus, the region was not only more exposed than ever, but fears grew that the Kremlin might open a second front in an attempt to further destabilise the alliance.

Of all countries, it was neither France nor Germany but the UK which stepped up. It actively released intelligence to disrupt the Kremlin's plans and it was the first in Europe to ferry large quantities of anti-tank weapons to Kyiv. Indeed, by September 2022, Britain had provided more military support to Ukraine than any other country other than the US,[26] to the extent that the Ukrainians came to see the British, alongside the Poles, as their most significant European partner.[27] While Emmanuel Macron of France and Germany's Olaf Scholz attempted to reach out to Moscow or prevaricated, Britain's Boris Johnson paid successive visits to Kyiv during the spring and summer of 2022 to show decisive political support for the Ukrainian cause.

The UK also moved to firm up NATO defences in the Baltic region. It pushed for the reinforcement of the Enhanced Forward

Presence; the British deployments to Poland and Estonia were quickly, though temporarily, doubled.[28] When Finland and Sweden, long of the view that membership of the EU would be sufficient for their defence needs, applied for NATO membership, it was Britain which issued security assurances for the interim period until both nations joined the alliance.[29] Significantly, they did not seek similar guarantees from any other European country.

As 'modern' geopolitics has returned to Europe, and the Baltic in particular, the UK has been drawn back into the region. During the Cold War, until the late 1980s, the UK was the linchpin in the defence of the northern flank of NATO. Today, for all the talk of 'Global Britain' and the Indo-Pacific 'tilt'—which are not opposed to the centrality of the Euro-Atlantic to British interests—the UK remains critical to the security of the Baltic region. Due to its awesome power, the US may be more favoured as a Baltic ally, but Britain once again leads among European countries.

19

THE GEOPOLITICAL SIGNIFICANCE OF
KALININGRAD AND THE SUWAŁKI GAP

Professor Raimundas Lopata

The origin and originality of the problem often referred to as the Kaliningrad puzzle are geopolitical. What follows is a concise description of the region's peculiarities and its problems.

The part of East Prussia taken by the Soviet Union after the Second World War was transformed into a gigantic Soviet military base. It performed the functions of an outpost against the West on the one hand; and on the other hand, a barrier which helped the USSR to ensure the dependence of the Eastern Baltics and domination in Poland. After the Cold War, Kaliningrad Oblast, a territory of 15,000 square kilometres with a population of nearly one million people, owned by the Russian Federation as its most westerly territory, became isolated from the motherland and turned into an exclave. Gradually the exclave found itself first at the crossroads of different security structures and, later, surrounded by one of them. These changes to the situation gave rise to the so-called Kaliningrad discourse. This focused upon political decisions, academic discussions and research, which are influenced by the internal transformation in the USSR and the Russian Federation (RF). It has also been devoted to the role of this Russian-owned exclave in East-West relations as well as its place in Russian interior and foreign politics.

Strategic Capacity of Russia's Government and the Need to Rule Over the Exclave

This factor, of strategic capacity, is employed to describe the value of Kaliningrad Oblast as a security object to the Russian Federation. After the Cold War the value of the exclave territory was determined by a combination of several symbolic and strategic aspects.

The symbolic factors were formally reflected in Russian political rhetoric regarding Kaliningrad/Konigsberg as a World War II trophy that had justly come to belong to Russia. However, such rhetoric is rooted in the complications of the status of Kaliningrad Oblast from the standpoint of international law and, as a direct consequence, the impact of the Potsdam Conference.

The strategic reasons were revealed in Moscow's efforts to utilize the geopolitical significance of the region, i.e., the desire to either retain the exclave as a military outpost against the West, or to turn it into the window which would enable Russia's structural integration with the West, or to prepare grounds for it to become Russia's geopolitical platform ('a passing pawn') in the European Union.

It is noteworthy that any practical implementation of the geopolitical significance of the Oblast was inseparable, not only from Moscow attempts at legitimizing the World War II gain, but also from attempts at effective governing, i.e., enhancing an institutional base that would warrant political, legal, and economic stability of the exclave.[1]

Legitimization of Judicial Dependence on Russia

Following the collapse of the Soviet Union, the exclave position of Kaliningrad Oblast brought about specific political, economic, and psychological tensions. The situation was particularly complicated by the fact that geopolitical changes provoked the debate not only over the unique nature of the state fragment, but also over the status of international recognition thereof to Russia.

In the latter case it was claimed that the ties between Kaliningrad Oblast and Russia historically shared a very limited context. The former East Prussia and Konigsberg were annexed to the Soviet Union after World War II as a tool ensuring the dependence of the Eastern Baltics on the Soviet Union. Otherwise, Moscow had no historical rights to the territory. In other words, the issue of Kaliningrad Oblast was inseparable from the issue of the political future of the Oblast, given the fact that the judicial dependence of the Oblast on the Russian Federation was non-final and fixed term (there was no sovereignty, since at the Potsdam Conference part of East Prussia was annexed to the USSR for temporary administration until peace had been established).

After the 'Iron Curtain' fell down, these explanations were reflected in miscellaneous internationalization (divisions, condominiums, exterritoriality, decolonization, autonomation, independence, etc.) plans emerging in the West and neighbouring countries.

On the other hand, the debates were accompanied by Moscow's conscious attempts at initiating and agitating such discussions. European states were provoked to restrain officially from internationalization plans. Neighbouring (intermediate) states, primarily Lithuania, signed contracts and agreements to provide guarantees relating to conditions to secure the sustenance (*zhizneobespechenie*) of Kaliningrad Oblast, at the same time documenting 'the special interest' in the development of the exclave. In this way the motherland sought to enhance the political argument concerning the organic link of the Oblast with continental Russia, and to substitute the problem of the political future of the Oblast for 'technical' issues dealing with the economic and social development of the region.

It should be pointed out that Moscow viewed the issue of the future of Kaliningrad Oblast, not only in terms of the influence of the Potsdam Conference in relations with the West. It also framed it in terms of the dependence of the Kuril Islands, which Russia claimed in 1945, in relations with Japan, as well as the influence of this issue on Russia's strategy in the Far East in general. In other words, Russia realized that, as was the case with the Kurils, absolute territorial legitimacy was unattainable. Moscow hoped to resolve this problem by creating a favourable balance. In the East, it tried to offset claims related to the legitimacy of its eastern borders, harboured by Japan (supported by the USA) and by the Chinese. In the West, Kaliningrad Oblast remained highly dependent on western European states. By managing the situation in this way, the Kremlin sought not only to maintain the status quo at its western and the eastern flanks, but also to keep the way open to gains in politics, diplomacy, and its sphere of influence, as well as gains of a territorial nature.[2]

Efficiency of Governing

From the standpoint of international law, attempts to neutralize the controversy of the Oblast's status by means of maintaining a power balance have had a direct influence on the way Moscow has approached the practical side of running the exclave.

The Kremlin sought to create the image of Kaliningrad Oblast as an independent subject of the Russian Federation. Although practical implementations of such image varied (for instance, governor Yuri Matochkin and the 'Yantar' Free Economic Zone (FEZ) in 1991–5, governor Leonid Gorbenko and the 'Yantar' Special Economic Zone (SEZ) in 1996–2000, governor ex-Admiral Vladimir Yegorov, and 'the pilot region' in 2000–5, the present, 'appointed' governor Georgi Boos and 'mini-state' plans), these forms unveiled Moscow's strategy: imitating the potential independence of the Oblast to convince the local political elite that the federal centre has a plan to develop the Oblast, and oversees the levers for its implementation, both internally and externally.

Seeking to maintain the Oblast and, in due course, to use it as a tool to influence Euro-integration processes, the Kremlin opted to utilize only the methods which would ensure the implementation a particular central strategy, regardless of whether they corresponded to or contradicted the vital interests of the Oblast. On the other hand, to ensure the legitimacy of its actions, the motherland was forced to consider the practical side. The absence of efforts intended to stimulate the Oblast's development, taking note of its particular situation, could result in fermenting anti-federal moods. This is why state documents have always emphasized the objective to ensure the development of the Oblast as an inalienable part of the Russian Federation, while the federal centre regularly did its best to resolve Kaliningrad's problems with local politicians. This was done to emphasize that the constant attention given to the province was coincidental to Moscow's attempts to resolve strategic issues. This circumstance is illustrated by both the peripeteia concerning the fate of the specific economic regime in the Oblast and by issues of Russian transit, as well as the role of the military elite of the Oblast.[3]

Military Function of the Exclave

From a formal standpoint, this function aims to enhance the guarantee of the Kaliningrad Oblast's dependence on the Russian Federation in terms of both internal and external aspects.

Speaking of the internal aspect, the militarization of the Oblast assists Moscow in overseeing the behaviour of the region's political elite. For example, in 1994–5, the restriction and abolition of the FEZ regime in the Oblast was accompanied by the establishment of a special defence region under the supervision of Russia's Baltic Fleet, directly answerable to the Ministry of Defence and the General Headquarters. During the governor's elections in 2000, the Kremlin almost openly supported Russia's Baltic Fleet Commander, Admiral Vladimir Yegorov who was popular in the circles of the local political elite and personally loyal to Vladimir Putin (he has been the only admiral-governor in the history of the Russian Federation). In late 2005, chiefs of Russia's Baltic Fleet, headed by Admiral Vladimir Valuyev, unambiguously warned the new governor Boos of the fact that the military elite of the Oblast disapproves of efforts to enhance economic and cultural cooperation between the Oblast and foreign countries, on the grounds that they would facilitate non-violent secession of Kaliningrad Oblast from the Russian Federation.

Meanwhile, speaking of the external aspect, the military potential of the Oblast is a tool used by the Kremlin in dialogue with western Europe (and the USA) concerning maintaining the balance of forces. The suppressing function of the Russian military stretches beyond the borders of the Oblast and embraces at least the eastern Baltic region. For example, in 1993–5 as well as spring 2001, Moscow sought to exploit the issue of Russian military transit to and from Kaliningrad via Lithuanian territory in order not only to hinder the process of Lithuania's integration into NATO, but also, through political agreements necessary to legitimize this transit, to retain Lithuania within its zone of influence. On a broader scale, Russia aspired to control the process of expansion of Western structures into the East, coincidentally exerting influence on the geopolitical situation of Central and Eastern Europe. It should be pointed out that during this time, France and Germany in particular, adopted a position of non-interference and even expressed favourable attitudes towards Russia with respect to these tendencies.[4]

Role of Other Countries and International Institutions in the Kaliningrad Issue

After the end of the Cold War, a number of Western countries turned their attention to the Kaliningrad issue. It must be noted that none of them reminded Russia of the complicated legal and political aspects of Kaliningrad Oblast and chose not to raise the issue of escalating separatist tendencies regarding the Oblast. This Western standpoint can be understood as an attempt, in the course of time, to connect Russia structurally with the West as opposed to alienating it. The position gave Moscow the opportunity to freely balance the western flank, allowing it to replace concerns of the exclave's political and legal problems, with less severe 'technical' issues regarding the socio-economic development of the Oblast. This approach would ensure that the Western states as well as the EU would view Kaliningrad Oblast in terms of Moscow. Finally the 'humble' behaviour of the West enabled Russia, which at the time was drawing a direct geopolitical line between Moscow and Kaliningrad, to use it as a tool to hinder the development and integration of Western structures (for instance, by demanding specific declarations regarding the Oblast as part of the Russian Federation), in other words, turning the exclave into a geopolitical hostage in relations between the East and the West.

Neighbouring (intermediate) countries, Lithuania and Poland, tried to question this formula of Kaliningrad geopolitics, as they were significantly engaged in the issue of the Oblast, particularly as they made their own practical decisions on how to gravitate westward. They repeatedly tried to draw the West's attention to Russian foreign policy, which aimed to revise the ratio of powers under the influence of Euro-Atlantic integration. Lithuania and Poland complained that this was being done at the expense of the interests of intermediary states, such as themselves, and that the Kaliningrad issue might be exploited in this respect.

As a result, in 1993–5, Lithuania was supported by the USA and Great Britain in withstanding Russia's pressure to legitimize military transit through Lithuanian territory. In 2001, the official paradigm 'to turn the issue of Kaliningrad Oblast into a priority', formulated in Vilnius in 1998, was approved by the European Commission and several northern European states. It must be noted that Moscow initially had no objections to this paradigm, as it viewed Lithuania's membership of the EU as a distant priority and was more concerned with driving a wedge between the USA and Europe as well as fostering mutual relations with the large EU states.

However, having realized the mistake it had made in its assessment of the scope, rate and success of Euro-Atlantic integration, whilst lacking the means to stop this process, Moscow attempted to openly balance the conflict. Russia argued that, in terms of Kaliningrad, that EU expansion was an external issue, Brussels was responsible for communication with continental Russia about the changes made to Kaliningrad's situation that it was causing. Russia therefore sought to modify the structure of the dialogue on the development of Kaliningrad Oblast by eliminating 'intermediaries' and negotiating on issues relating to the exclave directly with the large EU states and Brussels.

Seeking to neutralize the influence of the Russian influence on their national interest of Euro-Atlantic integration, Poland and

Lithuania tended to reduce their engagement in this dialogue. Announcing themselves as 'non-transit' states, they enabled Russia to focus on one target—the territory of the Lithuanian Republic.

Alongside other Russian interests in Lithuanian territory, Moscow demanded an exterritorial corridor, preventing Vilnius from becoming an obstacle to the development of the exclave. Russia simultaneously used its relations with the large EU states and, seeking to receive privileges and compensations to all citizens of the Russian Federation, exerted pressure on and even overtly blackmailed the European Commission. After the expansion of the EU, Russia demanded that a special negotiating format be designed for Kaliningrad-related issues.

The diplomatic relations between the EU and Russia revealed that, formally, the former accepted the rules proposed by the latter. Brussels refused to assume political responsibility for the development of the Oblast and agreed to focus only on those problems which came as a direct consequence of EU expansion. The EU did not object to opening European funds for the economic growth of the exclave in accordance with Russia's terms (the new SEZ law, redistribution of European financial aid to Kaliningrad Oblast in Moscow, and the allocation of that aid to economic subjects in the exclave as defined by Moscow).

Nevertheless, the essentially new perspective on Kaliningrad Oblast, which did not allow the exclave to be distanced from the motherland and projected onto it the role of Russian geopolitical maneuvering against Euro-integration, was made possible thanks to Moscow's direct strategic contact with the West, specifically, with the most important counteragent, Berlin. Specific manifestations of this contact may be observed both in the North European Gas Pipeline project through the Baltic Sea, as well as in the instituting of new air transport routes with flights to Moscow and Saint Petersburg, supplemented in 2006 with direct flights between Kaliningrad and Berlin (several more routes connecting the exclave to Hamburg and Frankfurt are to appear in the near future).

Alternatively, such EU steps may be regarded as attempts to involve Russia in strategic partnership (without rejecting the eventual structural transformation of the latter) by making use of Kaliningrad Oblast.[5]

Securing the Link Between the Exclave and the Motherland (Issues of Military, Passenger, and Cargo Transit)

Russia has employed other means in its bid to avoid isolation of the exclave from continental Russia, with the aim of guaranteeing the dependence of the Oblast and increasing influence on the EU integration processes. Manipulating the idea of the exclave as 'the pilot region', Russia began to strengthen the mechanisms of control over the Oblast from the centre. It initiated a new law on SEZ, which welcomed large capital from the motherland and injected investments from abroad, and, at the same time, changed the political leadership of the Oblast. Boos, the newly appointed governor, undertook radical reconstruction in the administration of the exclave, developed specific projects of socio-economic transformation and received the Kremlin's approval for unconventional plans for modernization. Recently, threatening forecasts have argued that, upon the implementation of these initiatives, the concentration of significant Russian capital in the exclave will enable Moscow to interfere further in the economic life of neighbouring countries. Initiatives to mechanically increase the population in Kaliningrad may influence identity construction in Kaliningrad whilst also making the territory more populous than Estonia and Latvia. Meanwhile, transit through Lithuanian territory would intensify.

Bearing in mind that, after the end of the Cold War, many forecasts regarding Kaliningrad Oblast remained unfulfilled and

Russia's numerous modernization plans were not implemented for various reasons, it may be expected that, in order to increase the region's dependence, Moscow will choose to rely on traditional measures. This approach involves strengthening the link to Kaliningrad by using Lithuanian territory for military, passenger, and cargo transit.

The issue of Russian military transit to and from Kaliningrad Oblast through Lithuanian territory has been the most sensitive one, raising noticeable pressure between Moscow and Vilnius. The essence of the problem is that Russia sought specific conditions for its military transit through Lithuania and tried to legitimize this transit by providing it with the settlement status. Meanwhile Lithuania regarded these endeavours of Russia's foreign policy as a threat to its sovereignty and integration into NATO. As a result, at the beginning of 1995, a compromise on the issue was reached, which, while retaining Moscow's ability to use the transit territory, preserved Lithuania's sovereignty. The established procedure for Russian military transit did not, in the end, hinder Lithuania's integration into North-Atlantic structures.

As Lithuania was integrating into the EU, a question arose regarding the transit of citizens of the Russian Federation to and from Kaliningrad Oblast. It was resolved by a compromise which involved the participation of the EU as well as Lithuania and Russia.

Despite Russia's efforts to institutionalize the issue of cargo transit to and from Kaliningrad Oblast in a specific way, decisions regarding Russian transit of this kind revolve around technical matters.

It is noteworthy that Moscow puts a lot of effort into linking all three types of transit. It thus seeks to apply specific passenger transit conventions to cargo transit and eventually to military transit to and from Kaliningrad Oblast through the Lithuanian territory.

To summarize, it should be noted that Moscow has been consistently stoking tensions through its two strategies in the Kaliningrad region ('*zagranichnaya* Russia') since the Cold War. First is the strategy of maintaining Kaliningrad as a military outpost, which regards the region as of special strategic significance and characterizing it as a bridgehead where Western influence can be slowed or stopped. The second strategy is to make the Oblast a testing ground for economic reforms that could provide a geopolitical link connecting Russia with the West, due to its favorable geographical position.

In certain periods there have been quite reasonable hopes that Moscow's vision of the Kaliningrad region as a testing ground for economic reforms could gradually prevail. It was even called a 'pilot project' in diplomatic documents agreed by the West and Russia. Moscow itself did not tire of giving hope to the region that it would gain a new political and economic status, in compensation for its former enslavement to the Soviet Union. Obviously, today it is clear that, at the time, Moscow actually did not have a strategic plan on how to ensure stable socio-economic development of the area and did not realize immediately the scale and speed of international processes, primarily Euro-Atlantic integration. As the West did not have a strategic vision for Kaliningrad region either, the freedom to maneuver opened up for Moscow to balance the power on the so-called western flank. This allowed the political problems of the exclave to be replaced by 'technical' economic-social problems in regional development issues and ensured that the attitude of Western countries towards the EU have to take account of Russia. In this way, the Kremlin perceived that there were some advantages that could be taken from the Euro-Atlantic integration process.

About fifteen years ago in Moscow it was decided that the fact that the region lagged behind its neighbours economically, primarily Poland and Lithuania, could be disastrous. Therefore, an attempt was made to search for new instruments and new operating spaces. Federal funds to 'stabilize' the economic gap with Kaliningrad's neighbours were implemented under the slogan of Kaliningrad being Russia's window to Europe. In other words, the area was not to become a territory, which the Europeans could exploit as an easy way to penetrate into Russia markets, but rather it was announced that Russian business would attempt to integrate into European markets in order to modernize the management of the area. This even involved a break in the tradition of only remembering the history of Kaliningrad since 1945, acknowledging instead historical continuity whilst also sweetly receiving EU financial support, which of course, was redistributed in Moscow.

Thus, in diplomatic practice, the Kaliningrad region turned into a hostage, used in strategic exchanges between Russia and the West, based on deterrence (withholding)—a tactic of reassurance and relatability for the West. In the initial process of cession, Kaliningrad became incorporated into Russia as war booty. The territory has since been used to maintain its own hostage situation and to force other countries, as well as international authorities, to refrain from releasing it either directly or indirectly. At the same time, the exclave will depend on whether Russia's regional policy can transform it for use by the centre as a bridgehead to increase its influence in the EU without actually opening the Kaliningrad region up to EU influence.

It should be emphasised that Moscow linked the question of the future of the Kaliningrad Region not only to overcoming the legacy of the Potsdam Conference in Moscow's relations with the West, but also to the situation of the Kuril dependencies in Moscow's relations with Japan and, more broadly, with the impact of this dispute on Russia's strategy on the Far East in general. In other words, Russia has realised that absolute territorial legitimacy is unattainable, both in the Kuril Islands and, perhaps to a lesser extent, in the Kaliningrad Region. Moscow hopes to solve this problem by gaining political leverage in two ways: by playing the Chinese card to counterbalance the legitimacy of its eastern borders being questioned by Japan and the US, on the one hand; and by playing the eastern European card to leverage the dependency of the Kaliningrad Region. In fact, the Kremlin hopes that, by balancing the two, it will not only maintain the *status quo* on the western and eastern flanks, but also keep the way open for Russia's eventual political, diplomatic and territorial gains in its spheres of influence.

After the expansion of the West, the academic focus of Russia balancing in central and eastern Europe, using the Kaliningrad factor, has been suppressed. But after the Russian military's shift in the balance of power in the Baltic Sea region, which began with the intervention in Ukraine—there has been an enforced reevaluation of Kaliningrad's political, economic and military status, as well as its place in the new security architecture.

Moscow has tightened its control in socio-economic and political processes in Kaliningrad. The Oblast has become a metropolis for financial subsidies, economic status changes and attempts to stabilize the socio-economic situation with infrastructural projects, in order to maintain the vitality of the Kaliningrad region under conditions of isolation and transit restriction. Political control is ensured with Moscow's proteges in the regional command and the dominance of the 'United Russia' Party in the so-called elected institutions.

After the war against Georgia, from around 2009, Russia took serious organizational measures for the mobilization of military forces. These measures affected the Kaliningrad region, which was already turned into a formidable military bastion from 2016. Considering all of the Russian military forces' development measures applied in the Western Military District, it can be said that in 2015–16, Moscow had gained a complete superiority of conventional weapons over NATO. The Kaliningrad region played an important role in this process.[6]

Under such circumstances, we can see a strategically new Kaliningrad field perspective. Kaliningrad has not only become the centre of the Russian A2/AD 'bubble', raising security challenges for the Baltic States and Poland, but also as a mitigating factor for the geopolitical role of Belarus.

Russia's closest military ally, Belarus, is situated at a critical geographic position alongside the Suwałki Gap (or Corridor). Named after a town in northeastern Poland, the Suwałki Gap is the area surrounding the 104-kilometre Polish–Lithuanian land border, sandwiched between the Russian exclave of Kaliningrad and Belarus. The Suwałki Gap is strategically important because it connects continental European NATO with the Baltic States, making it the only land bridge that NATO ground forces can use to reinforce the Baltic States from Poland in the case of a military contingency involving Russia while Finland has not yet formally become a member of NATO.

The logic is that Russia and Belarus could close the gap through physical occupation or long-range interdiction to prevent those reinforcements from reaching the Baltic States, thus isolating them, and that this could increase the chances of a major territorial fait accompli at their expense. The scenario was simulated during joint strategic military exercise of the armed forces of the Russian Federation and Belarus.[7]

With the Ukraine invasion, the Suwałki Gap gains a new position as NATO's biggest vulnerability in Europe and an easy way for Russia to cut the Baltic States off if needed.[8]

On the other hand, after the failure of the Russian 'blitzkrieg' plans in Ukraine, the argument that critically assessed Russia's ability to use both the Kaliningrad and Suwałki Gap cards in the confrontation with the West gained new meaning. Recent Chatham House research 'Myths and Misconceptions Around Russian Military Intent' confirms it.[9]

The Chatham House research challenges some ideas about Russian military power and doctrine in general, specifically on issues of the strategic significance of Kaliningrad and the Suwałki Gap. Research proved that the real strategic values of both is limited because military escalation in the region holds more dangers for Russia than for NATO. The perceived strategic importance of the Suwałki Gap follows on from a misunderstanding of its military value and vulnerability. The border between Poland and Lithuania does not matter strategically and any attempt to seize territory there would constitute an Article 5 emergency.

* * *

Before the open and brutal Russian invasion of Ukraine, several strategic scenarios related to the Kaliningrad factor were under consideration.

The constant remilitarization of the Kaliningrad region challenged not only regional but also transatlantic state relationships. For Moscow, the military potential of the exclave is a tool in the strategic dialogue with the West for maintaining the balance of power. It is noteworthy that the factor of remilitarizing the Kurils is treated by Moscow as an anti-US geopolitical tool aimed at increasing Russia's strategic influence in the Far East, southeast Asia and the Pacific Ocean basin, in a similar way.

At the same time, we cannot rule out the possibility that Kaliningrad could have been a 'transitional pawn' in the geopolitical chess game between the West and Russia after a change of international circumstances. Moscow may have been encouraged to reconsider its policy in Kaliningrad by negotiations with the EU on a visa-free regime (as Kaliningrad transformed into a so-called 'pilot region'); the EU by Eurasian Economic Union negotiations on a free trade space 'from Lisbon to Vladivostok.'

Russian aggression has turned its back on this method of strategic thinking.

20

THE MARITIME GEOPOLITICS OF THE BALTIC SEA

Professor Basil Germond

The Baltic Sea stretches from the Danish Straits in the west to St Petersburg in the east, and from the German and Polish coasts in the south to near the Arctic Circle in the north. Riparian states are diverse in size and power, yet the Baltic Sea is a nearly landlocked sea, which has functioned as a bridge between them. In other words, 'geography has shaped the development of societies around the Baltic Sea'.[1] Indeed, the Sea has historically played an important economic and geopolitical role in the region whether for the Nordic countries, the three Baltic States, or even the two big continental powers: Russia and Germany. It has a disproportionate importance for Russia as an access route to the global sea lanes of communication. It has also been instrumental in the development of Prussia and other states of the pre-unification German Confederation. Germany's Navy Command is located in Rostock and its Maritime Operations Centre in Glücksburg, both on the Baltic, not the Atlantic, coast.

The maritime geopolitics of the Baltic Sea has been defined by push and pull factors, by connectivity and confrontation. Indeed, riparian states are geo-economically interdependent, which creates incentives for political integration (whether the Hanseatic League or the EU) but also generates political contention and competition. In the twenty-first century, this dynamic is dominated by the opposition between Russia and all the other riparian states, which are closely aligned within the EU and NATO. The geopolitics of the Baltic Sea has always had a strong maritime dimension, which is the focus of this chapter.

The Concept of Maritime Geopolitics

Human and states' agency is constrained by geography, 'for geography does not argue. It simply is.'[2] This is not to say that 'politics and policies are determined by geography but that geographical factors need to be taken into account in the list of explanatory factors along with other material, structural and ideational factors.'[3] Geographical 'permanencies' impact on decision-making processes but decision-makers also take advantage of geography to achieve economic, political or security goals, either by pursuing geo-power politics or, at the ideational level, by promoting geo-informed narratives and representations that influence discourses and practices.

Geological factors, such the length and shape of their coastline, have affected states' ability to develop a navy as well as their propensity to adopt a maritime culture.[4] Access to the global sea lanes of communication is instrumental from an economic and military perspective. For example, Russia's location on the global grid has historically prevented unhindered access to 'warm waters', since sea lanes are either via choke points and bottlenecks commanded by competitors (e.g. Danish Straits, Turkish Straits, Sea of Japan) or via hostile waters in the Arctic. On the other hand, if one's coastline is easily accessible, it represents an opportunity for enemies to launch an assault from the sea. There is thus a 'strategic ambivalence' of the coastline.[5] That said, geography and politics are intertwined, which is accounted for by the concept of geopolitics. In other words, geographical factors cannot be separated from political circumstances, which are subject to change. For example, due to the presence of land competitors, continental states such as Germany and China have historically been committed to securing their land borders at the expense of developing maritime power.

Historians and strategists, from Alfred Mahan and Halford Mackinder to Colin Gray and Andrew Lambert, have emphasised the preponderance of seapower over land power.[6] Maritime powers can exploit their control of the global supply chain to exercise long-term strategic effects, resulting in their eventual preponderance in long wars (such as WWII and the Cold War). On the battlefield, agile thinking and the adoption of a maritime mindset enable even those states that do not possess powerful naval forces to exert effects from the sea in support of land-based objectives. A recent example is the unexpected military successes of Ukraine in the maritime domain, which results from Kyiv's endorsement of a Western strategy that fosters creative thinking and grants the Black Sea theatre of operations a much greater importance than Russia expected.[7] In sum, this shows that seapower is not a simple outcome of geographical determinants, but the result of the adoption of a maritime mindset, which is dependent on a sustained maritime culture.[8]

Although never the sole factor, geography influences the development of a maritime identity and, down the line, a maritime culture. Continental powers are naturally turned landward, which prevents them from sustaining a maritime strategic culture. An example is Russia, whose naval strategy has remained constrained by a continental outlook. And even when, under the leadership of Admiral Gorshkov, the Soviet Navy achieved global reach capabilities it never managed to become more than 'a seaward extension of the Army,'[9] again something that has been made apparent by Russia's recent failure to exploit and maintain its initial control of the Black Sea.

Maritime geopolitics also has an ideational dimension. Critical geopolitics unravels the way geographical knowledge and representations are produced via discursive practices that constructs and naturalizes 'one' world and 'one' truth.[10] Geographical representations along an inside/us/threatened versus an outside/them/threatening dichotomy can be used to reinforce binary identities and then to normalise policies such as the projection of security and norms to tackle the threats as far away from home as possible, for which maritime power projection and good order at sea play an important role (e.g. humanitarian operations, foreign interventions, counter-piracy). In other words, the practice and narrative of sea control and maritime power is based on the importance of controlling the sea in order to control the land.[11] Sea control has both an economic and a military dimension, which are intertwined as the sea is first and foremost a lane of communication and, as such, a 'great enabler'[12] in war and peace.

Maritime Geo-Economics of the Baltic Sea

The maritime domain has a significant economic value. Industrial activities linked to the sea and its resources (including fisheries, tourism, and offshore energy production) account for about 5% of the world's GDP. Furthermore, the global supply chain is highly dependent on maritime transportation. About 90% of the world's trade is by sea. Interruptions of shipping flows are often unexpected and have direct and serious consequences. Recent disruptions of the supply chain have resulted from accidents (e.g. the closure of the Suez Canal in 2021), workforce shortage in Chinese ports due to the Covid-19 pandemic, or wars (e.g. the global food crisis in 2022 resulting from Russia's blockade of Ukrainian ports).

The Baltic Sea plays an important economic role for riparian states. However, the geo-economic dimension of the Baltic Sea goes beyond being a sea lane of communication between the region and the rest of the world; the Sea represents a shared economic space that has historically incentivised intra-regional trade as well as political integration. Maritime transport has traditionally been the cheapest and safest option for merchants. Maritime trade has played a crucial role both in terms of power politics and in consolidating states around the Baltic Sea, from the Vikings in the early Middle Ages to the German Teutonic Knights and the Hanseatic League until the sixteenth century, to the Scandinavian kingdoms of Sweden and Denmark until the eighteenth century, and eventually Russia and Germany in the nineteenth and twentieth centuries.

The Hanseatic League is a case in point. It was not a state but a network of seafaring/trading cities that had fostered the sense of a common belonging and cooperative behaviours via intercity trade. That eventually contributed to the consolidation of political power around the Baltic rim.[13] What had started as a guild of merchants based in Lübeck and other North German towns, who shared a common (economic) interest in cooperating, became a confederation of several dozens of cities around the Baltic rim, able to speak out to stronger political power. The relationships between the Hanse and more established polities were reciprocal though, with rulers benefiting from a flourishing trade that was not limited to the Baltic rim, as the Hanse dominated the trade between the Baltic region and Western Europe.

Indeed, what characterises the importance of Baltic Sea trade through time is not just its intra-Baltic (regional) dimension but its out-of-area element. As a result, extra-regional dynamics have always played an important role in Baltic politics.

From the seventeenth century, the rise of modern (nation-) states eroded the power and relevance of the Hanse.[14] Since then, struggles to dominate the Baltic Sea have constituted a constant feature of the region. Control passed from the United Provinces to Denmark and Sweden, then from Russia to Germany. However, since the Napoleonic Wars, tensions in the Baltic region have not so much reflected regional rivalries but rather the power struggles taking place outside and beyond the region.[15] Powerful actors strove to secure control of the Baltic Sea, but this remained either limited in time or incomplete, and the Baltic Sea never became anybody's *mare nostrum*. Indeed, complete control of its shores has never been achieved, even by Nazi Germany during the Second World War.[16]

In the twenty-first century, the geopolitical structure of the Baltic Sea region borrows from the Hanse as well as from the modern nation-state era. All riparian states but Russia are highly connected, not only as trading partners but as members of two interrelated political, economic and security communities, namely the EU and NATO. This further creates a sense of economic interdependence and shared objectives. Furthermore, until 2014, there was hope that, in the spirit of the Hanse, economic cooperation with Russia would generate trust, reciprocal interests, and enduring political cooperation. As such, the Baltic Sea was considered as a unifying element to reach out to Russia via trade.

The European integration process had another impact on the economic value of the Baltic Sea, which is located at the periphery of Europe and lacks ports deep enough to accommodate big container ships that have become the international norm. Thus, with the liberalisation of trade within the EU, Baltic maritime trade has lost its importance for EU members.[17] Indeed, land transportation from Copenhagen or Antwerp to the Baltic region has become both relevant and efficient enough thanks to European integration mechanisms and common market institutions. Nevertheless, more than half a billion tonnes of cargo each year transit through Baltic ports. The traffic is dense in relation to the surface of the sea and because sea lanes are concentrated due to bottlenecks, shallow waters, and other navigational hazards. There is also an important fishing industry operating in the Baltic Sea. In addition, the sea plays a role as part of the critical infrastructure of the Baltic region: for energy security (in particular undersea gas pipelines from Russia although this reliance is likely to stop in the foreseeable future and for as long as there is no regime change in Russia) as well as for data/internet cables.[18]

For Russia, the Baltic Sea remains an important sea lane of communication, which is a key component of Russia's network of access to 'warm waters' (and thus to global trade). Until the Ukraine war in 2022, it was a gateway to the EU for trade but also institutional cooperation for marine safety and marine environment protection. Indeed, riparian states have cooperated under the auspices of the Helsinki Commission (Helcom) to address those issues well before the end of the Cold War. Also, the Council of the Baltic States (CBS) tackles sustainable development and environmental issues as well as human trafficking. However, Helcom meetings were suspended following Ukraine's invasion, and Russia was suspended from the CBS. In this context, the environmental security of the Baltic Sea is more precarious than ever with pressing issues such as eutrophication and fishing quotas requiring effective cooperative mechanisms.

Relationships between Putin's Russia and European states (in the Baltic Sea region and beyond) have been damaged beyond repair. But the Baltic Sea remains nonetheless crucial for Russia's economy, viz. import/export, including export of crude oil and petroleum products, and supply of Kaliningrad. Whereas this will not be sufficient to normalise economic relations and institutional cooperation between Russia and the West, this continues to influence Russia's strategic objectives and naval planning in the region, albeit in an antagonistic way.

The Maritime Dimension of the Baltic Sea Geopolitics

During the Cold War period, the Baltic Sea region was divided into not two but three zones: the NATO one (West Germany, Denmark, and Norway), the Warsaw Pact one (the USSR, Poland, and East Germany), and the 'neutral' one (Finland and Sweden).[19] The end of the Cold War signified the end of this geopolitical heterogeneity. With the simultaneous end of the Soviet threat, liberalisation of the Russian economy, rise of the EU as both an economic and a political block, and survival of NATO as the main provider of collective security in Europe, the Baltic Sea region embarked on a process of integration under Western structures.

The transition of Yeltsin's Russia to market economy during the 1990s as well as the accession of Poland and the Baltic States to both NATO and the EU, gave hope that a pan-European cooperative security architecture could be put in place and that Russia would be integrated within this institutional structure (e.g. CBS, Helcom, Partnership and Cooperation Agreement with the EU) and work positively to address common challenges such as environmental pollution and organised crime. Until the 2008 Georgian War, Russia was also considered as a partner of both NATO and the EU rather than a revisionist power,[20] and a conventional war in Europe was almost unthinkable. However, Russia's easy acceptance of the Baltic States' accession to NATO in 2004 had rather come as a surprise to academics at the time,[21] especially given the enduring strategic importance of the Baltic Sea for Moscow.

In 2022, all riparian states but Russia are more integrated than ever within Western institutions, but the Baltic Sea has not become an 'EU lake'. Putin's Russia has stopped any meaningful cooperation with the EU and has demonstrated a complete lack of respect for liberal values as well as the rule of law that are core elements of the EU's project. Now, with the planned accession of Finland and Sweden, some commentators have claimed that the Baltic Sea is about to become a 'NATO lake.'[22] In fact, in the context of the new Cold War between the West and Russia, the Baltic Sea is anything but a 'NATO lake'. Yet, the 'NATO lake' narrative is used to construct the Baltic Sea as a non-Russian space and to foster unity in face of the growing Russian threat. However, such a narrative can be counterproductive and misleading when it comes to securing long-term NATO investments in the region, since 'if it is a "NATO lake" already, why bother?'[23] This exemplifies how the manipulation of geopolitical representations can have concrete effects. The symbolic construction of the Baltic Sea as someone's *mare nostrum* is a powerful narrative with practical consequences on both sides of the current divide.

The Baltic Sea region is strongly unified within Western structures and values, but there is also more risk of it becoming the focal point of a NATO-Russia conflict. As relations between Russia and the West deteriorate, the geostrategic importance of the Baltic Sea increases. Indeed, it is a space of very close proximity between antagonists;[24] it is a zone of possible encounters that is of high strategic value. As mentioned above, the Baltic Sea is crucial for Russia's access to the global sea lanes of communication. Furthermore, in case of conflict, it would become a key strategic approach to Russia, especially to its major demographic and economic centres. Its strategic value also comes from Kaliningrad, which is (with Sebastopol in the Black Sea) the only all-year ice-free naval base for the Russian navy. In addition, the Baltic Sea route is key to connecting the exclave of Kaliningrad to mainland Russia without having to cross NATO airspace or territory: a strategic feature that has recently been emphasised by Lithuania's enforcement of the EU transit ban of military and dual-use goods from mainland Russia to Kaliningrad.

Since 2014, Russia has been growingly confrontational in the Baltic Sea. Moscow has become expert in 'covert, but deniable activities that test resilience and spread unease.'[25] Hybrid warfare and grey zone operations, such as harassing civilian activities by 'conducting military operations within other countries' exclusive economic zones [...] challenge NATO's solidarity'[26] as much as it asserts Russia's status as a Baltic Sea power. For example, in June 2022, Russian warships entered Danish territorial waters without authorisation. This can be put in relation with the fact that Denmark is one of the countries supplying Kyiv with antiship Harpoon missiles, which have played a key role in preventing Russia from maintaining control of the north western Black Sea. However, as a result of the Ukraine war, the solidarity of Western Baltic riparian states has strengthened to a degree rarely, if ever, experienced since the end of the Cold War. Moscow's gesticulations and propaganda are having less impact than before. And Western nations, well aware of the risk of hybrid warfare, can devote more resources to securing the grey zone, e.g. peacetime presence at sea and early warning capabilities.[27]

Naval Balance in the Baltic Sea

Russia's Baltic Fleet is ageing and far from balanced.[28] According to the *Military Balance 2022*, the Baltic Fleet consists of one Kilo-class diesel-electric submarine, one destroyer, five frigates, 30 patrol and coastal combatants, 11 mine warfare vessels, four medium amphibious ships, and various small crafts and support ships.[29] While this fleet can, on paper, easily be outclassed by NATO, this would be contingent on reinforcement from outside the Baltic region. So, even if the Baltic Fleet is outsmarted by Western regional navies in terms of operationality, weapon systems and sailors' morale and skills (a balance which is unlikely to change in the foreseeable future, especially considering the current sanctions that impact on Russia's military complex), in quantitative terms, it remains the dominant force in the region.

In case of a full-scale conflict, the Baltic Sea lanes of communication would need to be secured,[30] especially in order for NATO reinforcement to reach the region. War operations in the Black Sea in 2022 showed that even though Russia initially secured control of the north-western Black Sea, it was then not able to maintain it, let alone to exploit it to produce strategic effects. While the naval balance in the Baltic Sea is even less favourable to Russia than it was in the Black Sea, NATO cannot be complacent. Indeed, the Baltic Fleet, for all its shortcomings, is backed by air and A2/AD capabilities in mainland Russia and Kaliningrad,[31] which includes land-based naval aviation, surface-to-air as well as antiship missiles.[32] Missiles based in Kaliningrad (including nuclear-capable surface-to-surface Iskander short-range ballistic missiles) can target NATO warships penetrating the Baltic Sea via the Danish Straits.

However, the extent to which Russia's A2/AD poses a threat has recently been deconstructed.[33] Furthermore, Russian ships and Kaliningrad's installations are also threatened by NATO long-range strikes.[34] And sea routes from St Petersburg to Kaliningrad are extremely vulnerable to NATO attacks.[35] With Sweden and Finland joining NATO, Russian warships will further be at the mercy of the Alliance's coastal defence. Ukraine's great success rate of sinking Russian warships with land-based missiles in the Black Sea would be replicated by NATO in the Baltic Sea even more efficiently, especially in the Gulf of Finland that commands access to St Petersburg.[36]

The Russian invasion of Ukraine is likely to result in further investments in naval assets (whether warships, weapon systems, land-based missiles, or patrol aircraft) by Baltic Sea countries. Military analysts have long recognised the need to address the vulnerabilities of the three Baltic States. Indeed, in case of a Russian attack, they might quickly be cut off from the rest of NATO and Russia can use land-based missiles to lock NATO reinforcement out for longer. Furthermore, a conflict between Russia and NATO is unlikely to be limited to the Baltic Sea, and thus NATO naval assets might be employed elsewhere. At a political level, reassurance is key, hence the planned increased commitment of NATO permanent naval presence (as approved at the June 2022 Madrid Summit) and the frequent conduct of large-scale joint exercises (which also contribute to operational readiness and interoperability). At the operational level, it is also crucial to increase Baltic States' operational capabilities in terms of coastal defence (beyond their comparative advantage in mine warfare that complements other NATO navies very well), which requires developing a targeted procurement strategy.[37] In sum, there are two priorities: strengthening NATO's overall commitment to the defence of the region and at the same time developing regional capacities for immediate response, in particular decreasing reliance on external NATO assets for coastal defence and regional sea control.

Conclusion

During the Cold War the Baltic Sea was considered as a 'no-man's land on the periphery of the main axis of confrontation.'[38] Today, Russia is again the defined enemy and a disruptive actor in the region. However, all the other riparian states are highly integrated both politically, militarily, and economically. So long as there is no open war between NATO and Russia, the Baltic Sea will remain a space of thriving economic activities at the heart of Northern Europe. Russia's grey zone activities in the maritime domain will regularly disrupt the repose of the region, but overall, the sea will remain a unifying factor. However, its strategic value in case of war means that Western nations must prepare for the worst. This requires naval procurement plans and the allocation of resources to the region's defence, but also a better understanding of Russia's Achilles' heel that is its lack of seapower mindset and its deficient maritime strategy as illustrated by its recent failures in the Black Sea.

NOTES

1. THE IMPORTANCE OF THE BALTIC

1. https://www.cfg.polis.cam.ac.uk/programmes/baltic
2. This section draws heavily upon an article written by Charles Clarke and Professor Brendan Simms for the *New Statesman* at the time of the launch of the Baltic Geopolitics Programme, https://www.newstatesman.com/politics/scotland/2021/02/why-britain-matters-europe
3. HMSO CP 403, https://assets.publishing.service.gov.uk/government/uploads/system/uploads/attachment_data/file/975077/Global_Britain_in_a_Competitive_Age-_the_Integrated_Review_of_Security__Defence__Development_and_Foreign_Policy.pdf
4. http://en.kremlin.ru/events/president/news/66181

3. THE BALTIC STATES, RUSSIA AND EUROPE'S ORDER, 1917–1991–2022

1. Robert D. McFadden, 'Leaders Gather in New York to Chart a World Order', *New York Times [NYT]*, 31 Jan. 1992; Michael Wines, 'Bush and Yeltsin Declare Formal End to Cold War', *NYT*, 2 Feb. 1992.
2. Wines, 'Bush and Yeltsin Declare Formal End to Cold War'.
3. George H. W. Bush, 'Remarks to the Citizens in Mainz, Federal Republic of Germany', 31 May 1989, available at: The American Presidency Project, https://www.presidency.ucsb.edu/documents/remarks-the-citizens-mainz-federal-republic-germany
4. 'Address by the President of the Russian Federation', 24 Feb. 2022, http://en.kremlin.ru/events/president/news/67843

5. Guntis Šmidchens, *The Power of Song: Nonviolent National Culture in the Baltic Singing Revolution* (Univ. of Washington Press, 2014).

6. Kristina Spohr, *Post Wall, Post Square: Rebuilding the World after 1989* (William Collins, 2019), introduction and ch. 7.

7. Ibid., 'Between Political Rhetoric and *Realpolitik* Calculations: Western Diplomacy and the Baltic Independence Struggle in the Cold War Endgame', *Cold War History* 6, 1 (2006), pp. 1–42.

8. Holly Ellyatt, 'Fears Grow among Russia's Neighbors that Putin Might not Stop at Ukraine', *CNBC*, 8 March 2022. See also Mark Episkopos, 'Putin Invokes Peter the Great as Russia Prepares for Long War', *The National Interest*, 12 June 2022; Robert Coalson, 'Putin Pledges to Protect all Ethnic Russians Anywhere. So, Where Are They?', *RFERL*, 10 April 2014.

9. Neville Chamberlain, 27 September 1938.

10. Sajid Javid, 14 March 2022.

11. Kristina Spohr, 'Finland and the Baltic States, 1914–1945', in Robert Gerwarth, ed., *Twisted Paths: Europe, 1914–1945* (OUP, 2007), pp. 271–96.

12. Ibid.

13. See, for example, Magnus Ilmjärv, *Silent Submission: Formation of Foreign Policy in Estonia, Latvia and Lithuania, 1920–1940* (Almqvist & Wiksell, 2004); Kaarel Piirimäe, *Roosevelt, Churchill, and the Baltic Question: Allied Relations during the Second World War* (Palgrave Macmillan, 2014); Kaarel Piirimäe, James S. Corum, and Olaf Mertelsmann, eds, *The Second World War and the Baltic States* (Peter Lang, 2014).

14. See, for example, Kari Alenius, *Viron, Latvian ja Liettuan historia* (Atena Kustannus Oy, 2000); Violeta Davoliūtė and Tomas Balkelis, eds, *Narratives of Exile and Identity: Soviet Deportation Memoirs from the Baltic States* (CEU Press, 2018). On 'Russification', see Sonia B. Green, 'Language of Lullabies: The Russification and De-Russification of the Baltic States', *Michigan Journal of International Law* 19, 219 (1997), pp. 219–75.

15. See Richard C. M. Mole, *The Baltic States from the Soviet Union to the European Union: Identity, Discourse and Power in the Post-Communist*

Transition of Estonia, Latvia and Lithuania (Routledge, 2012); Timofey Agarin, *A Cat's Lick: Democratisation and Minority Communities in the Post-Soviet Baltic* (Rodopi, 2010), chs 2–3; Graham Smith, *The Baltic States: The National Self-Determination of Estonia, Latvia and Lithuania* (Palgrave Macmillan, 1996); Rogers Brubaker, 'Nationhood and the National Question in the Soviet Union and Post-Soviet Eurasia: An Institutionalist Account', *Theory and Society* 23, 1 (Feb., 1994), pp. 47–78.

16. Kaarel Piirimäe, 'Gorbachev's New Thinking and How its Interaction with Perestroika in the Republics Catalysed the Soviet Collapse', *Scandinavian Journal of History* (Aug. 2020), online DOI: 10.1080/03468755.2020.1784268; Kristina Spohr, *Germany and the Baltic Problem after the Cold War: The Development of a new Ostpolitik, 1989–2000* (Routledge, 2004), ch. 1; John Hiden, Vahur Made, David J. Smith, eds, *The Baltic Question during the Cold War* (Routledge, 2008). For the U.S. Non-Recognition Policy, see https://digitalarchive.wilsoncenter.org/collection/279/united-states-non-recognition-policy. See also Lauri Mälksoo, *Illegal Annexation and State Continuity: The Case of the Incorporation of the Baltic States by the USSR* (Brill, 2022, 2nd revised edn).

17. Ibid; 'Between Political Rhetoric and *Realpolitik* Calculations'. See also 'The Baltic Question in West German Politics, 1949–90', *Journal of Baltic Studies* 38, 2 (June 2007), pp. 153–78.

18. See, for example, Una Bergmane, "Is This the End of Perestroika?' International Reactions to the Soviet Use of Force in the Baltic Republics in January 1991', *Journal of Cold War Studies* 22, 2 (Spring 2020), pp. 26–57; Ainius Lasas, 'Bloody Sunday: What did Gorbachev know about the January 1991 Events in Vilnius and Riga?', *Journal of Baltic Studies* 38, 2 (June 2007), pp. 179–94.

19. Spohr, *Post Wall, Post Square*, ch. 7. See also Vladislav Zubok, *Collapse: The Fall of the Soviet Union* (Yale UP, 2021). Cf. Serhii Plokhy, *The Last Empire: The Final Days of the Soviet Union* (Oneworld, 2015). On Soviet disintegration, see also Vladislav Zubok, Kristina Spohr, et al., Forum—'A Cold War Endgame or an Opportunity Missed? Analysing the Soviet Collapse Thirty Years Later', *Cold War History* 21, 4, pp. 541–99.

20. Edijs Bošs, *Aligning with the Unipole: Alliance Policies of Estonia, Latvia and Lithuania, 1988–1998* (unpublished doctoral thesis, Cambridge University, 2011).

21. Spohr, *Germany and the Baltic Problem after the Cold War*, ch. 5. Stephen Holmes and Ivan Krastev, *The Light that Failed: A Reckoning* (Penguin, 2020).

22. See, for example, George Soroka and Tomasz Stępniewski, 'Russia and the Rest: Permeable Sovereignty and the Former Soviet Socialist Republics', *Journal of Soviet and Post-Soviet Politics and Society* 6, 2 (2020), pp. 3–12; Willliam Safire, 'On Language—The Near Abroad', *NYT*, 22 May 1994.

23. Putin's speech of 25 April 2005 'Poslaniye Federal'nomu Sobraniyu Rossiiskoy Federatsii', http://kremlin.ru/events/president/transcripts/22931.

24. On Putin's obsession with Western betrayal, see 'Putin's Munich Speech 15 Years Later: What Prophecies Have Come True?', *Tass*, 10 Feb. 2022; Putin's 'Speech and the Following Discussion at the Munich Conference on Security Policy', Munich Security Conference, 10 Feb. 2007, http://en.kremlin.ru/events/president/transcripts/copy/24034; 'Putin: There Were Five Waves of NATO Expansion', *Deusche Welle*, 23 Dec. 2021. Cf. Kristina Spohr, 'Russia's war against Ukraine is not only a challenge to territorial borders. It is Putin's war to change Europe's order', LSE British Policy and Politics Blog, 25 Feb. 2022, https://blogs.lse.ac.uk/politicsandpolicy/putins-war-against-european-order/; 'Die Geschichte der NATO-Osterweiterung', *Dekoder*, 10 Feb. 2022, https://www.dekoder.org/de/gnose/nato-osterweiterung-debatte-versprechen; Kristina Spohr with Kaarel Piirimäe, 'With or without Russia? The Boris, Bill and Helmut Bromance and the Harsh Realities of Securing Europe in the Post-Wall World, 1990–1994', *Diplomacy & Statecraft*, 33, 1 (2022), pp. 158–193. See also Daniel S. Hamilton and Kristina Spohr, eds, *Open Door: NATO and Euro-Atlantic Security After the Cold War* (Brookings Institution Press, 2019) as well as Spohr, 'Precedent-setting or Precluded? The 'NATO Enlargement Question' in the Triangular Bonn-Washington-Moscow Diplomacy of 1990–1991', *Journal of Cold War Studies* 14, 4 (2012), pp. 4–54. See also

Chatham House Report, 'Myths and Misconceptions in the Debate on Russia', 13 May 2021, https://www.chathamhouse.org/2021/05/myths-and-misconceptions-debate-russia/myth-03-russia-was-promised-nato-would-not-enlarge

25. Lukas Milevski, 'Baltic Prudence or Paranoia, Redux: What Does Zapad-2017 Mean for the Baltic States?', *Baltic Bulletin* (August 2017); Alexandra Wiktorek Sarlo, 'Fighting Disinformation in the Baltic States', *Baltic Bulletin* (July 2017).

26. Oren Liebermann, Frederik Pleitgen and Vasco Cotovio, 'New Satellite Images Suggest Military Buildup in Russia's Strategic Baltic Enclave', *CNN*, 17 Oct. 2018; Warsaw Institute, 'Drones, Battle Tanks, Aircraft and Iskanders: Russia Advances Military Buildup in Kaliningrad', *Russia Monitor*, 16 Dec. 2019; Rodion Ebbighausen, 'China and Russia Combine Naval Forces in the Baltic Sea', *Deutsche Welle*, 24 July 2017.

27. See, for example, Fiona Hill and Clifford G. Gaddy, *Mr. Putin: Operative in the Kremlin* (Brookings Institution Press, 2015 edn), esp. ch. 4: 'The History Man'; Igor Torbakov, 'Vladimir Putin's Twisted Politics of History', 30 June 2020, https://eurasianet.org/perspectives-vladimir-putins-twisted-politics-of-history; Anna Reid, 'Putin's War on History: The Thousand-Year Struggle Over Ukraine', *Foreign Affairs* (May/June 2022), https://www.foreignaffairs.com/articles/ukraine/2022-04-06/putins-war-history-ukraine-russia; Mark Edele, 'Fighting Russia's History Wars: Vladimir Putin and the Codification of World War II', *History and Memory* 29, 2 (Fall/Winter 2017), pp. 90–124; Christopher Clark, 'Krieg in der Ukraine—Zar Putin der Große', *Süddeutsche Zeitung*, 1 July 2022. See also 'Vladimir Putin's Historical Disinformation', *U.S. Department of State*, 6 May 2022, https://www.state.gov/disarming-disinformation/vladimir-putins-historical-disinformation/

28. 'Putin Shows Off Russia's Naval Might with Major Parade', *AFP*, 30 July 2017.

29. 'Putin Slams Lenin for Laying 'Atomic Bomb' Under Russia', *The Moscow Times*, 21 Jan. 2016.

30. 'Address by the President of the Russian Federation', 21 Feb. 2022, http://en.kremlin.ru/events/president/news/67828; and 'Security

Council Meeting', 21 Feb. 2022, http://en.kremlin.ru/events/president/news/67825

31. In December 2021, Putin—in an interview aired as part of a new state TV documentary 'Russia-New History'—not merely lamented the demise of 'historical Russia under the name of the Soviet Union', but the loss of '40% of our territory', much of 'what had been built up over 1000 years.' See 'Russian President Vladimir Putin Says He Moonlighted as a Taxi Driver in the 1990s', *ABC News* (Australia), 13 Dec. 2022 and Steve Rosenberg, 'What is Russia's Vladimir Putin Planning?', BBC News, 20 Dec. 2022. Cf. Putin: 'On the Historical Unity of Russians and Ukrainians', 12 July 2021, http://en.kremlin.ru/events/president/news/66181; 'Putin Calls Ukrainian Statehood a Fiction—History Suggests Otherwise', *NYT*, 21 Feb. 2022.

32. 'Vladimir Putin: The Real Lessons of the 75th Anniversary of World War II', 18 June 2020, *The National Interest*, https://nationalinterest.org/feature/vladimir-putin-real-lessons-75th-anniversary-world-war-ii-162982; Una Bergmane, 'How Putin is Rehabilitating the Nazi-Soviet Pact', *Baltic Bulletin* (July 2020).

33. See 'Putin rasskazal ob otnoshenii k lozungu "Mozhem povtorit"'. *Izvestia*, 10 March 2022.

34. See, for example, 'Vladimir Putin's Victory Day Speech in Full', Moscow, 9 May 2022, available at https://www.spectator.co.uk/article/read-vladimir-putin-s-victory-day-speech-in-full. Cf. Anne Applebaum, World War II Is All that Putin Has Left', *The Atlantic*, 11 May 2022.

35. Andrew Roth, 'Putin Compares Himself to Peter the Great in Quest to Take Back Russian Lands', *The Guardian*, 10 June 2022; Ishaan Tharoor, 'Putin Makes his Imperial Pretensions Clear', *Washington Post [WP]*, 13 June 2022; and 'Putin Asserts Strong, Sovereign Russia against Sanctions "Blitzkrieg"', *Reuters*, 17 June 2022.

36. 'Baerbock: Sweden and Finland Will Strengthen NATO', *Deutschland.de*, 29 June 2022, https://www.deutschland.de/en/news/baerbock-sweden-and-finland-will-strengthen-nato. See also Carl Bildt, 'What NATO's Northern Expansion Means', *Project Syndicate*, 21 April 2022.

37. Most recently, tensions in the Baltic region grew over the blown up

Nord Stream gas pipelines. See Jan M. Olsen, 'NATO Believes Baltic Sea Gas Pipeline Leaks Were Sabotage', *WP*, 29 Sept. 2022.

4. ATTAINING BALTIC INDEPENDENCE: IN SEARCH OF A HELPING HAND

1. *Dokumenty vneshnei politiki SSSR*, Vol. 2, eed. G. Deev et al. (Moscow: Pol. Lit., 1958) docs. 188, 214 and 384. Estonia and Lithuania were settled by treaty in November 1919; Latvia in June 1920.

2. Jonathan Haslam, *The Spectre of War: International Communism and the Origins of World War II* (Princeton: Princeton University Press, 2021), chapter 12.

3. For the story: Tom Bower, *The Red Web* (London: Mandarin, 1993).

4. Vysshaya Shkola Komiteta Gosudarstvennoi Bezopasnosti pri Soviete Ministrov SSSR imeni F.E. Dzerzhinskogo, No 001580, ed. Colonel Markelov et al. *Angliiskaya Razvedka* (Moscow 1963) pp. 38–39. This is a highly classified textbook for KGB training that was published in a closed edition; subsequently released in the Baltic after scanning.

5. Personal knowledge. I got to know her while serving as temporary clerk to the foreign and security policy sub-committee of the EU Committee of the House of Lords for nine months in 2002.

6. Personal knowledge. I knew him while working in Washington DC in 1985.

7. Haslam, *Russia's Cold War: Soviet Foreign Policy from the October Revolution to the Fall of the Wall.* Dashichev was my guest in Cambridge for a week in May 1989, where he told me the entire story.

8. Krister Wahlbäck, 'De baltiska staternas självständigheet från svensk säkerhetspolitisk synpunkt, 16 September 1991': *Ett imperium implodera. Rapporterna och analyser från svenska dipllomater i Sovietunionen och dess lydstater med tonvikt på Baltikum åren 1989–1991* (Stockholm: Utrikesdepartmentet, 2011). Neither the documents nor the pages therein are numbered.

9. Lars Fredén, *Återkomster: svensk säkerhetspolitik och de baltiska ländernas första år i självständighet: 1991–1994* (Stockholm: Atlantis, 2006) p. 28. Fredén represented Sweden in Lithuania and Latvia from the summer of 1989 to the summer of 1991. He is a trained Sinologist, served in

Moscow and eventually became ambassador to Sweden. The fact that he was at one time security policy adviser to the Prime Minister and acted as go-between in the negotiations for the withdrawal of the Russians from the Baltic does suggest that he had skills well beyond average for the Utrikesdepartmentet.

10. 'Skrunda-1: Exploring a Soviet Ghost Town in the Forests of Latvia': https://www.exutopia.com/skrunda-1-exploring-a-soviet-ghost-town-in-the-forests-of-latvia/

11. Hans Olsson, 1st department, Utrikesdepartementet, 'Baltikum', 6 February 1991: *Ett imperium imploderar.*

12. Igor Korotchenko, 'Organy gosbezopasnosti v bob'be s natsionalizmom i separatizmom', *Natsional'naya oborona*, 18 March 2021.

13. Fréden (Riga) to Olsson (Stockholm), 12 February 1991. The Swedish General Consulate in Leningrad had opened an office in Riga a few months before: *Ett imperium imploderar.*

14. 'Läget i Baltikum i december 1989', Dag Sebastian Ahlander (Leningrad) to the Utrikesdepartementet (Stockholm), 5 December 1989: *Ett imperium imploderar.*

15. Örjan Berner, 'Sovjet och Europa—januari 1991', 7 January 1991: ibid.

16. Blech (Moscow) to Ausamt (Bonn), 18 May 1990: *Akten zur Auswärtigen Politik der Bundesrepublik Deutschland 1990*, ed. T. Geiger et al., (Oldenbourg: De Gruyter, 2021) doc. 144.

17. 'Gespräch des Bundeskanzler Kohl mit dem britischen Aussenminister Hurd', 30 January 1991: *Akten zur Auswärtigen Politik der Bundesrepublik Deutschland 1991*, ed. M. Peter et al., (Oldenbourg: De Gruyter, 2022) doc. 174.

18. 'Brent Scowcroft Oral History Part II', Presidential Oral Histories, Miller Center, University of Virginia: https://millercenter.org/the-presidency/presidential-oral-histories/brent-scowcroft-oral-history-part-ii

19. 'Mikhail Golovanov: 'Iz okon my nablyudali, kak padayut grazhdanskie', *Otkrytye Mediya*, 19 September 2019; 'Ot Litauen', Ahlander (Riga) to the Utrikesdepartementet (Stockholm), 13 January 1991: *Ett imperium imploderar.*

20. Ahlander (Leningrad) to the Utrikesdepartementet (Stockholm), 15 March 1991: ibid.

5. BALTIC LIBERATION, THE BALTIC SEA REGIONAL CONTEXT
AND SWEDEN DURING THE END OF THE COLD WAR

1. Kuldkepp, Mart. 'Swedish Political Attitudes towards Baltic Independence in the Short Twentieth Century' *Ajalooline Ajakiri*, no. 3/4 (2016), pp. 397–430.

2. Doeser, Fredrik. *In Search of Security after the Collapse of the Soviet Union: Foreign Policy Change in Denmark, Finland and Sweden, 1988–1993.* Stockholm: Stockholm University, 2008, pp. 216–17, p. 221.

3. Lundén, Thomas, and Torbjörn Nilsson. *Sverige och Baltikums frigörelse: Två vittnesseminarier om storpolitik kring Östersjön 1989–1994.* Huddinge: CBEES, Centre for Baltic and East European Studies, 2008, p. 17.

4. Kuldkepp, 'Swedish Political Attitudes towards Baltic Independence in the Short Twentieth Century', p. 420.

5. Lundén and Nilsson. *Sverige och Baltikums frigörelse: Två vittnesseminarier om storpolitik kring Östersjön 1989–1994*, p. 26.

6. Bergman, Annika. 'Adjacent Internationalism: The Concept of Solidarity and Post-Cold War Nordic–Baltic Relations.' *Cooperation and Conflict* 41, no. 1 (2006), pp. 73–97.

7. Mart Kuldkepp (2022) 'Baltic liberation first-hand: Sweden's pro-Baltic foreign policy shift and Swedish diplomatic reporting in 1989–1991', *Scandinavian Journal of History*, 47:3, pp. 325–346.

6. THE MICE THAT ROARED

1. This chapter draws heavily on Kristian Gerner and Stefan Hedlund, *The Baltic States and the End of the Soviet Empire* (London: Routledge, 1993).

2. Mare Taagepera, 'The Ecological and Political Problems of Phosphorite Mining in Estonia,' *Journal of Baltic Studies*, vol. 20, no. 2 (1989), pp. 165–74.

3. Ulo Ignats, *Fosforitbrytningen i Estland* (Göteborg: MH Publishing, 1989, p. 27).

4. Toomas Ilves, 'Baltic Area SR/3,' *Radio Free Europe Research*, 8 May 1987, p. 10.

5. Toomas Ilves, 'Baltic Area SR/2,' *Radio Free Europe Research*, 20 March 1987, pp. 4–5.

6. Rein Taagepera, 'Estonia's Road to Independence,' *Problems of Communism*, vol. 38, no. 6 (1989), p. 18.

7. *Edasi*, 26 September 1987. Ulo Ignats, *Estland: Den sjungande revolutionen* (Göteborg: MH Publishing, 1989), pp. 33–4.

8. Igor Klyamkin, 'Pochemu trudno govorit pravdu,' *Novyi Mir*, no. 2, 1989, pp. 221–24, p. 237.

9. Saulius Girnius, 'Baltic Area SR/8,' *Radio Free Europe Research*, 4 August 1988, pp. 19–23.

10. Ignats, 1989, op. cit., pp. 71–2.

11. Alfred E. Senn, *Lithuania Awakening* (Berkeley, CA: University of California Press), pp. 6–7.

12. *Izvestiya*, 22 October 1988.

13. The rather strange wording reflected how conflicted the issue was: 'Do you consider necessary the preservation of the Union of Soviet Socialist Republics as a renewed federation of equal sovereign republics, in which the rights and freedoms of an individual of any nationality will be guaranteed?' (Sheehy, Ann, 'Referendum on the Preservation of the Union,' *Report on the USSR*, vol. 3, no. 7 (1991), p. 6).

7. CONTRIBUTIONS OF THE BALTIC INDEPENDENCE CAMPAIGNS TO SOVIET COLLAPSE

1. For an interpretation of complexity and its application, Walter C. Clemens, *The Baltic Transformed: Complexity theory and European security* (Lanham, MD: Rowman & Littlefield, 2001).

2. Jack F. Matlock, *Autopsy on an Empire: The American ambassador's account of the Soviet Union* (New York: Random House, 1995), 648.

3. Archie Brown, *Seven years that changed the world: Perestroika in perspective* (Oxford; New York: Oxford University Press, 2007), 221.

4. Laurien Crump and Simon Godard, 'Reassessing Communist International Organisations: A Comparative Analysis of COMECON and the Warsaw Pact in relation to their Cold War Competitors', *Contemporary European History* 27, no. 1 (2018): 85–109.

5. Fritz Bartel, 'Fugitive leverage: Commercial Banks, Sovereign Debt, and Cold War Crisis in Poland, 1980–1982', *Enterprise & Society* 18, no. 1 (2017): 72–107.

6. Valdis Blūzma, Tālavs Jundzis, and Jānis Riekstiņs, *Regaining Independence: Non-violent resistance in Latvia 1945–1991* (Riga: Latvian Academy of Sciences, 2009), 582–586.

7. Critical remarks by Elie Kedourie, Sidney Hook, Hugh Trevor-Roper and Milovan Djilas about the rise of nationalist movements in Eastern Europe, G. R. Urban, *The End of Empire: The demise of the Soviet Union, G.R. Urban in conversation with leading thinkers of our time* (Washington, D.C.: University Publishing Association, 1993), 113, 36, 86, 193–194. On Western orientalism toward eastern Europe, Larry Wolff, *Inventing Eastern Europe: The map of civilization on the mind of the enlightenment* (Stanford, Calif.: Stanford University Press, 1994); Merje Kuus, 'Europe's eastern expansion and the reinscription of otherness in East-Central Europe,' *Progress in Human Geography* 28, no. 4 (2004): 472–489.

8. Ainius Lasas, 'Guilt, sympathy, and cooperation: EU—Baltic relations in the early 1990s,' *East European Politics and Societies* 22, no. 2 (2008): 347–372. The European Parliament suggested raising the Baltic question at the United Nations' Decolonization subcommittee but this UN body never discussed it.

9. Archie Brown, *The Gorbachev Factor* (Oxford; New York: Oxford University Press, 1996); Timothy J. Colton, *Yeltsin: A life* (New York: Basic Books, 2008).

10. Giovanni Capoccia and R. Daniel Kelemen, 'The study of critical junctures: Theory, narrative, and counterfactuals in historical institutionalism', *World Politics* 59, no. 3 (2007): 341–369.

11. John Lewis Gaddis, *The Cold War* (London: Penguin, 2007); Robert Service, *The End of the Cold War, 1985–1991* (London: Macmillan 2015).

12. See Mark Kramer, 'The collapse of East European communism and the repercussions within the Soviet Union (Part 3)', *Journal of Cold War Studies* 7, no. 1 (2005): 3–96, and the two earlier parts of the three-part article appearing in the same journal.

13. Alex Pravda, 'The Collapse of the Soviet Union, 1990–1991', in *The Cambridge History of the Cold War. Vol. 3. Endings*, ed. Melvyn Leffler (Cambridge: Cambridge University Press, 2010), 356–377.

14. Serhii Plokhy, *The Last Empire: The Final Days of the Soviet Union* (New York: Basic Books, 2014),

15. Vladislav M. Zubok, *Collapse: The fall of the Soviet Union* (New Haven: Yale University Press, 2021).

16. Aleksándr Vladímirovič Ostróvskij, *Glupost' ili izmena? Rassledovanie gibeli SSSR* (M.: Krymskij most 9-D Forum, 2011).

17. R. H. Simonian, 'Pribaltika i raspad SSSR', Dzhakson T.N., Komarov A.A., Mikhailova Iu.L., Nazarova E.L. (Ed.), *Rossiia i Pribaltiiskii region v XIX—XX vv.: Problemy vzaimootnoshenii v meniaiushchemsia mire* (Moskva, 2012), 207–227.

18. Talavs Jundzis, 'Regaining the independence of Latvia', *Latvia and Latvians: Collection of scholarly articles* ed Jānis Stradiņš et al (Riga: Latvian Academy of Sciences, 2018), 54–92; Mati Graf, *Ühe impeeriumi lõpp ja Eesti taasiseseisvumine 1988–1991* (Tallinn: Argo, 2012).

19. Pravda, 'The Collapse of the Soviet Union, 1990–1991', 364.

20. Ibid.

21. Lars Fredrik Stöcker, *Bridging the Baltic Sea: Networks of resistance and opposition during the Cold War Era* (Lanham, MD: Lexington Books, 2018).

22. J. R. Jamieson, 'Visit to Tallinn 25–27 September', 13 October 1981, FCO 28/4603, National Archives (United Kingdom).

23. William Risch, 'A Soviet West: Nationhood, Regionalism, and Empire in the Annexed Western Borderlands', *Nationalities Papers* 43, no. 1 (2015): 63–81, arguing that the Soviet West produced a sense of difference, which was not inherently anti-Soviet but had the potential to became so in the era of glasnost (p. 78).

24. Oliver Pagel, 'Lucrative Business for Moscow: Foreign Currency Revenues from Finnish Tourism in the Estonian SSR 1965–1980', *Ajalooline ajakiri–The Estonian Historical Journal* (2015), no 1–2: 159–87; Oliver Pagel, 'Finnish Foreign Tourism in the Estonian SSR during the Cold War, 1955–1980' in Tõnu Tannberg (ed.), *Behind the Iron Curtain: Soviet Estonia in the era of the Cold War* (Frankfurt: Peter Lang, 2015), 295–315.

25. Marek Miil, 'The Communist Party's Fight Against "Bourgeois Television" 1968–1988' in Tõnu Tannberg (ed.), *Behind the Iron Curtain: Soviet Estonia in the Era of the Cold War* (Frankfurt: Peter Lang, 2015): 317–358.

26. Martin Klesment, Allan Puur and Jaak Valge, *Childbearing and Macro-Economic Trends in Estonia in the 20th Century* (Tallinn: Estonian Interuniversity Population Research, 2010).

27. Mark R. Beissinger, *Nationalist Mobilization and the Collapse of the Soviet State* (Cambridge; New York: Cambridge University Press, 2002), 441.

28. Andrus Park, *End of An Empire? A conceptualization of the Soviet disintegration crisis, 1985–1991* (Tartu: Tartu University Press), 165–167.

29. Beissinger, *Nationalist Mobilization*, 385–442.

30. Rein Taagepera, 'Estonia in September 1988: Stalinists, *Centrists and Restorationists*', *Journal of Baltic Studies* 20, no. 2 (1989): 175–190.

31. Joseph Enge, 'Why the Soviet Coercive use of Force in the Baltic Republics Failed in 1990–1991 and Led to the End of the Soviet Union', in *The Baltic States and the End of the Cold War*, ed. Kaarel Piirimäe and Olaf Mertelsmann (Frankfurt: Peter Lang, 2018), 269–292.

32. Beissinger, *Nationalist Mobilization*, 162.

33. Nils R. Muiznieks, 'The Influence of the Baltic Popular Movements on the Process of Soviet Disintegration', *Europe-Asia Studies* 47, no. 1 (1995): 3–25; *Towards Independence: The Baltic Popular Movements*, ed. Jan Arveds Trapans (Boulder, Col.: Westview, 1991).

34. Keiji Sato, 'The Molotov-Ribbentrop Commission and Claims of Post-Soviet Secessionist Territories to Sovereignty', *Demokratizatsiya* 18, no. 2 (2010): 148–159.

35. Jaak Rakfeldt, 'Home Environments, Memories, and Life Stories: Preservation of Estonian National Identity', *Journal of Baltic Studies* 46, no. 4 (2015): 511–542.

36. Una Bergmane, *Politics of Uncertainty: the US, The Baltic Question and the collapse of the USSR* (Oxford University Press, forthcoming), 69.

37. Lauri Mälksoo, *Illegal Annexation and State Continuity: The case of the incorporation of the Baltic States by the USSR* (Leiden; Boston: Brill Nijhoff), 59–60.

38. Kaarel Piirimäe, 'The Peace Treaty of Tartu: The Postcolonial Situation 100 Years Later', *Ajalooline Ajakiri. The Estonian Historical Journal* 173, no. 3/4 (2020): 189–196.

39. Juhan Saharov 'An Economic Innovation as an Icebreaker: The Contractual Work Experiment in Soviet Estonia in 1985', *The Baltic States and the End of the Cold War*, ed. Kaarel Piirimäe and Olaf Mertelsmann (Frankfurt: Peter Lang, 2018): 65–84; Juhan Saharov,

'From an Economic Term to a Political Concept: The Conceptual Innovation of 'Self-Management' in Soviet Estonia', *Contributions to the History of Concepts* 16, no. 1 (2021): 116–140; Juhan Saharov, 'From Future Scenarios to Sovereignty Declarations: Estonian Cyberspeak and the Breakup of the Soviet Union', *Europe-Asia Studies* (2022): 1–23.

40. Park, *End of an Empire?*, 186, referring to the 'war of the laws' between the republics and the centre.

41. Graf, *Impeeriumi lõpp*, 77, points to the Interregional Group's decision to adopt the system of collective leadership from the Estonian Popular Front.

42. Alexei Yurchak, *Everything Was Forever, Until It Was No More: The last Soviet generation* (Princeton: Princeton University Press, 2013); Hank Johnston and Aili Aarelaid-Tart, 'Generations, Microcohorts, and Long-Term Mobilization: The Estonian National Movement, 1940–1991', *Sociological Perspectives* 43, no. 4 (2000): 671–698.

43. J. K. Gordon, 'Meetings with Lennart Meri', 2 July 1981, FCO 28/4603, National Archives (United Kingdom).

44. G. Edgar (Soviet Department), 'Possible call by Estonian Foreign Minister', 1 October 1990, Foreign and Commonwealth Office, Freedom of Information Act 2000 Request—Ref: 0122–16 (Kaarel Piirimäe).

45. Zubok, *The Collapse*, 56–57.

46. For example, self-accounting was taken mainly from Hungarian discussions, the Popular Front probably from Russian debates.

47. David Manning, 'Taastatud vabadus: Briti diplomaadi mälestusi aastaist 1990–1991', *Välisministeeriumi aastaraamat 2008/2009* (Tallinn, 2009), 84–90 (89).

48. Trivimi Velliste, 'Kõne Lauluväljakul 11 septembril 1988. aastal' in *Eesti poliitilise mõtte ajaloost: valitud artiklid 1987–1991*, ed. H. Samel (Tallinn: Jaan Tõnissoni Instituut, 1988/1992), 21–24.

49. Eek-Pajuste (ed.), *Teine tulemine II: Välisministeeriumi taasloomise lugu* (Tallinn: välisministeerium, 2008), 166.

50. Hindrek Meri, *Tagasivaateid veerevast vagunist* (Tartu: Ilmamaa, 2008), 449–452.

51. Interview with Raivo Vare, Tallinn, 30 January 2019 (Kaarel Piirimäe).

52. Kaarel Piirimäe, 'Estonia "has not time": Existential Politics at the End

of Empire.' *Connexe: les espaces postcommunistes en question(s)* 6 (2020): 21–50.

53. Beissinger, *Nationalist Mobilization*, 93; Vadim A. V. Medvedev, *Komande Gorbačeva: Vzglâd iznutri* (Moskva: Bylina), 83.

54. Anatoly S. Chernyaev, *My Six Years With Gorbachev*; translated and edited by Robert D. English and Elizabeth Tucker (University Park: Pennsylvania State University Press, 2000), xix.

55. Una Bergmane, "'Is This the End of Perestroika?" International Reactions to the Soviet Use of Force in the Baltic Republics in January 1991', *Journal of Cold War Studies* 22, no. 2 (2020): 26–57.

56. Una Bergmane, 'French and US Reactions Facing the Disintegration of the USSR: The case of the Baltic states (1989–1991)' (Unpublished PhD Thesis: Sciences Po-Institut d'études politiques de Paris, 2016), 273.

57. This is borrowed from Stephen D. Krasner, *Sovereignty: Organized Hypocrisy* (Princeton, NJ: Princeton University Press, 1999).

58. Beth A. Fischer, 'Visions of Ending the Cold War: Triumphalism and U.S. Soviet policy', in *Visions of the End of the Cold War, 1945–1990*, ed. Frédéric Bozo, Marie-Pierre Rey, Bernd Rother and N. Piers Ludlow (New York: Berghahn, 2014), 294–308.

59. Bergmane, *Politics of Uncertainty* (forthcoming), 189, where she rightly points out that the only official and permanent diplomatic presence remained that of Sweden.

8. BALTIC EXCEPTIONALISM FROM VERSAILLES TO BELOVEZHSKAYA PUSCHA

1. Ernest Renan, 'What is a nation?' in *What is a nation? And other political writings.* Columbia University Press, 2018, p. 251.

2. Lisa Bortolotti and Kathleen Murphy-Hollies, 'Exceptionalism at the Time of Covid-19: Where Nationalism Meets Irrationality', *Danish Yearbook of Philosophy*, 2022, p. 1.

3. John A. Agnew, 'An excess of "national exceptionalism": towards a new political geography of American foreign policy', *Political Geography Quarterly*, Vol. 2, No. 2, 1983, p. 152.

4. Daniel J. Mitchell, 'The "Progressive" Threat to Baltic Exceptionalism', https://www.cato.org/blog/progressive-threat-baltic-exceptionalism

5. 'Baltic Exceptionalism? A Roundtable featuring Baltic Foreign Ministers and Prof. Anna Grzymala-Busse' https://library.stanford.edu/events/baltic-exceptionalism-roundtable-featuring-baltic-foreign-ministers-and-prof-anna-grzymala

6. Jurgis Jurgelis, 'Pavergtas protas', https://www.delfi.lt/news/ringas/lit/jurgis-jurgelis-pavergtas-protas.d?id=91177901

7. *Travaux du Comité d'études*. T.2: *Questions Européennes* (Paris: Imprimerie nationale, 1919), p. 352.

8. Ibid, p. 337–338, 354.

9. 'Outline of tentative report and recommendations', 21–01–1919, in David Hunter Miller, *My Diary at the Conference of Paris, with Documents*, Vol. 4. Doc. 246, p. 219–225.

10. 'Courland, Livonia and Estonia'. *Handbook prepared under the direction of the Historical Section of the Foreign Office (No. 50)* (London: H.M. Stationery Office, 1920), p. 27.

11. *Russian Poland, Lithuania and White Russia. Handbook prepared under the direction of the Historical Section of the Foreign Office (No. 44)* (London: H.M. Stationery Office, 1920), p. 46, 60.

12. Link (ed.), Arthur S., *The Deliberations of the Council of Four (March 24-June 28, 1919): Notes of the Official Interpreter, Paul Mantoux*, Vol. 2 (Princeton: Princeton University Press, 1992), p. 325–326.

13. Ibid, Vol. 1, 02–05–1919 entry, p. 459.

14. Session no. 44 of the Lithuanian delegation in Paris, 30–05–1919, Lietuvos Centrinis Valstybes Archyvas, 383/7/1, p. 67.

15. *Rossiya i soyuzniki / Pravitel'stvennii vestnik*, 19–09–1919, p. 2.

16. А. Н. Сахаров (ed.), *Istoriya Rossii s drevneishikh vremen do nashikh dnyei*. T. 2. Moscow: Prospect, 2019, p. 234.

17. Andrei Kozyrev, *The Firebird: The Elusive Fate of Russian Democracy*. Pittsburg, PA: University of Pittsburg Press, 2019, p. 46–47.

18. Colin Powell, *A Soldier's Way: An Autobiography*. Hutchinson: London, 1995, p. 450.

19. Vladimir Zhirinovsky speech at the roundtable '300 lyet vstupleniya Pribaltiki v sostav Rossii', 30–08–2021, https://www.youtube.com/watch?v=ssUC_Gpb0YQ

20. Mark Galeotti, 'The Baltic States as Targets and Levers: The Role of

the Region in Russian Strategy', https://www.marshallcenter.org/en/
publications/security-insights/baltic-states-targets-and-levers-role-
region-russian-strategy-0

9. CONTEXT, CROSS-PRESSURES AND COMPROMISE: THE ROLES OF GORBACHEV AND YELTSIN

1. Serhii Plokhy, *The Last Empire: The Final Days of the Soviet Union* (Basic Books, New York, 2014), pp. 400–401.
2. There was no compulsion. Six of the fifteen republics refused to hold the referendum—Estonia, Latvia, Lithuania, Georgia, Armenia and Moldova (Archie Brown, *The Human Factor: Gorbachev, Reagan, and Thatcher, and the End of the Cold War* (Oxford University Press, Oxford and New York, 2020, paperback, 2022), p. 347.
3. Archie Brown, *The Gorbachev Factor* (Oxford University Press, Oxford and New York, 1996), pp. 10–11 and 321.
4. *Reytingi Boris El'tsina i Mikhaila Gorbacheva po 10-bal'noy shkale* [Ratings of Boris Yeltsin and Mikhail Gorbachev on a 10-point scale] (VTsIOM, Moscow, 1993).
5. Brown, *The Human Factor*, pp. 241–246.
6. Pavel Palazchenko, *My Years with Gorbachev and Shevardnadze: The Memoirs of a Soviet Interpreter* (Pennsylvania State University Press, University Park, PA, 1997), p. 267.
7. Vladislav Zubok, *Collapse: The Fall of the Soviet Union* (Yale University Press, New Haven and London, 2021), p.105.
8. Ibid.
9. In addition to his highest party post, Gorbachev was, from March 1990, President of the USSR, having been indirectly elected to that office by the Soviet legislature.
10. Jeffrey A. Engel, *When the World Seemed New: George H.W. Bush and the End of the Cold War* (Houghton Mifflin Harcourt, Boston and New York, 2017), p. 371.
11. Charles Moore, *Margaret Thatcher: The Authorized Biography. Volume Three: Herself Alone* (Allen Lane, London, 2019), pp. 537–538.
12. Brown, *The Gorbachev Factor*, p. 295.
13. Aleksandr Yakovlev, *Sumerki* (2003), pp. 519–520; and Brown, *The Human Factor*, p. 346.

14. Rodric Braithwaite, unpublished Moscow diaries, entry for 18 July 1991; and Braithwaite, *Across the Moscow River: The World Turned Upside Down* (Yale University Press, New Haven and London, 2002), p. 147.

15. Archie Brown, *Seven Years that Changed the World: Perestroika in Perspective* (Oxford University Press, Oxford and New York, 2007), pp. 319–324.

10. THE HOUSE DIVIDED

1. Vladislav Zubok, *Collapse: The Fall of the Soviet Union* (Yale University Press, 2021).

14. BRITISH POLICY TOWARDS THE BALTIC STATES IN 1991

1. John Hiden and Patrick Salmon, *The Baltic Nations and Europe: Estonia, Latvia and Lithuania in the Twentieth Century*, revised edition, London and New York: Longman, 1993, p. 188.

2. All documentary references are to this series; all are from the year 1991.

3. Sir David Logan ended his career as Ambassador to Turkey (1997–2001); Sir David Manning as Ambassador to the United States (2003–7). Sir Tim Barrow served as Ambassador to Russia (2011–16), Permanent Representative and Ambassador to the EU (2017–20) and Second Permanent Secretary and Political Director at the Foreign, Commonwealth and Development Office (FCDO). He was appointed National Security Adviser in September 2022. Sian MacLeod has been Ambassador to Serbia since 2019. Braithwaite, Manning and MacLeod have all contributed eyewitness accounts to *The Last Days of the Soviet Union: Reporting from the British Embassy, Moscow* (History Note No, 24: FCDO Historians, 2021), https://issuu.com/fcohistorians/docs/last_days_of_the_soviet_union_fcdo_hn_24; Logan's recording for the British Diplomatic Oral History Programme (BDOHP), https://archives.chu.cam.ac.uk/wp-content/uploads/sites/2/2022/01/Logan_David.pdf, pp. 51–7, contains an account of his time in Moscow.

4. Moscow tel. 64, 10 January, FCO 28/11046.

5. Tel. 54 to Moscow, 11 January, ibid.

6. Tel. 52 to Moscow; Prentice minute to Lyne, both 11 January, ibid.

7. Moscow tel. 71, 11 January, ibid.

8. Moscow tel. 76, 12 January, FCO 28/11047.

9. Moscow tel. 79, 13 January, ibid.

10. Tel. 69 to Moscow, 14 January, ibid.

11. Moscow tel. 129, 17 January, ibid.

12. BDOHP (note 3 above), pp. 51–2.

13. Moscow tel. 118, 17 January, FCO 28/11047.

14. Moscow tel. 129, 17 January, ibid.

15. Tel. 54 to UKMIS New York, 18 January, ibid.

16. Lyne submission, 18 January, FCO 28/11048.

17. Braithwaite to Lyne, 24 January, FCO 28/11049.

18. Moscow tel. 206, 28 January, ibid.

19. Moscow tel. 253, FCO 28/11050.

20. Moscow tel. 299, 7 February, ibid.

21. https://johnmajorarchive.org.uk/1991/03/05/mr-majors-press-conference-in-moscow-5-march-1991/ (accessed 14 August 2022).

22. Minutes by Richard Bone (Head of Library and Records), 14 February, FCO 28/11051, and Heather Yasamee (Historical Branch), 24 June, FCO 28/11052.

23. MacLeod to Miller, 27 March; Miller to MacLeod, 4 April, FCO 28/11051.

24. Minute by Simon Fraser (PPS), 5 April, ibid.

25. Braithwaite to Lyne, 24 April, ibid.

26. Lyne minute, 4 July, ibid.

27. FCO 28/11053.

28. Simon Gass to Stephen Wall (private secretary to the prime minister), 23 August, ibid. Lyne wrote in the margin: 'Why, for years, did the lawyers tell us that Ministers could not visit the Baltic!!!'

29. 23 August, ibid.

30. Moscow tel. 1784, 25 August, ibid.

31. Moscow tels. 1784, 1785, 25 August, ibid.

32. Moscow tel. 1786, 25 August, ibid.

33. Moscow tel. 1791, 26 August, ibid.

34. Moscow tel. 1792, 26 August, ibid.

35. Moscow tel. 1811, 28 August, ibid.

36. Moscow tel. 1898, 2 September, ibid.
37. 9 September, ibid.
38. Ibid.
39. Covering letter from Gass to Wall, 11 October, ibid.
40. Notes of meetings forwarded by Sian MacLeod to George Fergusson (Soviet Department), 14 October, FCO 28/11054.
41. Keith Hamilton, *Transformational Diplomacy after the Cold War: Britain's Know How Fund in Post-Communist Europe, 1989–2003*, London and New York: Routledge, 2013, pp. 70–4.

16. HISTORICAL PROPAGANDA IN PRO-KREMLIN MEDIA: THE CASE OF THE COLLAPSE OF THE SOVIET UNION

1. Jade McGlynn. (2021). 'Moscow Is Using Memory Diplomacy to Export Its Narrative to the World', *Foreign Policy*, https://foreignpolicy.com/2021/06/25/russia-puting-ww2-soviet-ussr-memory-diplomacy-history-narrative/
2. Ibid.
3. Ibid.
4. Ivo Juurvee, Vladimir Sazonov, Kati Parppei, Edgars Engizers, Ieva Pałasz, Malgorzata Zawadzka. (2020). 'Falsification of History as A Tool of Influence', NATO Strategic Communications Centre of Excellence, Riga.
5. Full version of the media analysis report: https://www.debunkeu.org/pro-kremlin-media-uses-30th-anniversary-of-ussr-collapse-to-ignite-nostalgia-towards-the-soviet-era
6. 'Russia: excerpts from Putin's State-of-the-Nation Speech', 25 April 2005, https://www.rferl.org/a/1058630.html
7. According to similarweb.com data, 20/01/2022
8. According to similarweb.com data, 20/01/2022
9. https://www.debunkeu.org/pro-kremlin-media-uses-30th-anniversary-of-ussr-collapse-to-ignite-nostalgia-towards-the-soviet-era
10. 'Russia's Top Five Persistent Disinformation Narratives'. U.S. Department of State, 20.01.2022, https://www.state.gov/russias-top-five-persistent-disinformation-narratives/
11. Ibid.

12. Igor Lossev. 'Bandera-phobia in the Russian Consciousness', International Centre for Defence and Security, (04/11/2014), https://icds.ee/en/bandera-phobia-in-the-russian-consciousness/

13. Lukas Andriukaitis. (2020). 'Russian Propaganda Efforts in the Baltics and the Wider Region', Vilnius Institute for Policy Analysis. https://vilniusinstitute.lt/wp-content/uploads/2020/05/VIPA_Andriukaitis_2020_Iv4-1%D0%B5.pdf

14. Tatiana Zhurzhenko. 'Russia's never-ending war against "fascism": Memory politics in the Russian-Ukrainian conflict', Eurozine (08.05.2015), https://www.eurozine.com/russias-never-ending-war-against-fascism/

15. Ibid.

16. Ibid.

17. Lossev, 'Bandera-phobia in the Russian Consciousness'.

18. Lukas Andriukaitis. (2020). 'Russian Propaganda Efforts in the Baltics and the Wider Region'.

19. Rodgers, Alexandr. 'Pochemu vyrodilas' KPSS'. Al'ternativa, (28.09.2021), http://alternatio.org/articles/articles/item/95246-pochemu-vyrodilas-kpss

20. Samsonov, Alexandr. 'Natsional'niy vopros–ugroza budushchemu Rossii'. Voennoye obozreniye, (03.11.2021), https://topwar.ru/187624-nacionalnyj-vopros-ugroza-buduschemu-rossii.html

21. Ibid.

22. Anastasiya Mishina A. 'Zakat imperii. Kak Pribaltika pokidala Sovietskiy Soyuz'. Baltnews, (18.08.2021), https://lv.baltnews.com/Saeima_elections/20210818/1025030258/Zakat-imperii-Kak-Pribaltika-pokidala-Sovetskiy-Soyuz.html

17. THE UKRAINIAN DIMENSION

1. Serhii Plokhy, *The Last Empire: The Final Days of the Soviet Union*, (New York: Basic Books, 2014), pp. 400–401.

2. 'Considerations on the Government of Poland and on its Proposed Reformation'; www.files.ethz.ch/isn/125482/5016_Rousseau_Considerations_on_the_Government_of_Poland.pdf

3. Nils R. Muiznieks, 'The influence of the Baltic popular movements on

process of Soviet disintegration', *Europe-Asia Studies*, vol. 47, no. 1, 1995, pp. 3–25.

4. Taras Kuzio and Andrew Wilson, *Ukraine: Perestroika to Independence*, (Houndmills: Macmillan, 1994).

5. See the review of the memoirs of Bohdan Horyn, *Ne til'ky pro sebe*, (Kyiv: Pul'sary, 2006) by Alla Yaroshinskaya, 'Narodnyi Rukh na sluzhbe KGB', *Rosbalt.ru*, 9 December 2010; www.rosbalt.ru/ukraina/2010/12/09/798964.html. Horyn was in a more radical group than Rukh, the Ukrainian Helsinki Union.

6. Vladimir Paniotto, 'The Ukrainian movement for *perestroika*—Rukh': A sociological survey', *Soviet Studies*, vol. 43, no. 1, 1991, pp. 177–181, at p. 178.

7. See the presentation of documents by the Security Services of Ukraine in 'Rozsekrecheno dokumenty KHB pro Narodnyi rukh Ukraïny', *Kharkiv Human Rights Protection Group*, 3 September 2009; https://khpg.org/1252007024. This source and that in note 5 are in Zubok, *Collapse*, pp. 86 and 450–1, n. 53; but the discussion is different.

8. Kuzio and Wilson, *Ukraine*, p. 110.

9. Oleksii Haran, 'Do voli—cherez natsional'nyi kongres', *Moloda hvardiia*, 12 October 1990.

10. Andrew Wilson, *Ukrainian Nationalism in the 1990s: A Minority Faith*, (Cambridge: Cambridge University Press, 1997), p. 72.

11. Kamil Kłysiński, 'The celebration of the 100th anniversary of the proclamation of the Belarusian People's Republic', *OSW*, 28 March 2018; www.osw.waw.pl/en/publikacje/analyses/2018–03–28/celebration-100th-anniversary-proclamation-belarusian-peoples

12. See also 'Nasha Revoliutsiia 1917–1921', www.dsnews.ua/nasha_revolyutsiya_1917

13. 'Metodychni rekomendatsiï do 100-richchia Ukraïns'koï revoliutsiï 1917–1921 rokiv', *Ukrainian Institute of National Memory (uinp.gov.ua/)*, 6 March 2017; https://uinp.gov.ua/informaciyni-materialy/vchytelyam/metodychni-rekomendaciyi/metodychni-rekomendaciyi-do-100-richchya-ukrayinskoyi-revolyuciyi-1917-1921-rokiv

14. Plokhy, *The Last Empire*, p. 198.

15. Plokhy, *The Last Empire*, chapter three.

16. Plokhy, *The Last Empire*, pp. 260–7.
17. Denys Kazanskyi and Maryna Vorotyntseva, *Yak Ukraïna vtrachala Donbas*, (Kyiv: Chorna hora, 2020), pp. 14–17.
18. Vladislav Zubok, *Collapse: The Fall of the Soviet Union*, (New Haven and London: Yale University Press, 2021), pp. 323–6.
19. Plokhy, *The Last Empire*, p. 259.
20. Plokhy, *The Last Empire*, p. 259.
21. Plokhy, *The Last Empire*, pp. 177–8.
22. Vladislav Zubok, 'The post-Soviet roots of the war in Ukraine', *Spectator*, 26 February 2022; www.spectator.co.uk/article/the-post-soviet-roots-of-the-war-in-ukraine
23. James Sherr, 'Nothing new under the sun? Continuity and change in Russian policy towards Ukraine', *International Centre for Defence and Security*, 10 July 2020; https://icds.ee/en/nothing-new-under-the-sun-continuity-and-change-in-russian-policy-towards-ukraine/
24. Zubok, 'The post-Soviet roots of the war in Ukraine'.
25. Paul D'Anieri, *Ukraine and Russia: From Civilised Divorce to Uncivil War*, (Cambridge, UK: Cambridge University Press, 2019).
26. Vera Tolz, 'Rethinking Russian–Ukrainian relations: a new trend in nation-building in post-communist Russia?', *Nations and Nationalism*, vol. 4, 2002, pp. 235–53.
27. Anders Åslund, 'Russia's invasion has highlighted Ukraine's nation-building progress', *Ukraine Alert*, 14 August 2022; www.atlanticcouncil.org/blogs/ukrainealert/russias-invasion-has-highlighted-ukraines-nation-building-progress/
28. Neil A. Abrams and M. Steven Fish, 'Policies first, institutions second: lessons from Estonia's economic reforms', *Post-Soviet Affairs*, vol. 31, no. 6, 2015, pp. 491–513.
29. Nataliia Aliushyna, 'Viina yak chans dlia restartu', *Obozrevatel*, 15 August 2022; https://news.obozrevatel.com/ukr/society/vijna-yak-shans-dlya-restartu.htm?fbclid=IwAR194pdQ72iTiRXx1EAiGTqUNzVHt2h01CjQywMYxCIcuG1SehipMJaB6_o
30. Jadwiga Rogoża, 'Ukraine: from decommunisation to derussification', *OSW Commentary*, 17 June 2022; www.osw.waw.pl/en/publikacje/osw-commentary/2022–06–17/ukraine-decommunisation-to-derussification

31. Leonid Kuchma, *Ukraïna—ne Rossiya*, (Moscow: Vremya, 2004).

32. Ostap Kushnir (ed.), *The Intermarium as the Polish–Ukrainian Linchpin in Baltic–Black Sea Cooperation*, (Cambridge: Cambridge Scholars, 2019).

33. Sevgil Musayeva and Alim Aliyev (interview), 'Yaroslav Hrytsak: Ukraïna stane novym tsentral'noyevropeis'kym tyhrom', *Ukraïns'ka pravda*, 1 May 2022, www.pravda.com.ua/articles/2022/05/1/7343225/

18. THE BALTIC GEOPOLITICS CHALLENGES FOR TODAY

1. Robert Cooper, 'The post-modern state and the world order', Demos, 21/02/2003, https://www.demos.co.uk/files/postmodernstate.pdf

2. In the aftermath of the Russian financial crisis in 1998, Russia's GDP shrank to a mere US$209 billion in 1999, comparable to the economic yield of London. See: 'World Economic Outlook Database: Russia GDP 1990–2005', International Monetary Fund, undated, https://www.imf.org/en/Publications/WEO/weo-database/2022/April/weo-report?c=92 2,&s=NGDPD,&sy=1990&ey=2005&ssm=0&scsm=1&scc=0&ssd=1 &ssc=0&sic=0&sort=country&ds=.&br=1

3. Dmitri Trenin, *Baltic Chance: The Baltic States, Russia and the West in the Emerging Greater Europe* (New York, NY: Carnegie Endowment for International Peace, 1997).

4. Patrick Wintour, Ian Traynor and Tom Whitehouse, 'Russian and British troops in tense Pristina stand-off', *The Guardian*, 13/06/1999, https://www.theguardian.com/world/1999/jun/13/balkans5

5. For the general question of the EU and defence in the region, see: Alyson J.K. Bailes, Gunilla Herolf, Bengt Sundelius and Stockholm International Peace Research Institute (eds), *The Nordic countries and the European security and defence policy* (Oxford: Oxford University Press, 2006).

6. Mary E. Sarrotte, *Not One Inch: America, Russia, and the Making of Post-Cold War Stalemate* (London: Yale University Press, 2021).

7. Vladimir Putin, Speech: 'Speech and the Following Discussion at the Munich Conference on Security Policy', The Kremlin, 10/02/2007, http://en.kremlin.ru/events/president/transcripts/copy/24034

8. 'Strategic Concept 2010', The North Atlantic Treaty Organisation, 03/02/2012, https://www.nato.int/cps/en/natohq/topics_82705.htm

9. Esme Kirk-Wade and Sanjana Balakrishnan, 'Defence spending pledges by NATO members since Russia invaded Ukraine', House of Commons Library, 11/08/2022, https://commonslibrary.parliament.uk/defence-spending-pledges-by-nato-members-since-russia-invaded-ukraine/

10. 'The strategic defence and security review: securing Britain in an age of uncertainty', Cabinet Office, 19/11/2020, https://www.gov.uk/government/publications/the-strategic-defence-and-security-review-securing-britain-in-an-age-of-uncertainty

11. Ibid.

12. The Centre for Geopolitics, Cambridge, and the Hanns-Seidel Foundation organised a colloquium on 'The function and fate of NATO's Enhanced Forward presence' at Cambridge on 30 June 2022, which was attended by academics and practitioners. Also, see: Ann-Sofie Dahl and Anders Fogh Rasmussen, *Strategic Challenges in the Baltic Sea Region* (Washington, DC: Georgetown University Press, 2018).

13. See: Andrew Foxall, 'How Russia "positions" the United Kingdom', Council on Geostrategy, 07/04/2021, https://www.geostrategy.org.uk/research/how-russia-positions-the-united-kingdom/

14. 'Shipping in the Baltic Sea', Baltic Lines, 15/02/2017, https://vasab.org/wp-content/uploads/2018/06/Baltic-LINes-Shipping_Report-20122016.pdf

15. James Rogers, 'Geopolitics and the "Wider North": The United Kingdom as a "Strategic Pivot"', *RUSI Journal*, 157:6 (2012), pp. 42–53.

16. Brendan Simms, 'The world after Brexit', *The New Statesman*, 01/03/2017, https://www.newstatesman.com/world/2017/03/world-after-brexit

17. James Rogers and Ugis Romanovs, 'Brexit: military implications for the Baltic States', Coping with Complexity in the Euro-Atlantic Community and Beyond: The Riga Conference Papers 2016 (Latvian Institute of International Affairs, 2016), pp. 50–61.

18. Riina Kaljurand, Tony Lawrence, Pauli Järvenpää and Tomas Jermalavičius, 'Brexit and Baltic Sea Security', International Centre for Defence and Security, 05/12/2016, https://icds.ee/en/brexit-and-baltic-sea-security/

19. 'Nordic Baltic policy statement', External Affairs Directorate of the Scottish Government, 29/09/2017, https://www.gov.scot/publications/points-north-scottish-governments-nordic-baltic-policy-statement/

20. 'UK to maintain military presence in Germany', British Ministry of Defence, 30/09/2018, https://www.gov.uk/government/news/uk-to-maintain-military-presence-in-germany

21. 'Thousands of troops from UK-led force begin milestone maritime training deployment', Ministry of Defence, 24/05/2019, https://www.gov.uk/government/news/thousands-of-troops-from-uk-led-force-begin-milestone-maritime-training-deployment

22. For more on the UK's role in securing Estonian independence, see: Patrick Maldre, 'The United Kingdom and Estonia's achievement of independence', *Estonian World*, 23/02/2021, https://estonianworld.com/security/the-uk-and-estonias-achievement-of-independence/

23. Anna Wieslander and Viktor Lundquist, 'The UK, France and the United States in Sweden's Vicinity: Strategic Interests and Military Activities', Atlantic Council Europe Centre, 29/06/2021, https://www.atlanticcouncil.org/wp-content/uploads/2021/08/The-UK-France-and-the-United-States-in-Swedens-vicinity.pdf

24. 'UK to provide engineering support to Poland amid border pressures', Ministry of Defence, 09/12/2021, https://www.gov.uk/government/news/uk-to-provide-engineering-support-to-poland-amid-border-pressures

25. See: Boris Johnson, Speech: 'PM speech to the Lord Mayor's Banquet', 10 Downing Street, 15/11/2021, https://www.gov.uk/government/speeches/pm-speech-to-the-lord-mayors-banquet-15-november-2021 (last accessed: 03/11/2022) and Liz Truss, 'We must stand together for freedom and democracy', *Daily Telegraph*, 13/11/2021, https://www.telegraph.co.uk/news/2021/11/13/must-stand-together-freedom-democracy/

26. 'Ukraine Support Tracker', Kiel Institute, 18/08/2022, https://www.ifw-kiel.de/topics/war-against-ukraine/ukraine-support-tracker/

27. See: 'Ukrainians doubt at least two EU countries are "friendly"—survey', *European Pravda*, https://www.eurointegration.com.ua/eng/news/2022/03/20/7136286/

28. 'British troops and equipment on the way to bolster NATO in Estonia', *The British Army*, 18/02/2022, https://www.army.mod.uk/news-and-events/news/2022/02/exercise-iron-surge-bolsters-nato/

29. Alexander Lanoszka and James Rogers, '"Global Britain" extends to Northern Europe', *Britain's World*, 12/05/2022, https://www.geostrategy.org.uk/britains-world/security-assurances-global-britain-extends-to-northern-europe/

19. THE GEOPOLITICAL SIGNIFICANCE OF KALININGRAD AND THE SUWAŁKI GAP

1. Raimundas Lopata, Sirutavičius Vladas, 'Lithuania and Kaliningrad Oblast: A Clearer Frame for Cooperation', *Lithuanian Foreign Policy Review*, 1999, no. 3, p. 51–66; Česlovas Laurinavičius, Raimundas Lopata, Sirutavičius Vladas, 'Military Transit of the Russian Federation Through the Territory of the Republic of Lithuania', *Lithuanian Political Science Yearbook*, 2001, Vilnius, p. 131–158.

2. Raimundas Lopata, 'Geopolitical Hostage: the Case of Kaliningrad Oblast of the Russian Federation', *Lithuanian Annual Strategic Review 2003*, Vilnius, 2004, p. 203–220.

3. Raimundas Lopata, *Anatomy of a Hostage: Kaliningrad Anniversary Case*. Tartu: Baltic Defence College, 2006, p. 86–108.

4. Raimundas Lopata, 'Kaliningrad otage géopolitique de la Russie: Un point de vue lituanien', *Le courier des pays de l'Est*, 2005, No. 1048, p. 30–39.

5. Raimundas Lopata, 'Kaliningrad Anniversary: the First Steps of Georgy Boos', *Lithuanian Foreign Policy Review*, 2005, No. 1–2 (13–14), p. 127–152.

6. Raimundas Lopata, 'Kaliningrad in the European Security Architecture after the Annexation of Crimea', *Lithuanian Annual Strategic Review*, Volume 16, Issue 1 (2018), p. 303–328.

7. Daivis Petraitis, 'The Anatomy of Zapad-2017: Certain Features of Russian Military Planning', *Lithuanian Annual Strategic Review*, Volume 16, Issue 1 (2018), p. 229–267.

8. Steven Erlanger, 'With the Ukraine Invasion, NATO is Suddenly Vulnerable', *International New York Times*, 26 February 2022; Richard Spencer, 'Baltic Countries Mind the Gap', *The Times*, 5 March 2022.

9. 'Myths and Misconceptions Around Russian Military Intent: How They Affect Western Policy, and What Can Be Done', 14 July 2022, https://www.chathamhouse.org/2022/07/myths-and-misconceptions-around-russian-military-intent/myth-2-suwalki-gap-matters

20. THE MARITIME GEOPOLITICS OF THE BALTIC SEA

1. Gunnar Åselius (2018), 'Continuity and change—lessons from 1000 years of geopolitics in the Baltic Sea area', *Global Affairs*, Vol. 4, No. 4–5, p. 467.
2. Nicholas J. Spykman (1938), 'Geography and foreign policy, II', *American Political Science Review*, Vol. 32, No. 2, p. 236.
3. Basil Germond (2015), 'The geopolitical dimension of maritime security', *Marine Policy*, Vol. 54, p. 138.
4. Jakub Grygiel (2012), 'Geography and seapower', in Peter Dutton, Robert Ross, and Tunsjø, Øystein. (eds), *Twenty-First Century Seapower: Cooperation and Conflict at Sea*, Routledge, Abingdon, New York, p. 35; Michael S. Lindberg (1998), *Geographical Impact on Coastal Defence Navies*, Macmillan, Basingstoke, p. 38; Alfred Thayer Mahan (2007), *The Influence of Sea Power Upon History, 1660–1783*, Cosimo Classics, New York (Original edition: Prentice-Hall, Englewood Cliffs, 1890), pp. 29–81.
5. Eric Grove (1990), *The Future of Sea Power*, Naval Institute Press, Annapolis, p. 48.
6. Colin S. Gray (1992), *The Leverage of Sea Power: The Strategic Advantage of Navies in War*, The Free Press (Macmillan), New York; Andrew Lambert (2018), *SeapowerStates*, Yale University Press, New Haven and London; H.J. Mackinder (1904), 'The Geographical Pivot of History', *The Geographical Journal*, Vol. 23, No. 4, pp. 421–437; Mahan, *op.cit.*
7. Basil Germond (2022), 'Ukraine War: How Kyiv's Southern Offensive Will Exploit Russia's Naval Vulnerabilities', *The Conversation*, 31 August 2022, https://theconversation.com/ukraine-war-how-kyivs-southern-offensive-will-exploit-russias-naval-vulnerabilities-189651
8. Basil Germond (2022), 'The Solidaristic Society of Maritime Nations', *Australian Naval Review*, Vol. 2022, No. 1, pp. 72–85; Lambert, *op.cit.*
9. Norman Friedman (2007), 'Naval Strategy', in Tan, Andrew T.H. (ed), *The Politics of Maritime Power*, Routledge, London, p. 41.

10. Gearóid Ó Tuathail and John Agnew (1992), 'Geopolitics and Discourse: Practical Geopolitical Reasoning in American Foreign Policy', *Political Geography*, Vol. 11, No. 2, p. 192.

11. Basil Germond (2015), *The Maritime Dimension of European Security: Seapower and the European Union*, Palgrave MacMillan, London.

12. Colin S. Gray (1994), *The Navy in the post-Cold War World: The Uses and Value of Strategic Sea Power*, The Pennsylvania State University Press, University Park (PA), p. 13.

13. Lincoln Paine (2013), *The Sea and Civilization: A Maritime History of the World*, Atlantic Books, London, p. 333.

14. *Ibid*, p. 335.

15. Åselius, *op.cit.*

16. Craig L. Symonds (2018), *World War II at Sea: A Global History*, OUP, Oxford.

17. Åselius, *op.cit.*, p. 471.

18. Heinrich Lange, William Combes, Tomas Jermalavičius and Tony Lawrence (2019), *To the Seas Again: Maritime Defence and Deterrence in the Baltic Region*, International Centre for Defence and Security, Tallinn, pp. 4–6.

19. Gediminas Vitkus (2002), *Changing Security Regime in the Baltic Sea Region*, NATO Euro-Atlantic Partnership Council, Individual Research Fellowship, 2000–2002 Programme, Final Report, https://www.nato.int/acad/fellow/99–01/Vitkus.pdf, p. 4.

20. Lange et al., *op.cit.*, p. 2.

21. Rikard Bengtsson (2000), 'Towards a Stable Peace in the Baltic Sea Region?', *Cooperation and Conflict*, Vol. 35, No. 4, p. 374; Adrian Hyde-Price (2000), *NATO and the Baltic Sea Region: Towards Regional Security Governance?*, NATO Research Fellowship Scheme 1998–2000, Final Report, https://www.nato.int/acad/fellow/98–00/hyde.pdf, p. 9.

22. See for example Robin Häggblom (2022), 'Finnish-Estonian Cooperation Turning Baltic Sea Into A NATO-Lake', *Naval News*, 25 August 2022, https://www.navalnews.com/naval-news/2022/08/finnish-estonian-cooperation-turning-baltic-sea-into-a-nato-lake/

23. Julian Pawlak (2022), 'No, Don't Call the Baltic a "NATO Lake"', *RUSI Commentary*, 5 September 2022, https://www.rusi.org/explore-our-research/publications/commentary/no-dont-call-baltic-nato-lake

24. Lange et al., *op.cit.*, p. 2.
25. *Ibid*, p. 16.
26. Matthew Thomas (2020), 'Maritime Security Issues in the Baltic Sea Region', *Baltic Bulletin*, Foreign Policy Research Institute, 22 June 2020, https://www.fpri.org/article/2020/07/maritime-security-issues-in-the-baltic-sea-region/
27. Martin N. Murphy and Gary Schaub (2017), 'The Baltic: Grey-Zone Threats on Nato's Northern Flank', *Center for International Maritime Security*, 29 March 2017, https://cimsec.org/baltic-grey-zone-threats-natos-northern-flank/
28. Jonas Kjellén (2021), *The Russia Baltic Fleet: Organisation and role within the Armed Forces in 2020*, Swedish Defence Research Agency, FOI-R—5119—SE, https://www.foi.se/en/foi/news-and-pressroom/news/2021-03-17-russias-baltic-fleet-has-one-foot-on-land.html
29. IISS (2022), *The Military Balance 2022*, IISS, Routledge, London, pp. 202–203.
30. Lange et al., *op.cit.*, p. 3.
31. Kjellén, *op.cit.*; Thomas, *op.cit.*
32. IISS, op.cit., p. 203.
33. Robin Häggblom (2022), 'Myth 5: "Russia creates impenetrable 'A2/AD bubbles'"', 'Myths and Misconceptions Around Russian Military Intent', Chatham House, https://www.chathamhouse.org/2022/06/myths-and-misconceptions-around-russian-military-intent/myth-5-russia-creates-impenetrable
34. Åselius, *op.cit.*, p. 472.
35. Lange et al., *op.cit.*, p. 20.
36. Häggblom, *op.cit.*
37. Lange et al., *op.cit.*; Thomas, *op.cit.*
38. Hyde-Price, *op.cit.*, p. 2.

THE AUTHORS

Sir Rodric Braithwaite, British Ambassador to the Soviet Union 1988–1991 and to Russia 1991–2, and author, *Russia: Myths and Realities*

Professor Archie Brown FBA, Emeritus Professor of Politics, University of Oxford, and author, *The Human Factor: Gorbachev, Reagan, and Thatcher, and the end of the Cold War*

Rt Hon Charles Clarke, Joint Leader, Baltic Geopolitics Programme, University of Cambridge, and author, *The University Challenge*

Dr John Freeman, Research Assistant, Baltic Geopolitics Programme, University of Cambridge

Professor Basil Germond, Professor of International Security, Lancaster University, and author, *The Maritime Dimension of European Security: Seapower and the European Union*

Professor Jonathan Haslam FBA, Emeritus Professor of the History of International Relations, University of Cambridge, and author, *The Spectre of War: International Communism and the Origins of World War II*

Professor Stefan Hedlund, Professor at the Institute for Russian and Eurasian Studies, Uppsala University, and co-author (with

THE AUTHORS

Kristian Gerner), *The Baltic States and the End of the Soviet Empire*

Bridget Kendall, Hon FBA, Master of Peterhouse, University of Cambridge. BBC Moscow correspondent 1989–1994

Dr Mart Kuldkepp, Associate Professor, School for European Languages, Culture and Society at University College London, and author, *Baltic Crisis: Nordic and Baltic Countries During the End Stage of the Cold War*

Dr Donatas Kupčiūnas, Research Associate, Baltic Geopolitics Programme, Research Fellow, Wolfson College, University of Cambridge, author, '*The Vilnius Conflict in European Diplomacy, 1919–1923*'

Rt Hon Sir David Lidington, Chair of the Royal United Services Institute, UK Chairman of the Aurora Forum and Minister for Europe 2010–2016

Professor Raimundas Lopata, Member of the Lithuanian Seimas, Chair of Committee for the Future and Member of Committee on National Security and Defence of the Lithuanian Seimas, formerly Professor at the Institute of International Relations and Political Science Vilnius University, and author, *Anatomy of a Hostage: Kaliningrad Anniversary Case (2006, 2007)*

Professor Kaarel Piirimäe, Associate Professor of Contemporary History, University of Tartu and Project Researcher at Helsinki University, articles include 'Gorbachev's new thinking and how its interaction with perestroika in the republics catalysed the Soviet collapse' and 'Estonia "has no time"'

James Rogers, Co-Founder and Director of Research, Council on Geostrategy

Professor Patrick Salmon, Chief Historian at the Foreign,

Commonwealth and Development Office, and author, *The Baltic Nations and Europe: Estonia, Latvia and Lithuania in the Twentieth Century*

Sturla Sigurjónsson, Ambassador of Iceland to the United Kingdom

Professor Brendan Simms, Director, Centre for Geopolitics and Professor of the History of European International Relations University of Cambridge, and author, *Britain's Europe: A Thousand Years of Conflict and Cooperation*

Professor Kristina Spohr, Professor of International History, London School of Economics, and author, *Post Wall, Post Square: Rebuilding the World after 1989* and *Germany and The Baltic Problem After the Cold War*

Neil Taylor MBE, awarded MBE for outstanding contribution to the UK's bilateral relationship with Estonia, author, *Estonia: A Modern History and The Brandt Guide to Estonia*

Professor Andrew Wilson, University College London, and author, *Ukraine Crisis: What the West Needs to Know and The Ukrainians: Unexpected Nation*

Dr Inga Zakšauskienė, Assistant Professor, Faculty of History, University of Vilnius, and author, *Discovering the Secret Listener: Western Radio Broadcasts to Soviet Lithuania*

Professor Vladislav Zubok, Professor of International History, LSE, and author, *Collapse: The Fall of the Soviet Union*

INDEX

INDEX

INDEX

British Council, 204, 209
Brown, Archibald, 92, 182
Bucharest Summit (2008), 173
Bund, The, 23
Burbulis, Genady, 117–18
Bureau of Intelligence and
  Research (INR), 51
Bush, George Herbert Walker,
  54–5, 106, 128–9, 132, 144–8,
  150, 216, 246
  'Chicken Kiev' speech (1991),
    106, 246
  Malta Summit (1989), 57, 144
  new era declaration (1992), 35
  Reagan, relationship with, 54
  Rüütel and Meri meeting
    (1991), 147
Byzantine Empire (330–1453), 155

Cambridge University, 3
Cameron, David, 266, 268
Carlsson, Ingvar, 67, 68
Catherine II, Empress of Russia,
  7, 23, 160
Catholic League, 7
Catholicism, 15, 30, 39, 41, 156
Central Asia, 185–6, 208, 241,
  251
Central Intelligence Agency
  (CIA), 51, 55, 231
Centre for Baltic Studies, 209
Centre for Geopolitics, 212
Cēsis, Latvia, 19–20
Chamberlain, Arthur Neville, 37
Chatham House, 287

Chechnya, 186, 261
Chernenko, Konstantin, 123
Chernovetskiy, Leonid, 253
Chernyaev, Anatoly, 51, 105, 202
China, 44, 276, 286, 291, 293
Christianity
  Catholicism, 15, 30, 39, 41, 156
  Orthodoxy, 15, 18, 117, 155–6
  Protestantism, 7, 15, 18, 81, 117
Churchill, Winston, 100
Clemenceau, Georges, 114
Clinton, William 'Bill', 246, 262
CNN, 149
Cold War (1947–91), 5, 35, 36, 41,
  43, 91–2, 95, 106, 128, 150, 272
  maritime geopolitics and, 291
  neutrality, 61–2, 63, 64, 65, 66,
    68, 69, 70, 296
colonialism, 53, 93
'Colour Revolutions', 232
COMECON (1949–91), 92
Commission on Security and
  Cooperation in Europe
  (CSCE), 43, 63
Common European Home, 76,
  149
Commonwealth of Independent
  States (CIS), 90, 118, 193
Communist International, 49
Communist Party of Estonia, 82,
  103
Communist Party of Lithuania,
  86, 241
Communist Party of the Soviet
  Union, 40, 81, 82, 85, 88, 89–90,
  249

INDEX

INDEX

INDEX

INDEX

INDEX

INDEX

INDEX

INDEX

INDEX

INDEX

INDEX

INDEX

INDEX

INDEX

INDEX

INDEX

INDEX

INDEX

INDEX

INDEX

INDEX

INDEX

Russian annexation (1797), 160
  University of, 160
Vilnius University, 15
Visegrad Group, 166
Vistula river, 8
Vladimir, Grand Prince of Kiev, 155
Voennaya mysl', 51
Voice of America, 100
Voldemaras, Augustinas, 114
Volyn, Ukraine, 249
Voshchanov, Pavel, 250

Wannsee Conference (1942), 28
War on Terror (2001–), 263
warm waters, 290–91, 295
Warsaw Pact, 54, 164, 166, 167,
  175, 179, 199, 213, 264, 296
Warsaw, Poland, 8, 17, 160
  NATO Summit (2016), 267
Watts, Arthur, 204
Weber, Maximilian, 81
Weimar Republic (1918–33), 27
Welles Declaration (1940), 242
West Germany (1949–90), 22, 42
Weston, John, 199, 208
White Sea Canal, 268
Wieslander, Anna, 270
Wilczyńska, Magdalena, 221
Wilson, Woodrow, 112
World War I (1914–18), 19–20,
  38, 64, 66
World War II (1939–45), 8, 11, 22,
  23–4, 27–9, 46, 51, 118–19, 163,
  165, 184

Baltic Sea and, 294
German invasion of Russia
  (1941–5), 46, 51, 163
Holocaust (1941–5), 23–4, 28
Kaliningrad and, 273, 274, 275
maritime geopolitics and, 291
Molotov-Ribbentrop Pact
  (1939), *see* Molotov-
  Ribbentrop Pact
Potsdam Conference (1945),
  274, 275, 276, 285
Yalta Conference (1945), 166
Wright, Patrick, 203

Yakovlev, Aleksandr, 101, 131, 141–
  2, 229
Yalta Conference (1945), 166
Yanaev, Gennadiy, 130
Yantar, Kaliningrad, 277
Yazov, Dmitrii, 58, 129, 146, 147
Yegorov, Vladimir, 277, 278
Yeltsin, Boris, 93, 99, 123–6, 214,
  296
  Baltic independence declara-
    tions (1991), 149, 151, 164,
    205
  Belovezha Accords (1991), 90,
    117–18, 234
  Bush, relationship with, 147–8,
    150
  coup attempt (1991), 90, 94, 149
  Extraordinary Party Congress
    (1990), 87
  Gorbachev, relationship with,